CONSCIENCELESS
ACTS
SOCIETAL
MAYHEM

CONSCIENCELESS
ACTS
SOCIETAL
MAYHEM

*Uncontrollable, Unreachable Youth and
Today's Desensitized World*

FOSTER W. CLINE, M.D.

The Love and Logic
PRESS INC.
Golden, Colorado

First edition
First printing, 1995
Printed in the United States of America

This publication is designed to provide authoritative information in
regard to the subject matter. Based on the professional and personal
experiences of the author, the various therapeutic techniques
described within are meant to be implemented by trained professionals
only. As always, good judgment on the part of any professional who
works with disturbed children is of the utmost importance.

Library of Congress Cataloging-in-Publication Data

Cline, Foster.
    Conscienceless acts, societal mayhem : uncontrollable, unreachable
youth and today's desensitized world / by Foster W. Cline.
        p.   cm.
    Includes index.
    ISBN 0-944634-19-2 (hardcover) : $21.95 ($27.95 Can.)
    1. Attachment behavior in children. 2. Antisocial personality
disorders—Etiology. 3. Interpersonal confrontation—Therapeutic
use. 4. Conduct disorders in children. 5. Conduct disorders in
adolescence. 6. Problem children—Rehabilitation. 7. Problem youth—
Rehabilitation. I. Title.
RJ507.A77C56   1995
618.92'8582—dc20   94-42238
                                                        CIP

This book is dedicated to America's lawmakers, who, like young parents, generally take on their task with care, concern, and good intentions. They attempt, as do parents, to deal effectively with the demands and needs of those under their authority. And like young parents, they must inevitably discover that the more that is given without reservation—the more that is provided prior to self-improvement or change on the recipients' part—the greater the demands, dependence, and disability of those recipients. Legislators must learn, as do parents, that to give first and then require change leads to a spoiled, demanding, and disabled population. As wise parents, legislators must learn to say, "I do care. But you must first *show* that you want to change. Only then will I match your self-help."

CONTENTS

ACKNOWLEDGMENTS

No individual is born wise. All therapists learn from their own teachers—primarily their patients, those whom they aid in the struggle to become effective, capable, and loving human beings. Looking back on my years helping others, I have been lucky to have been surrounded by supportive and thoughtful professionals such as those at Evergreen Consultants. And I have been blessed to know patients who have taught me of the struggle and flight of the human spirit.

It was from such patients that I learned of the essential effect that the first year of life has on the development of personality. It was from their struggle to overcome very early abuse and neglect that I, like John Bowlby so many years before, rediscovered that when society abets mere children in having, and then destroying, their own children, society does so at the risk of destroying itself.

INTRODUCTION

There is a growing cancer in America. It has been growing silently for a long time, deep inside the body. In the last few years, it has produced painful symptoms that have been ignored or glossed over because we fear what such aches and pains might really mean. Left unchecked, this cancer will eat away at society until the final, excruciating death throes.

In 1991, more than 24,000 Americans were killed by their brethren, up 5.4 percent over the year before. A Senate Judiciary Committee report sanguinely stated that the trend "will continue for many years to come." In that year, and in every year now, it is estimated that more than 1.5 million Americans are victims of assault, more than 650,000 women are raped. Homicide is now the second leading cause of death among 15-to-24-year-olds, and it is the leading cause among 15-to-34-year-old African American males.

The violence is becoming increasingly senseless. A man riding a suburban commuter train opens fire and kills and wounds dozens. A young child is abducted from in front of her house in a "safe" neighborhood, to be found dead later in nearby woods. A teenager murders a motorist, just to take her car for a joyride.

Kill a person for a joyride? What's going on here? Years ago, when some of us in the psychiatric field saw that government policies were starting to promote lawlessness, we joked that it would not be long before people wouldn't feel safe going out at night. Now people are afraid in the daytime, and not just outside, either. Some citizens are virtual prisoners in their homes, shying away from windows because random gunfire jeopardizes them. Although most robberies still occur when folks aren't home, thugs are more often entering homes when the occupants are present—

1

posing as service people, simply pushing open the door—and attacking the occupants at dinner. Their purpose may not even be to rob, but just "for the fun of it."

What's going on is that we are raising a generation of severely disturbed children, many of whom are in their teens and beyond. As statistics show, these children are becoming drug users, purse-snatchers, rapists, and murderers at an earlier and earlier age. And it doesn't look as if anything that the government—or the psychological profession—is doing is helping one whit.

Every day, thousands of young children are abused—beaten physically or verbally, often by young parents who were abused themselves. Drug and alcohol use by our young people is growing steadily, and the substances they use are ever more available and deadly. Every year, a larger percentage of the prison population is made up of adolescents, and the total number incarcerated in the United States—more than a million souls—if put together in one place, would make the tenth-largest city in the country.

In his 1991 book, *Save the Family, Save the Child*, Dr. Vincent Fontana, medical director of the New York Foundling Hospital, noted that the number of newborn babies abandoned to die in New York City increased more than 42 percent from 1986 to 1989, from 1,128 to 1,606. The reasons for this increase? Fontana says starkly: "Crack and AIDS."

Fontana goes on to tell the effects of drugs, and especially crack, on newborns, their families, and society. He reports that in 1987, 73 percent of fatalities attributed to child abuse were drug related, and the number of drug-related cases of child abuse and neglect tripled between 1986 and 1988.

And it gets worse. Around the country, the number of babies exposed to cocaine in the womb is rising precipitously: in Philadelphia; in Florida; in Boise, Idaho; even in Peoria, Illinois. The cases cross all economic and racial lines.

Why the concern over this "recreational" drug? Why should society be worried about what individuals put in their bodies?

Society must be concerned because, more and more, the people who are putting cocaine into their bodies are young, pregnant girls.

Since cocaine is one of the most dangerous substances for a baby in the womb, this drug use is creating a swarm of sick children whose chances for having productive lives are being shortened before they are born. In addition, continued use of cocaine breaks up families. Mothers, who have for years been seen as the backbone of the family, give up their family roles when they get on crack. They don't care about raising children—they are consumed with getting crack, with staying high. They leave their infants so they can sell themselves or steal to get money for crack. They endanger their children's lives by taking them into the free-fire zones that are our nation's street-corner drug bazaars. So tens of thousands of crack babies, disadvantaged at birth, are further traumatized by a frightening, insecure infancy. Without parental care, these children are practically guaranteed to grow up to be threats to themselves, their neighbors, and society at large.

Deepening the effects of drugs on the country is creeping poverty. After two decades of decline, the number of Americans living below the poverty line began rising in 1980. There are now more than 33 million Americans officially considered "poor," or about the same number as there were in 1965, when the federal government's "war on poverty" began. In the 1980s, the number of children living in poverty increased by 22 percent. Fatherless families are growing across the board, up 80 percent in all races since 1970. One million teenage girls become pregnant each year in America. Only one third of the young mothers who give birth marry the child's father; this is significant for the babies, for poverty occurs in over 33 percent of single-parent families, but in only 6 percent of two-parent families. America's response to the problem? Throw more money and programs at it. But the problem grows worse.

Although the increase in crime, child abuse, and drug use is terrible enough, there are more ominous, insidious signs of problems ahead. Many young people entering adulthood are the vanguard of a vast number of Americans who suffer from the subtle effects of drugs in pregnancy, early abuse and neglect, and the breakup of the family. These Americans cannot meet the responsibilities required by society. Beyond this group is the mass of Americans who are simply tuning out society. The network news shows have lost millions of viewers since the 1980s, and those viewers have not migrated to cable or public television. Newspaper readership has also declined steadily. The news media, scrambling to hold on to its audience, has been increasing the amount of "soft news" and reports of celebrity scandals to the detriment of in-depth reporting on major national and international issues.

Voter totals are down—rarely do more than 50 percent of registered voters cast their ballots despite major efforts to make voting easier. It is becoming more and more difficult to fill jury pools, and many people see this civic duty as an undesirable chore to be avoided at all costs. Another civic responsibility, paying taxes for public services, is almost universally derided. An entire industry has grown up to help citizens hide their money from the tax collector.

Superficial answers to this seeming decay abound. Some commentators decry the "age of indifference" or a decrease in morality. While these ideas may be close to the truth, few of us want to face the harsh reality: Americans as a group appear to engage in less thoughtful planning, are less intelligent, have weaker conscience, and are less caring than they used to be. *All of these point to the loss of basic ego strengths built on genetics, perinatal events, and infantile and early childhood care.*

It might be said that by many measures, Americans are losing the ability to think and to love with commitment. As we look around us, it appears that responsible behavior, traditional values, and fortitude are being lost, and Americans are losing the ability to concentrate, plan ahead, and think causally. Average scores on widely accepted tests such as the Scholastic Aptitude Test (SAT) show a steady decline over the last quarter century. In 1965, the "average" student scored 500 on the SAT; in 1994, the "average" student still scored 500, but the test had been "dumbed down" over the years. The pupils of 1965 were simply smarter than their counterparts today.

The loss of the ability to think and love accounts for the breakup of the family, acceptance of media nonsense, lack of governmental backbone, law enforcement problems, and high school graduates who cannot achieve at the sixth-grade level. The loss of the ability to love and to think so pervades our culture that it scares us to even consider it. Instead, we chase after simple solutions that cure the symptoms but do not touch the underlying disease.

Some tell us that our salvation lies in teaching values. But even when these values are cloaked in popular music and advanced by teen idols, it appears that youngsters do not listen. As one research firm found out, our children "are more afraid of being ostracized by their peers than they are of dying from AIDS or drug use" (Cyntia Tucker, *Denver Post*, June 13, 1992).

Some feel that making fathers financially responsible for their children will help. But as those of us in the field know, many mothers have sex with so many men that they themselves are unsure of the paternity of the child. And if the father can be found, he very often has a profound problem earning enough money for him to live on, let alone to support a family. He may be unable to get or hold a job, or may not even care about it. Those who don't care for themselves rarely care for their children.

Others state that poverty must be the problem. Giving people economic opportunity will take care of society's headaches. But this assumes that if we stamp out poverty, we will suddenly have a large group of newly responsible adults who contemplate the long-term consequences of their sexual appetites, think carefully about how many children they can afford, take loving care of their infants, and form loving relationships with their spouses.

Education, then. Make educators accountable, retrain teachers to teach better. However, today's teachers are actually better prepared than they have ever been. Young, enthusiastic teachers are first surprised, then shocked, then grow calloused as they face classrooms of children who threaten them with knives, refuse to involve themselves in learning, and slash their car tires.

Law enforcement? Maybe our police could spend more time locking up criminals? More actual dollars and a larger percentage of gross national product is being spent on law enforcement than ever in American history. Jails are overflowing—dangerous people are being released on parole because of the crowding. Criminals are being apprehended in record numbers. The problem is not that the cops aren't doing their jobs, but that our society is creating too many violent criminals. The cops just can't keep up.

The real problem rests not with education, law enforcement, or even families per se. It rests with how we care for our infants, toddlers, and young children. Most thinking Americans realize what abysmal care American children receive; some of them even link this, in an unfocused way, to the deterioriation of society. Yet these well-meaning citizens generally do not wish to recognize that unless widespread societal and therapeutic changes are made *now*, civilization as we know it will be endangered.

Society responds perversely, insisting on creating its own problems while offering only phony solutions. The result is a codependent society composed of those who need help and those who give it. Ineffective remedies are repeatedly offered for emerging and more profound difficulties. Cocaine-addicted mothers are "rehabilitated," and then go on to produce more unhealthy children. A loving father who had his mentally retarded daughter sterilized in the 1960s is sued by the daughter and civil rights attorneys in the 1980s. After surgical correction, the daughter produces children that neither grandfather nor foster homes can handle, and institutionalization is recommended. Severely disturbed children are continually treated in play therapy without good results. Protective services remove children from foster care because parents are "too strict," but offer no alternatives. And when these children are placed in new homes, they generally become more disturbed.

What is the cause of these ills? What are the results we shall reap? For years, Americans have relied on government to find the answers—or more appropriately, to fund the answers. Our well-meaning representatives have given us program after program, all intended to correct one symptom or another. And yet the disease continues to spread.

I believe that both cause and result are bound up in an area that we have been loathe to look at—how we raise our children. Not during adolescence or the teen years, when children become unreachable. The topic that I will discuss is how children are cared for in their first year of life, and how government actually encourages people who destroy their children to have more children.

Because of the drug epidemic, because of the blossoming ranks of teenage mothers and fathers, because of the numbers of abusive families, our society is producing a generation of severely disturbed children who lack conscience. (Some analysts would say we are well into our second and even third generation of such children, and the numbers increase geometrically as each group of damaged children more than replaces itself with its own offspring.) For a number of reasons, which this book shall discuss, these children grow up unattached—incapable of caring about themselves and others, unable to distinguish right and wrong, unable to form loving relationships with anyone, unable to accept responsibility. They take what they want, when they want it, without thought to the pain or inconvenience they cause others, or the consequences for themselves. If they are apprehended for some crime, whether it be shoplifting or manslaughter, they show no remorse, no sense that what they have done is wrong or should be punished. In a sad, frightening way, these people are not human—they cannot connect to others, cannot love, cannot care. The only ways in which they can deal with others are rage, manipulation, or violence.

And as a growing number of therapists are realizing, traditional methods of rehabilitating these individuals—traditional ways of thinking about these individuals—are failing. First, we are expending most of our resources trying to reach people—adolescents and teens—who are unreachable. These are very often the children who have been through the child protective and criminal justice systems already. We try to rehabilitate them. We try to give them a new start. Within a short time, they are in trouble again.

Second, we are not using the right methods with such individuals. The great majority of social service workers and therapists continue to be enablers for these individuals: the children fail, it is society's fault, and there is a program to help. The individual is never allowed to be responsible for his own actions; to feel the consequences, embarrassment, and pain that accompanies mistakes in the adult world.

These individuals must be allowed to fail and to feel the results of that failure. This is not to say that we should let all those who fail in life die in the streets, but they should know that they *could* end up that way. When they understand that, they will be more likely to want to help in reclaiming themselves.

Third, we are promulgating social policy that is worsening the problem. We are giving people monetary encouragement to have babies and to take drugs; we need to go the other way. One avenue is to legalize drugs. Now, the best and brightest in our inner cities (and many of our suburbs) are going into the drug trade because it is the best way to make a lot of money fast. Nicotine is one of the most addicting substances we know of, but it is legal, so no one gets killed selling or buying it.

This book explores *causes* and *cures* of conscienceless acts and societal mayhem on two levels. The first level is that of the disturbed children, and the kind of parenting that creates them. The second level concerns American society and the governmental policies that are promoting cultural disruption. The two levels are interlocked, and must be understood together.

We can reach severely disturbed children and stop the cycle of damaged adults raising damaged children, but only by changing how we treat severely disturbed individuals. The techniques discussed in this book are grouped under the name *intrusive therapy,* and have proven to be effective in case after case. I have been using this therapy for thirty years, and the theoretic basis for it goes back many more years than that.

What therapists like myself do—what more therapists should do—is stop enabling these disturbed youngsters, stop giving them an easy exit from their messes. The type of therapy I demonstrate in this book is confrontive—it makes the child responsible for his own behavior. It is hands-on therapy in the most basic sense: the parent or therapist involved actually holds the child, lovingly and safely, but as firmly as necessary, in order for the child to work through the anger, pain, and bad memories that keep him from recognizing what he needs to do to change his life.

What you will see in this book is a therapy that *works*. You will read about children whom you have probably met in one way or another—either as a parent or grandparent, a relative, or a neighbor. You will read about children who are "out of control," "animals," and "vicious," and their families' trials with them. And you will see how intrusive therapy and being responsible for one's own mistakes can make it possible for these children to pull back from the brink of disaster, to have hope for their future.

For various reasons, these techniques have been resisted and negated by the professional community. Despite this, they are the fastest, best way to get severely disturbed children started on their way to mental health; and thus the fastest way for a society sick with senseless crime to cure itself. The stark choice is best illustrated in this quote often attributed to Abraham Lincoln:

> A child is a person who is going to carry on what you have started. He is going to sit where you are sitting, and when you are gone, attend to those things which you think are important. You may adopt all the policies you please, but how they are carried out depends on him. He will assume control of your cities, states, and nations. He is going to move in and take over your churches, schools, universities, and corporations. All your books are going to be judged, praised, or condemned by him. The fate of humanity is in his hands.

Part 1

THE DANGERS OF CONSCIENCELESS CHILDREN

1

THE UNATTACHED CHILD

What are "unattached" children, and why do they pose a threat to society? A number of researchers dislike this term, claiming that children who live with anybody must have *some* attachment to others, although it may be hidden by defensive behavior resulting from years of abuse or neglect. Therefore, labels such as *insecurely attached* or *anxiously attached* are often heard at seminars and in learned papers. But after more than a quarter-century of working with these children at my clinic in Evergreen, Colorado, I am convinced that there are severely disturbed young children who are not acting defensively, who are not hiding an ambivalence toward intimacy. They are not insecure; nor are they anxious. These children really do not care. They are simply and happily unattached: unable to form intimate relationships with others, unwilling to try, and uncaring about their condition. They are lacking something that all humans need to function in society—a conscience.

Having a conscience is actually caring about other people. The first step for an infant is caring about mother or father. Early in life, behavior patterns are laid down for the infant: I do this, mom is happy. I do that, dad is angry. That's control for the infant—power to make the parent feel or do something. (Recent studies are showing that early interaction between parent and infant actually result in the chemistry of the brain being laid down in a proper or improper way.) Soon the child recognizes that when his parents are happy, good things happen—he gets fed, cuddled, and smiled on. Thus, the child learns that he has an investment in keeping his parents happy—he learns that other people are important in his life.

13

As he grows, the child's conscience is rounded out. At a certain point, he learns that if he does something "wrong," the result is unpleasant—a spanking or a scolding. Pretty soon, he does things that are right because that makes his parents happy and keeps away punishment. Finally, the child arrives at the well-formed conscience: he himself wants to do things that are right.

Another aspect of this early development is that the child develops trust. An infant experiences a need—for example, hunger. With no other way to express the need, the child cries as if in a rage. The parents arrive on the scene with food to relieve the child's need. As this pattern is repeated hundreds of times, the child begins to understand that his parents will come when he cries. The child begins to trust other people.

If something goes wrong at this early stage of life—up to ten months of age—conscience formation and trust in others is broken. This is a common occurrence with the children of teenage mothers and drug users, who are not able to provide for their children's needs, and is certainly a factor in how children who are abused or abandoned develop. These children never learn that other people are important to them, and never learn to trust other people. These children do not attach to parents or anyone else; they feel no closeness to anyone; they do not bond. Clinically, these children are diagnosed as having *reactive attachment disorder.*

It doesn't take much to break the chain of development. John Robertson, an outstanding therapist at the Tavistock Child Development Centre in England, wrote the following in 1953:

> If a child is taken from his mother's care at [eighteen to twenty-four months], when he is so possessively and passionately attached to her, it is indeed as if his world had been shattered. His intense need of her is unsatisfied, and the frustration and longing may send him frantic with grief. It takes an exercise of imagination to sense the intensity of this distress. He is as overwhelmed as any adult who has lost a beloved person by death. To the child of two with his lack of understanding and complete inability to tolerate frustration it is as if his mother had died. He does not know death, but only absence; and if the only person

who can satisfy his imperative need is absent, she might as well be dead, so overwhelming is his loss.

Infantile loss is a precursor to lasting and devastating personality changes as the loss is disguised by layers of anger, frustration, and rage.

Pattern in Development of Unattached Children

The development of people with reactive attachment disorder follows a well-defined pattern. (Children who exhibit one or two of the following behaviors are unlikely to be unattached. Only when most of these signs are present can such a diagnosis be made.) The first part of the pattern involves the lack of an internal guidance system. For some reason, and often for a variety of reasons, these children never develop conscience. In psychological terms, they have no internalized object, no identification with anyone outside themselves. For most children there is a progression in values from "I want it, so I take it" (about two-three years old) to "I would take it, but my parents wouldn't like it" to "I would take it, but I don't feel good about doing things like that" (by six-seven years old). Reactive-attachment-disordered children never internalize their parents—they steal unless they are watched at all times.

Early on, these children demonstrate an inability to give and receive affection—they become stiff or push away when hugged or held, and refuse cuddling and kissing. Not just occasionally, as normal children do, but all the time:

> When Jane was small, I tried to rock her, but she wouldn't let me. She would grab the rungs of the rocking chair and rock me to her rhythm. She simply wouldn't accept my rocking her at all.

> When Paul was small, I tried to hug him and he turned sideways. I tried to turn him around but he'd resist. Well, you just can't hug a little boy with an elbow, hip bone, or shoulder jabbing at you.

> Tommy was never able to accept holding and cuddling. This showed up even during feeding . . . he would not drink his bot-

tle unless it was propped. . . . I told my pediatrician that something was really wrong, that Tommy simply didn't love me. He was ten months old then, and my doctor laughed and said that Tommy was a happy little boy and for me not to worry. Then, two years later when Tommy was causing me nothing but trouble, the doctor said, "Tommy just has a rotten personality." Now that was a real help!

Even more remarkable are the self-destructive tendencies of these children. Their parents tell stories that tread a thin line between the pathetic and the comical:

> When Robert was two, he started really banging his head against the bedroom wall. Occasionally our other children had banged their heads in their cribs, but nothing like this. Robert would bang his head so hard way back in the bedroom that the living room wall clock would chime.

> Joe caught bees in his hand. I mean, no gloves, no nothing. His hand would be a mass of welts. He'd cry, and then go back and do it again.

> Paul's favorite stunt at four years of age was standing on the front steps and falling over backward, arching his back. His head would literally bounce, bump, bump, bump on the pavement.

Along with cruelty to themselves, unattached children are cruel to others—way beyond the childhood cruelty we see in normal children. These children can cause serious physical harm to other children, animals, even adults, with total disregard for the feelings of the injured person:

> When I took the cat out of the washer, I was in a rage. I was crying. It seemed so senseless and so cruel. There was no reason! And I knew that talking with Paul about scalding it to death would have been an exercise in frustration.

> Tommy would try to light his little sister's hair on fire. Luckily, she was two and could usually avoid him.

As a result, these children also lack long-term childhood friends, for other children won't tolerate their cruelty and violence. Perhaps one hardy child will keep on trying for a few months, but after a while all other children will avoid the unattached ones. As one father said, "Friends? Does he have any friends? How many times do you have to get hit in the back of the head with a steel dump truck to quit coming back?"

Unattached children typically come across as "phony," although that is more a descriptive used by parents than a clinical term. Since they have no real connection to other people, how they interact with others is based on what they think they should do or need to do to get what they want, rather than on what they feel or want to do:

> How can I tell you how unreal Doug is? Actually, he's phony. Every hug is a manipulation. Sometimes he says "I love you," but I know he says it only because I might want to hear it. I never feel he really says something because he means it.

The second part of the pattern concerns issues of trust. Since attachment-disordered children lack trust in others, they have great problems letting others control them. Everything must be done on their terms; any small conflict becomes a kicking, screaming control battle. A loving hand on the shoulder is shrugged off violently; hugs are repelled with great force. They must have their own way, even if that way is destructive and potentially life-threatening. These children are like an elderly patient I remember whose appendix had ruptured and who nearly died because he refused to let doctors operate. He fought against his restraints, and in reply to every attempt to explain the situation to him, he shouted, "Nobody's going to operate on old Jacobs!"

(After the successful operation, Jacobs was a new patient. He couldn't have been more pleasant to the staff. As you will see, this amazing, almost unbelievable reversal in attitude occurs when a nontrusting individual is forced to give total control to others, and everything turns out all right.)

One of the manifestations of this that parents notice early on is lack of eye contact. If the child is being charming or wants something from the parent, eye contact is terrific. The child has an amazing ability to do or be whatever is required to get what he wants. But if the parent asks the child to do something, or to do something in a specific way, eye contact is generally lost. The child has no interest in doing anything that someone else wants him to do.

The more severe the attachment disorder, the more the child resists control. Others might describe the child as obnoxious and bratty, but these mild labels are best reserved for the normal child who is frequently too demanding—a real-life Dennis the Menace. The depth of disturbed children's behavior patterns that result from their unwillingness to be controlled can be comprehended only by frontline observers—parents and teachers—who, bordering on hopelessness, plead with friends, school therapists, and others to try to comprehend the incomprehensible.

> After we adopted Eddie at five, he hit our home like a tornado. . . . I was exhausted, trailing after him and picking up the pieces. At first I thought, "Man, this can't go on forever. The kid can't last." But he did, and it got worse! Nothing anywhere in the house was safe from Eddie.
>
> At first I thought, "What a neat, independent little guy." But after a few months, the house was an absolute wreck and so was I. My husband and I couldn't go out. It just wasn't safe to leave Eddie. A babysitter would come once! That was it. . . . If it hadn't been for my own natural children, I would have thought I simply didn't know how to handle children at all.

Because these disturbed children are typically deprived early in life, they constantly feel as if they will be left out. This leads to extreme symptoms such as hoarding, stealing, and gorging. Children who lack loving providers (or who cannot appreciate such providers) find the food itself, not the people who give it to them, all-important. They cannot equate the giving of sweets or other food with love, for they do not reciprocate others' emotions. Although their hoarding usually involves food and sweets, it may generalize to toys and things stolen from their parents. With children who have suffered extreme deprivation before their first birthday, this behavior and the accompanying thought disorder can make for some messy situations:

> If there is a milligram of sugar in the house, John [six years old] sniffs it out. He's uncanny. We can't leave him for a minute. Yesterday was a typical example. My wife and I were outside for only a short time. When we came back in, John had somehow unlocked the pantry door and was sitting on the floor with food crumbs and open boxes and jars all spilled out. Food was all over his face and shirt. The pantry looked like some kind of animal cage, and I thought, "My God, he's an animal."

Children who steal food are not just hungry or in a "growth spurt." They have a chronic sense of emptiness that cannot be removed by giving more food. The more food, the greater the hoarding! A first-grade teacher wrote this account of a boy named Mitchell, who was abandoned by his mother when he was two years old:

> The problem surfaced at school when other children started complaining that food was missing from their lunches, which they left by the door each morning. . . . We could not solve the mystery until one morning an observant child saw Mitchell ransacking those lunches.
> Confronted with this testimony, Mitchell readily admitted guilt and led us to his private cache under a bush behind the school. He seldom ate the food he took, but often checked to make sure it was there.
> I talked with Mitchell about his taking the food and that it made the other children unhappy. I assured him that it was okay to want the food and told him I would put a box of graham crackers in the office with his name on it. Anytime he felt hungry he could go in and have a cracker. I thought this was a brilliant idea! Mitchell didn't. He continued to steal food from lunches.

Unattached children often have difficulty with speech. Surprisingly, this is often a trust and control issue. Normal young children have speech problems, too, especially if they are resisting something their parents want them to do. For example, when an average child is told to go to bed, the response is apt to be a whining "Do I hafago?" But otherwise, their speech is clear and articulate. Many children with attachment disorder talk this way continually, as if they are in perpetual disagreement. Not only are the sounds they make inarticulate, but their content is often jumbled.

The third part of the pattern concerns issues of self-control. These children have none, and parents and teachers often have severe battles with such children, with the child crying and raging for hours. Nothing the adult does or says seems to help, whether the parent is threatening punishment or complying with the child's wishes. The child might scream, cover her ears, kick out at the parent or others; even when the child is alone in her room, the raging continues. There may be lulls, but as soon as the offending party reappears, the child is off again.

At other times, the battles are more subtle, with the child coming out with shocking, disgusting, or wildly inappropriate statements or actions:

> At times, Nancy is a goof, but it's only when she wants something or she's being threatened. And she does such weird things to be the center of attention. Once we had a group of relative strangers over and John [Nancy's foster brother] had been sharing one of the things that he had done that really pleased him. Well, this group of strangers was laughing and talking about John's experience, and Nancy marched out into the middle of the room and said clear as a bell, "Last week Kenny took me down into the basement and pulled my pants down and played with me." Well, you can imagine the conversation came to a sudden, embarrassed, violent halt. . . . Then Nancy marched over to the sofa and sat there with this smug grin on her face which was a definite "I gotcha!" grin. And the other thing was that her speech was absolutely clear. And you know how Nancy usually talks in her babytalk way. When she said that, it came out clear as a bell!

In the end stage of the pattern, authority figures typically lose their ability to control the child. Parents alternate between cracking down and just giving up. The child lies pathologically. Just as the *Saturday Night Live* character would do, the child lies even when the truth would sound better. I call this type of behavior *primary process lying.* The child almost always knows the difference between the truth and a lie; she just acts as if she doesn't, and she often lies in the face of absolute, present reality. For example, the child may have her hand in her mother's purse. The mother, seeing this, says, "What are you doing with your hand in my purse?" The child answers, "My hand's not in your purse." If caught stealing food, the child says, "What food?" If told to let go of the dog's tail, the child says, "What dog?"

In addition, the child is in constant conflict with family, and indeed with anyone in society who tries to control him: teachers, police, social services, anyone. Rage builds within, and he blames everyone but himself. Yet, deep inside, he has an unconscious recognition that *he* is wrong, that he is the one who is fouled up. He begins to see himself as wrong, made wrong, *bad,* and at war with a world that is right. Very often, the child believes that since he is bad, he will try to be the worst he can be, and will pull outlandish stunts at every turn. He may even identify himself with the forces of evil—praying to the devil, wishing to be Satan's child, and preoccupied with death, fire, blood, and gore:

> It's not that Paula is curious about blood and death on the TV. It's more than that. It scares me. On one of the programs, a baby died. It showed the funeral and the closed casket. Over and over again, Paula asked, "Don't we get to see it? Don't we get to see it? I want to see the baby's dead body."

The child also shows a superficial attractiveness and friendliness with strangers, which is not a normal reaction of most children. She has an uncanny ability to appear bright, loving, helpless, lost, creative—whatever front suits her needs at any time. Strangers, helpful neighbors, and even therapists often see the parents as the problem, which is not only frustrating to the parents, but can put them in a legal bind when the manipulative child twists things so that the parents are accused of child abuse:

> Well, Susie is back home. She ran away and took Sarge [her puppy], and then found a police officer. She actually told him

that I kicked her out of the house and wouldn't let her have her puppy! He read me the riot act. He said that I had tortured her. She told him that we made her tell lies about talking to the devil.

He was so hooked! He tried to get me to promise I would not get rid of the puppy. All this on the phone, mind you. Sarge has been vomiting blood since Susie brought him home. I don't know what she fed the poor thing. I tried to tell the officer that there was a slight chance Sarge wouldn't make it if Susie kept him. I don't think he understood a bit.

One time when she ran away, I know she pulled her seductive act, because when the man brought her home, after questioning me as to my fitness as a mother, he kept looking at me with this surprised look, saying "Are you sure she's eleven? I can't believe that she's only eleven years old." Susie can stir up about any type of fantasy she wants to.

At this point, outsiders who see the family note that the parents are hostile, angry, and frustrated. For years they have been searching for answers that will help them escape the private hell they endure with the child. They have received well-meaning advice that seems to work with other people's children, but not with theirs. The problem has slowly worsened, despite all their efforts, and they have come to doubt their own competence. Added to this pain is the insult of not being believed by friends, teachers, and therapists.

Here is a letter I received from the mother of one such child in Wisconsin:

> I just finished reading an article in August's issue of *Good Housekeeping* magazine, "Kids Who Kill." You see, I'm scared, real scared. I have a fifteen-year-old daughter who has been having troubles since day one.
>
> Even as a toddler she was a very headstrong, defiant, and sneaky child. As she got older, her abusiveness toward herself and her family grew worse. She has attempted suicide four times, three of which she was hospitalized for. She has been known to play with matches at age four and older, and has started small fires.
>
> She has shoplifted and stolen from school, started in about fifth grade. She is a chronic runaway.

She has threatened me with a knife, kicked and knocked me around. She has threatened to kill her older sister and myself with scissors in our sleep. My six-month-old baby—she stated she wanted to harm her when I was pregnant with her. This she stated to hospital staff while she was hospitalized for one of her attempted suicides. She has four counts of battery against her. She has assaulted a police officer. Have you heard enough?

I've tried to get her help. She's been to counselors. One put her on Ritalin, saying she had attention deficit disorder. Her behavior was the same on the drug as it was when she was not taking it.

In May 1988, she ran away from a Shelter-care here in Kenosha. Climbed out of a second-story window. Took off for Chicago, where she was living as a prostitute. For six days I did not know her whereabouts. I began to think the worst. The next day she returned by train, which she was put on by the Chicago police. I've been in and out of court with her.

The last ten months she's been in and out of foster homes and shelter care. We had a hearing in June and the judge wants to return her to my home in August.

I believe they feel justice has been done because she has been out of my home for the past ten months. Also, the catch is I'm on AFDC, and even I can tell you that they're spending too much taxpayers' money on this kid.

Believe me, I dread that day. I look at my daughter and it's like I don't know her. I fear for my safety along with the rest of my family.

How can I even begin to trust a child like that around? I've tried so hard to get something done about her. But no one seems to listen. If she's so irresponsible with her own life, how can I trust her with anyone else's?

Will they believe me or listen when she takes someone else's life or her own?

It scares me so much and hurts me so bad because no one knows the hell that girl has put us through. No one else has lived it.

What can I do? Can I get any other help and get something done about this child? Please, if you can help me, let me know. The weeks before she returns to my home are passing fast. I live in fear for what could happen and because of what she's done in the past. I love her. She's my daughter. But I don't trust her to have her around. And because I know her and what she is capable of, it's hard to be close to her.

Please help me if you can.

Such parents go from therapist to therapist, from school to school, rarely finding long-term help. And as the child becomes older, it becomes ever more difficult to correct the problem. The child's feelings of mistrust are compounded, her rage against control becomes more intense. She is eventually thrust out onto an unsuspecting, too-forgiving society that will have to pay for her treatment, and what she does to others, for the rest of her often-violent life.

The following letter, from a clinical psychologist who recognizes that she was an unattached child, gives a unique perspective on what such a child's young life is like.

My mother and I never connected well. I was a strong-willed child. I was not a boy. I reminded her of her own mother. Although this may be hard for some people to believe, I have clear prenatal memories that she did not want me, resented my presence in her body, and wanted me to die. I had to get born early or else she would have poisoned me. (Not deliberately, but she was toxic from the pregnancy and that was poisoning me.) Following birth, mother was unable to produce enough milk to nurse me and I subsequently contracted a thrush infection which lasted for at least a month or two. Thereafter, my mother developed a serious kidney infection and she was ill for several months.

During the early months I was sometimes cared for by my maternal grandmother, a stiff, non-nurturing person who never felt comfortable holding me, or any of my siblings for that matter. Because of my mother's illness, and the need to care for my two-year-old sister and fifteen-month-old brother, Mom did not have time to hold and feed me. I became enraged and cried much of the time. In fact, I was so angry that when she did take time to hold and feed me, I would not allow her to comfort me. So, there was no early reciprocity. Thus began a cycle that persisted between the two of us for most of my life.

I remember deliberately frustrating my mother by not allowing her to comfort me because I was mad at her about something. Then she would become angry at me and when I cried out to be held, she would yell and refuse. There are movies of me as a small child (about twenty months old) refusing to allow anyone to take pictures of me and turning my back to the camera.

By age four or five I was pretty angry with the whole world and decided that it would serve everyone right if I did the opposite of what they wanted me to do. I set out on a course of behavior whose major purpose was to frustrate and anger as many adults as possible. Particularly adults in authority. With my teachers I was very oppositional. In first grade the teacher told me to write my name at the top of the page and I asked, "Why?" She said, "Because I said so." So I turned the page upside down and wrote my name on the bottom. She took the page from me and said, "I told you to write your name at the top of the page." So I wrote "Your name" at the top of the page.

By fifth grade I had figured out that adults couldn't be trusted and people were always trying to cheat me out of everything, so I was justified in taking whatever I wanted. I stole on a daily basis and taught myself to pick pockets. I had few friends. In seventh grade I was evaluated for therapy, which I felt was a joke. The therapist identified me as a "scapegoat," and although we were in therapy for eighteen months, I never did talk much in the sessions. My parents stopped going, as nothing was helping. This made me even more angry and I decided that I would devote my life to not allowing anyone to have control over me.

In short, I was a typical unattached child who felt *entitled* to do whatever I wanted to do because the world had screwed me over. I cut class and did other naughty things, never believing I could get caught. I often thought about taking one of my father's guns and going around shooting people because no one could catch me. God only knows what would have happened to me if I had continued this type of behavior. I think I would either be in prison or I would be dead.

We will return to this woman's story in a later chapter, as her's is a tale that gives hope to the hundreds of thousands of unattached children and their parents.

2

THE UNATTACHED ADOLESCENT AND ADULT

Hundreds of thousands of adults who were deprived in infancy and childhood, who are reactive attachment disordered, wander America's streets feeling deprived, knowing others have it better, wanting to fill their own void, commiting conscienceless and senseless crimes and mayhem. Typically, these people feel victimized by the world: "I work my fingers to the bone, but I never get back what I really deserve." Feeling this deficiency, these individuals are demanding and bossy. Of course, many people shun them, reinforcing their feelings of deprivation and lack of love. But others, including well-meaning social organizations and government agencies, buy into their victimization routine and provide more to try to fill the bottomless yearning. Ultimately, however, these attempts are futile, since the person with the victimization syndrome simply complains more loudly, "More! Give me more! Do more for me!"

Whatever these individuals do get can never be enough, can never be satisfying. They have sex without ever feeling real intimacy or attachment. They vaguely want a "touching relationship" that they never experienced in infancy. Many young mothers only want to be held; instead, they become pregnant. Others want a baby to love them. They bear child after child in an attempt to fill their own needs, and since they feel so needy, they spend precious little time taking care of the needs of their own children. This sets into motion a generational vicious cycle as their own touch-deprived infants grow to adolescence and produce more children.

Unattached Adolescents and the Criminal Personality

When they grow up, these individuals, when they come in contact with the psychiatric community, are often diagnosed as having Conduct Disorder (CD), Borderline Personality Disorder (BPD), or Antisocial Personality Disorder (APD). Such people end up on the wrong side of the criminal justice system.

A brief look at the characteristics of someone with APD (according to the American Psychiatric Association) gives a professional glimpse of what these teens will become:

Truancy
Run away
Initiation of physical fights
Use of a weapon in more than one fight
Force of another into sexual activity
Physical cruelty to animals or persons
Deliberate destruction of property (other than fire-setting)
Deliberate fire-setting
Frequent lying
Theft
Theft with victimization (e.g., mugging, extortion, armed
    robbery, purse-snatching)
Inconsistent work behavior
Failure to conform to social norms
Irritability and aggressiveness
Failure to honor financial obligations
Failure to plan ahead
Lies and "cons" others for personal profit or pleasure
Reckless regarding his or her own safety
If a parent, lacks ability to function responsibly, raising
    children that show one of the following:
        Malnutrition
        Illness from minimal hygiene
        Failure to obtain medical care when child is sick
        A child dependent on neighbors or relatives for
            food or shelter

> Failure to arrange caretaking when parent is away
> Never sustained a totally monogamous relationship for
>   more than a year
> Lacks remorse and feels justified in having hurt, mis-
>   treated, or stolen from another

Horrible as this may seem, the psychiatric evaluation of a criminal personality can be almost directly extrapolated from the type
of personality shown by even young children with reactive attachment disorder.

As attachment-disordered children become adolescents, they
show a heightened disregard for others and their feelings. Unlike
the fortunate woman whose story ended Chapter 1, most of these
people remain disturbed. They look healthy, but they behave in
threatening, dangerous, destructive ways. The more intelligent and
sneaky they are, the more dangerous they become. They lack conscience, a condition commonly seen in adult psychopaths. From
an early age, they are capable of seriously injuring others without
remorse. They often steal—not just from their parents—and engage
in other antisocial behavior, including running away from home,
setting fires, destroying property, fighting, and using weapons.

As they grow older, they become more difficult to treat, and at
a certain point may actually become unreachable. Their rage
against others becomes too intense to overcome, and even the
strongest methods do not work because the children are too large to
be controlled safely. Despite our best intentions, and the best efforts
of a benign society, these adolescents may simply be lost to us.

Since these teens have no conscience, no connection to other
humans, they are more likely to do serious damage to others. They
frequently go into criminal activity, quickly working their way up
to serious offenses. Since they have never developed a sense of values, they take things because they want them, without thought to
payment, others' loss, or danger to themselves. They are also more
likely to do serious damage to themselves through substance abuse
or other antisocial behavior. They don't care about anyone, themselves included.

One letter I received from a mother in 1990 shows what these teenagers are like. The anguish in this woman's life is obvious:

> Dr. Cline, my husband and I need advice desperately. We adopted a seven-year-old boy who was the son of a niece of ours. She died of cancer, was not married, and no one would take the little boy. Since we had raised four children, and they are all good family people, we thought we could do it one more time. The boy's name is Rusty and he will be fifteen years old on January 22.
>
> We knew Rusty had problems as soon as he came to live with us, so we began counseling immediately. We saw three different counselors during about four years, each one dismissing us, saying Rusty was doing fine and just let them know if we ever felt we needed them. Dr. Cline, the child was no better when we were dismissed than when we started.
>
> We finally found a counselor who helped Rusty and ourselves go through some real bad times, but still he could not get to the real source of things going on inside this child.
>
> When Rusty gave up his only parent, he didn't cry. He said he was glad she died! Of course, we can understand his hurt and pain, but he is almost fifteen years old now and he has never cried about anything! Since we have been raising him we have lost family members and several pets, and he seems to enjoy us crying over the losses we feel.
>
> I read the symptoms listed in the article ["Kids Who Kill"] displayed by most violent children, and Rusty has all of them. He will tell lies when the truth would be easier. Rusty could not cope with regular school, so last year we sent him to San Marcos Baptist Academy. We saw him every month, either we flew him home or we drove down there. We did not want him to feel we did not care! We really do care about this child!
>
> He liked the school last year and so we enrolled him again this year. Only two weeks into the school year we received a call that Rusty was being placed on probation; the reason was receiving and hiding stolen merchandise. One week after Thanksgiving we received a call from the school to come pick him up immediately because he was being dismissed. He had been found stealing money from the lockers in the gym. He stole money even though he had money for whatever he needed always.
>
> We picked him up and took him to our older son's home. Our older son has three sons and is going to try to care for Rusty

until we can place him somewhere. Dr. Cline, my health is very bad and I believe it's all because of the worry over Rusty.

The big problem came in the summer when Rusty was home on vacation. He fondled our five-year-old granddaughter, Wendy. She told her dad and mom. Our family is hurting over this so much. Of course, we are keeping her from him. The sad part is Rusty feels no guilt or remorse about this. On the contrary, he has an enormous amount of anger toward the little girl.

Yesterday while cleaning his room I found a cassette tape he made before he left for school. He starts the tape by saying his full name and date. He called the tape "Code Operation W," meaning, as he said, "to kill Wendy." On this tape he described how he plans to wait until he can get guns and ammo, then he is going to get rid of us, his parents. He talks about building bombs. He said after he gets rid of us, then he will kill Wendy and her parents. We have the tape in a safe place and we have only let our older son hear it. We did not tell Wendy's parents about the tape.

Please, Dr. Cline, who can we go to for help? This child needs more than what we have done so far. We are just average people with limited income. In fact, my husband will be retiring in two years, so our resources are not much.

We really need to know if this threat on the tape was a real mad boy talking or was it something that could spell danger for all of us. Do we have to wait until he really kills or hurts someone before something is done?

The agony of this mother's final question echoes in newspaper headlines. More often than not, parents do have to wait for the child to be prosecuted for a criminal act before "something is done." Very frequently, especially in areas where access to competent psychologists is lacking, the first time these teens are treated in any fashion is when they are put behind bars. And as we have learned, being arrested does not usually turn these kids around. They are taken off the streets, but their underlying character problems are not addressed. When they hit the streets again, they're the same disturbed individuals.

The callousness that these adolescents show about others' suffering is shocking. One recent newspaper article from Milpitas, California, reports a horrible incident that seems to fit the pattern:

A teenager allegedly bragged about killing his fourteen-year-old ex-girlfriend and showed off her corpse to more than a dozen high school classmates, but none of them contacted authorities, officials said Tuesday.

One student covered the body with leaves so it couldn't be seen from the road and others threw rocks at it, said police Sergeant Ron Icely.

Sheriff's Sergeant Gary Meeker, who worked with Icely on the case, said he had "never seen a group of people act so callous about death in my fifteen years of police work. What the hell has happened to these kids?"

Detective Icely, who interviewed thirteen students who went to the site, said the youths were callous and cold, with no apparent feelings for [the victim].

But why should these teenagers care? They have no attachment to anyone else—they don't care about anyone else. Their anger and rage is primary, and very often their initial reaction is to strike out at whatever or whomever frustrates them. And they make no distinction between minor and major grievances—they are just as likely to kill someone over a minor disagreement or for a few dollars as they are when in the midst of a major dispute or crime.

This is why the violent acts of these people seem so senseless. An old woman is found raped and killed in her apartment, and nothing is stolen. One teenager gets into an argument with another at a party, goes home, gets a gun, and comes back and shoots up the party, killing three people. Unknown snipers stand on highway overpasses in Florida and New York and shoot at passing motorists, injuring and killing several. A seventeen-year-old in Baltimore guns down a passerby because he "just wanted to shoot someone."

It is not just the increased incidence of juvenile homicide that reflects this unattached behavior. Conscienceless adolescents and adults are dangerous in other ways. Since nothing that they ever get is enough to fill the void they feel inside, they can never have a lasting relationship with another person. They will suck another person dry—emotionally as well as financially—and then fairly skip down the street to whomever else will take them. Believing always that the other person is at fault, the unattached will tell the new partner massive lies about how the old partner wouldn't listen, wouldn't love, and ruined the relationship. And since it takes painful personal experience to teach the unwary that what you see of the unattached is most certainly not what you get, the unattached have a virtually limitless supply of new victims. In fact, the victims usually don't even know what hit them, and very often end up believing that they, not the unattached, were at fault.

This inability to have a lasting relationship means that the unattached do not hold jobs or live in one place for very long. Eventually, usually sooner rather than later, the unattached pick a fight with a supervisor or landlord, and they are either fired or leave on their own. Unfortunately, this does not put an end to the disagreement, as the unattached may harass their antagonists for some time afterward—vandalizing property, making vicious phone calls, smearing reputations, threatening lawsuits. The victims are first appalled, then angered, and then frightened for their safety as it becomes clear that this person who looked so normal a few months ago is really crazy, and that they have almost no defense against him.

Ted Bundy—An Attachment-Disordered Adult

Ted Bundy, serial killer, is almost a classic case of what can happen when an attachment-disordered child grows up. (Not all unattached children grow up to be killers, but almost all killers evidence the characteristics of the unattached.) Bundy, who charmingly conned more than thirty women into spending their last moments in horror, always saw the problem as lying outside himself. Just before he was executed for his crimes, he blamed pornography for his problems. His interviewer, James Dobson, believed him; many people believed him. He was a very convincing fellow!

What really happened? Before his death, Bundy brushed off his childhood, saying he didn't exactly grow up in a *Leave It to Beaver* family. Indeed! He was left in a foundling home by his mother. He was later told that his mother was his sister and that his grandparents were his parents. When he was three years old, his mother kidnapped him and took him to Seattle.

Ann Rule, an ex-police officer, wrote a book about Bundy called *The Stranger Beside Me*. She wrote of being torn between the facts as her friends on the police force told them, and her gut emotion that kept saying, "Ted couldn't be a killer." Rule told me that Bundy was a wonderful, charming man. "And imagine—I was locked in a building with him!" (At one time she staffed a crisis hotline with him.)

Then she had a dream about Bundy that made her see him as he was, and pointed to the genesis of the problem:

> It was that night, April 1, 1976, when I had the dream. It was very frightening, jarring me awake in a strange room in a strange city. I found myself in a large parking lot, with cars backing out and racing away. One of the cars ran over an infant, injuring it terribly, and I grabbed it up, knowing it was up to me to save it. [How many adoptive parents feel this way?] I had to get to a hospital, but no one would help. I carried the baby, wrapped almost completely in a gray blanket, into a car rental agency. They had plenty of cars, but they looked at the baby in my arms and refused to rent me one. I tried to get an ambulance, but the attendants turned me away. Finally, in desperation, I found a wagon, a child's wagon, and I put the injured infant in it, pulling it behind me for miles until I found an emergency room. I carried the baby, running, up to the desk. The admitting nurse glanced at the bundle in my arms. "No, we will not treat it." "But it's still alive! It's going to die if you don't do something." "It's better. Let it die. It will do no one any good to treat it." The nurse, the doctors, everyone, turned and moved away from me and the bleeding baby. And then I looked down at it. It was not an innocent baby; it was a demon. Even as I held it, it sunk its teeth into my hand and bit me. I did not have to be a Freudian scholar to understand my dream; it was all too clear. Had I been trying to save a monster, trying to protect something or someone who was too dangerous and evil to survive?

Michaud and Aynesworth, in their biography of Bundy, stated that the most accurate self-descriptive sentence they heard Bundy utter was one given to Pensacola police officers: "I'm the most cold-blooded son of a bitch you'll ever meet." In their book, Bundy's borderline personality traits come out strongly. His character is charming, and he is well-spoken. But this veneer hides the true monster within.

Here are Bundy's own words on his feeling of entitlement:

> The big payoff for me was actually possessing whatever it was I had stolen. It wasn't the act, necessarily. Ofttimes I would have to get intoxicated to get loose enough to be able to do it right. Apart from that, I really enjoyed having something on my wall or sitting in my apartment that I had wanted and gone out and taken.

On his lack of conscience:

> I mean, I don't feel guilty for anything! I feel less guilty now than I've felt in any time in my life. About anything. And it's not that I've forgotten anything, or else closed down part of my mind, or compartmentalized. I compartmentalize less now than I ever have.
>
> I guess I am in the enviable position of not having to deal with guilt. There's no reason for it. . . . I feel sorry for people who feel guilt.

But isn't Ted Bundy an extreme example? The danger to society can't be as great as that. Certainly not all unattached children grow up to be cold-blooded killers.

Unfortunately, only the results of Bundy's life are extreme. His early life followed patterns of abuse and neglect that are duplicated in every corner of our country. Every day, according to the Children's Defense Fund, 2,795 teenage girls become pregnant, 848 undersized children are born, 27 children die of poverty, 10 die from gunshots and 30 are wounded, 3 children die of abuse, 211 children are arrested for drug offenses, 1,512 drop out of school, 1,849 are abused or neglected, and 3,288 run away from home. There is an epidemic of children now entering our overburdened schools whose mothers used drugs during pregnancy, causing untold mental and physical damage to the children. Tens of thousands of children are living on the streets, often with no one to care for them. Even in more affluent homes, children are lacking parental guidance, as both parents (if there are two parents) work, leaving their children to be watched by others or by the television. Chapter 3 will discuss the ultimate costs to society of allowing children to grow up sick.

As these children reach childbearing age, those who are not removed from society by justice or violence will pass on what they have learned to their kids. (Although the reactive attachment disorder impairs an individual's capacity to form loving relationships, it does not in the least inhibit sexual desire. In fact, because of the shallowness of relationships and lack of conscience, coupled with the inability to plan ahead, the individual has more unprotected sex with more people, producing more children.) They will do to their children what was done to them. They will likely deprive their children at the worst possible time, whether to go buy drugs, or to go out with a friend, or just because they can't take the child's screaming anymore. Their children will probably grow up in poverty, feeling deprived, underserved by the government and other agencies, and starting a new cycle themselves. Thus, the crisis will be compounded as, generation by generation, the number (and percentage of the population) of people who are dangerously disturbed continues to grow. And we don't seem to be doing anything to stop the trend.

3

THE COST TO *YOU*

A generation of unattached children. What does it mean to society? And why should you be concerned?

Drain on Public Treasuries

There are compelling reasons why we should be worried about these children, on both a societal and a personal level. From the moment they are born, these children need special attention. Those who are born addicted to alcohol or cocaine are invariably far underweight, and neonatal intensive care units have to struggle to keep them alive during their withdrawal. Their health care must be heroic, involving high-technology, high-cost machines and monitors. The parents of many of these children are teenagers and poor, and have no means to pay for their infants' care. The cost is borne by the public.

When the children are released from the hospital, they generally face stressors such as hunger, neglect, abuse, and poverty, which have been found to exacerbate developmental problems. Thus, although these children might have been able to catch up with other children by age four given good nutrition, health, and stimulation, the lack of all three puts them farther behind their chronological mates.

When they are old enough to go to school, they require speech and other therapy to overcome disabilities, tutors, psychologists, and other professionals. In general, taxpayer dollars are spent to cover these costs, as these children are usually enrolled in public schools. In fact, many school districts, both urban and suburban, are being impoverished because laws mandate that these children be given the opportunity to learn. A single school district can spend millions of dollars trying (too often in vain) to correct the problems of unattached children, money that could otherwise be used to raise the educational standards of the rest of the students.

Unattached children also disrupt classes, ruining education for other children, and take up expensive administrative time. Teachers who have these children in their classes have to spend inordinate amounts of time with them, to the detriment of the other students. Most teachers cannot handle these children—they have no concept of their problems, and they may not be allowed to take the measures necessary to deal with them. Here is the story that one teacher who took my workshop on bonding techniques told me about a pair of first-graders:

Ashley lived with her father, stepmother, and stepsister. There was abuse in the family—sexual and physical—and the family drifted back and forth between Colorado and Oklahoma. Ashley would live at times with grandparents. Dad was frequently out of work.

Ashley had been an ongoing behavior problem at school when the following episode occurred. I had never heard of bonding therapy at the time, but I believe some of those techniques may have been used to diffuse the situation, out of instinct for survival rather than from knowledge.

In the principal's absence, Martha, the librarian, and I were designated "persons in charge." We both were skilled and successful with children in a school fraught with student discipline problems, and with abuse, neglect, crime, and illiteracy of the parents.

Ashley and her new friend Justin had been referred to the office by a substitute teacher because of disruptive behavior in their first-grade classroom. The principal was out of the building, and the school secretary was unable to keep the two children quiet or confined to a designated area of the office.

Martha had attempted to help by taking the children to the library to supervise them in separate areas of the room but within her vision. The children refused to stay seated or quiet, and Martha, appalled by her own lack of effectiveness, had called for my help.

When I walked into the situation, it was already out of control. Ashley was dancing through the checkout area, yelling, "I fucking well don't have to sit down. I can do as I fucking please, and you fucking well can't stop me, you fucking teachers."

Justin was running around the library trying to get the other children to join him. He was yelling, "This is my life, and I can live it as I fucking want to, and you fucking teachers can't stop me, and you better leave me alone, fucking girl."

Martha was adamant that no one should touch the children for risk of a lawsuit. At this point I asked her to call the principal back to school.

I took Ashley by the arm and asked her to sit down and wait with me for the principal. She told me to get my fucking hands off her. She ran to the outside door, opened it, and started to run outside. I stopped her and stood in front of the door so she couldn't leave. She kept trying to pull me away from the door so she could get out.

Justin had taken his belt off and ran across the library to hit me. On his second swing, I dragged the belt away and put it in the pocket of my blazer. He repeatedly charged at me and kept grabbing at my pocket to retrieve his belt, calling me "fucking bitch" and "fucking girl" and pulling at my clothes while I tried to keep Ashley from running out the door into the busy street. Martha stood by and watched, along with the three-hundred-pound custodian. The children ran from door to door trying to get out, but the three of us kept the doors blocked.

Justin tried to get Ashley to call 911 to get someone to "come out and get rid of these teachers." Several times both children threatened that they would "have our jobs."

Finally, the principal arrived. She tried to talk to the children in her usual stern and effective manner, but they were extremely disrespectful to her as well.

The first time Justin called her a "motherfucker," she grabbed him up in her arms and started toward the office. I took my cue from her and carried Ashley. They were both kicking and screaming obscenities, and teachers were peering out every classroom door along the way.

Jean held Justin while she called both their parents. He was kicking and stabbing her with his pencil. The custodian grabbed the pencil, and Justin threatened to "kick your penis off." Every time I tried to put Ashley down, she tried to run out of the room, so I held her on my lap. She was screaming so loudly that I held her very tightly and finally covered her mouth with my hand. I told her I wouldn't release my grip until she stopped struggling and screaming. To my surprise, after she did eventually stop, she passively sat on my lap until someone came in and relieved me so I could go back to my class.

After a three-day suspension, Ashley returned to school. Ashley's teacher made it a point to send Ashley to my classroom periodically on various pretenses. Ashley always entered the room very cautiously and visibly trembling, but after each initial contact she seemed to relax. Every time I saw her on the playground, she always spoke shyly and stood nearby. I can't help wondering now if this might have been the threshold of a bonding that could have taken place had I possessed the time, knowledge, and skill necessary.

I now can believe that perhaps I did do the right things that day, even though I'll never know for sure and the system would never support what I did. The "right thing" only works if there is adequate follow-up. I doubt if there was.

In conclusion, I find this incident comes back to haunt me periodically, perhaps because the idea of not being able to control a first-grader seems so ludicrous, or perhaps because the final outcome is unknown to me. But then, teachers are often not told what happens to children they refer for help. These cases have a way of disappearing into the great abyss of social service bureaucracy, and the scenario is repeated.

Ashley would be about eleven years old now, just about old enough to get pregnant and begin the cycle all over again.

These children drain our public treasuries in other ways. An unattached child may wreck one foster home and be shipped off to another, and then another. Each time this happens, government agencies incur expenses. Caseworkers must be paid salaries, and the more unattached children there are, the more caseworkers there will be. If the children run away, the police must track them down and bring them back, sometimes involving searches across state boundaries. Even if the children remain in one foster home, their cases must be followed by social workers and psychologists, with the concomitant stacks of paperwork that must be processed by teams of clerks and computers.

When these children become teenagers, many of them repeat

the life cycle of their parents. Angry at the world, with an aching need inside that can never be filled, they seek solace in drugs, alcohol, sex, and crime. They become teenage parents who are hooked on crack, uneducable, and unable and unwilling to work. Thus, they remain wards of the forgiving state, have children, and start the wheel of addiction, abuse, and dependency turning once again.

Government coffers are being drained at an astounding rate to feed, clothe, and house these teenage mothers and their children. From Aid to Families with Dependent Children (AFDC) to Social Security to Medicaid to drug rehab centers to social workers, these programs show the welfare state running wild. The "safety net" that politicians and bureaucrats are so fond of describing as catching only those "truly in need," each year is responsible for holding more people (and a larger percentage of the population). AFDC now totals more than $25 billion a year, and the food stamp program adds another $20 billion. Of the states' total expenditures of about $550 billion, approximately 24 percent, or some $132 billion, goes for welfare or corrections.

Of course, not all of this money is spent on the seriously disturbed, but as the number of these individuals grows, a larger share of the money will be appropriated either for helping them or for keeping them locked up. In the very near future, money will be siphoned from other useful programs to try to fill the bottomless pit that will be government programs related to the unattached.

At the same time that appropriations for this population are leapfrogging, expenses for other programs are growing, too. Our population is aging, and extra money is needed for Social Security, Medicare, and pension funds. Coming changes in the health care system will eat up not only money but bureaucratic attention. The long-neglected educational needs of the country must be addressed. And Americans, though seemingly resigned to higher income taxes in the short term, have never been willing to commit to tax rates that would fund all "necessary" programs to their requirements.

Therefore, the tens of billions of dollars needed to cope with the millions of conscienceless individuals who will be threatening our institutions in the twenty-first century will have to come at the expense of other elements in society. Innocent citizens will be victimized two ways: once by the uncaring beings stalking them in their cities and suburbs, and again by the loss of public funds that would otherwise benefit themselves or their children.

Here is the crux of the issue for government. One of its main functions is to distribute limited funds among competing interests. In a democracy like ours, those matters that are deemed most important by the voters (or their representatives) receive greater funding. Fighting crime continually appears near the top of the list of most desirable government activities in opinion polls; teaching (or enforcing) family planning and how to rear normal children garners scant attention. Expect more billions of dollars to flow toward the symptom—juvenile and adult crime—while the almost invisible cause of the symptom, poor early child care, goes untreated. Sadly, this will produce only spiraling law enforcement budgets, because although conviction rates are increasing and the police are becoming better at their jobs, by not reaching the infants at risk, far too many new criminals are being created every day for the system to keep up.

Think of the productive elements of society that could be helped with the money that will be spent coping with these destructive citizens. What advances in curing diseases such as cancer, AIDS, and multiple sclerosis could scientists make? How many thousands more high school graduates would be able to afford higher education through increased college loan programs? What number of job-retraining programs could be funded? On a state level, how much more money would be freed for primary education, or for public transportation, or for increased health coverage? Locally, how many more potholes could be filled? How many more parks could be upgraded? How many more day care centers could be opened?

Or look at it this way—how much lower would all of our taxes be if we didn't have to pay for the identification, care, therapy, apprehension, prosecution, and incarceration of millions of conscienceless people?

Unattached Individuals Make Us All Victims

Besides the monetary costs to us all, there are more personal costs that are harder to quantify. As described in Chapter 2, the personality of the attachment-disordered child is very close to that of someone with Antisocial Personality Disorder—a basic criminal personality type. Thus, the most visible effect on each of us of a generation of conscienceless children is the increase in crimes committed by these individuals—burglaries, carjackings, drug abuse, rapes, assaults, arson, and murders.

More and more Americans are becoming victims. In too many neighborhoods, being robbed or assaulted is almost a given. It is estimated that one out of every four women in the United States will be raped sometime in her life. The Federal Bureau of Investigation crime statistics show that about six of every one hundred Americans are victimized each year, and this rate has increased every year since 1982. A 1989 Department of Justice study showed that nine percent of children from ages twelve to nineteen reported being attacked *at school!*

And such attacks are increasingly violent. Senselessly violent. Instead of a simple carjacking, the victim is assaulted, too. Instead of a picked pocket, a man loses his wallet and is pushed in front of an oncoming car. Instead of just arguing with an ex-lover, a man buys a gun, stalks the woman, and then kills her.

We read these headlines and shake our heads in wonder. If a mugger wants to take money, why does he have to take a life, too? What drives a person to not only take someone else's possessions, but to destroy that person's life as well? And when these criminals are caught, how can they show no remorse? How can they smile for the cameras while their heinous deeds are catalogued in court?

The answer to these questions can be simply stated: These criminals are seriously disturbed people who don't care—cannot care—about anyone. They are enraged at society in general, and at just about anyone whom they meet. To them, there is no boundary between moral and immoral actions—there is no distinction between bad and worse. Killing is the same as knocking someone down; both are striking out against the hated enemy.

As these people have grown up, the effects of their lack of bonding in infancy have been accentuated by other life problems. These people don't have many friends, as they are generally anti-social or drive away those who would be friendly. They cannot handle another person having authority over them, and so have a difficult time in school and at work.

The disappointments in life add up. Some of them may actually be caused by other people: perhaps the disturbed individual deserved the promotion given to a co-worker, or maybe a lover embarrassed her in front of others. But most of the incidents will be of the individual's own manufacture. Having no ability to work with others, and no real desire to do so, they drift from job to job, with each firing being someone else's fault. Relationships never last long, and are never satisfying, for the other person can never fill the void felt by the individual with an attachment disorder. Soon, the other person realizes the problems the unattached individual has. Just as in childhood, when the disturbed child would chase away playmates with aggressive behavior, so are adult friends chased away by lies, manipulations, and erratic behavior. If the friend is lucky, he or she will escape with only a minimum of abuse. If unlucky, the friend will be stalked, harassed, perhaps beaten, and maybe killed.

This rage, this lack of feeling for other humans, translates into other costs for the rest of us. Because these people were essentially lost when they were infants, there are more stolen goods that must be replaced, more property damage that must be made good, more injured people who need emergency care and hospital beds, more people—victims as well as perpetrators—who require psychiatric help, more schools and businesses that must install expensive security apparatus. Sadly, these costs are becoming ingrained: instead of solving the root causes of our problems, we simply shoulder the burden as if it were the price we have to pay to live in modern America.

This is not a new phenomenon. In her book *Within Our Reach,*

Lisbeth Schorr cited University of Pennsylvania criminologist Marvin Wolfgang's studies of juvenile crime in Philadelphia. Wolfgang compared ten thousand children born in that city in 1945 to a similar group born in 1958. He found that about six percent of both groups were hard-core delinquents who committed more than fifty percent of the crimes of each group. The major difference between the groups was that those adolescents born in 1958 committed crimes that were far more serious than those of the group born in 1945. Those who became adolescents in the 1970s committed twice as many aggravated assaults and burglaries, three times as many murders, and five times as many robberies as their counterparts who came of age in the 1950s. As Wolfgang noted, whereas robbery victims previously escaped with slight injuries, now they are ending up dead or in the hospital: "People are getting their heads bashed in and seriously hurt in ways that didn't happen before."

Anecdotal evidence agrees with academic studies. Claude Brown, the author of *Manchild in the Promised Land,* said that the biggest difference between the Harlem of today and that of the 1950s, when he was growing up there, is the wanton violence. Returning to his neighborhood to try to learn the reasons for the senseless killings, Brown interviewed a number of teenagers. One sixteen-year-old told him, "That's what they do now. . . . You know, you take their stuff and you pop 'em." Stunned by these revelations, Brown wrote that the teenagers he talked with told him that "murder is in style now."

The long-range damage to neighborhoods is well-chronicled in the media: when an area is overrun by the unattached, good people who can leave get out. Those who can't leave imprison themselves behind barred windows and multilocked doors, venturing out only when necessary. Police make raid after raid, but the drugs and the crime keep coming back.

What violence caused by the seriously disturbed does to families and individuals cannot even be calculated. What happens to a person's psyche when his or her family is wiped out by drug use or gunfire? How does a young child change when he can't go to school without being shaken down for his lunch money or his jacket? What is it like to live in fear twenty-four hours a day?

A greater percentage of Americans are finding out the answer to the last question. Jan and Marcia Chaiken, who study crime for the Rand Corporation, write, "Crime, like television, has come into the living room—and into the church, the lobbies of public buildings, the parks, the shopping malls, the bus stations, the airport parking lots, the subways, the schools. . . . Crime and the fear of crime have spread from 'traditional' high crime areas into once-serene urban neighborhoods, from the central city to outlying suburbs and towns, and into summer resorts and college campuses." And *Washingon Post* editorial writer Ronald White has written, "Every time I realize that I have not enjoyed the cool night air nor marveled at a full moon, I know that one does not have to be robbed at gunpoint to be a victim of crime."

These questions cannot be shrugged off anymore as problems of the inner city, for the seriously disturbed are with all of us. Every state has its own Jeffrey Dahmer, its own Colin Ferguson. Every county has its own disruptive teens who go beyond mere juvenile delinquency. And every town has its own broken families, abusive parents, and drug users who are raising their own conscienceless children.

Law enforcement and the justice system are costing taxpayers billions of dollars. The FBI spends $2 billion a year out of a total Justice Department budget of about $8.5 billion, and this is nowhere near the total federal crime expenditure. Around the country, fully 750,000 Americans are employed by law enforcement agencies, meaning billions more in salaries, benefits, and pensions before the first traffic citation is issued. Conservative evaluations of the prison system state that it costs $20,000 a year to pay for the incarceration of each inmate when the costs of food, maintenance, guards' pay, and so on are factored in. Hundreds of millions of dollars are spent each year by federal and state authorities to build more jails for the ever-expanding prison population (now more than 1 million).

The reason for the explosive growth in prison population mirrors the reason for the growth in abandoned babies cited by Dr. Fontana—drugs. In 1981, about 113,000 people were put in jail altogether, and about 11,500 of these were for drug offenses. In 1989, of the 298,000 people put in jail, almost 88,000 were for drug offenses. And these figures tell only a fraction of the tale: of every 1,000 people arrested, only 70 go to jail.

When asked what problem they see coming toward them in the next few years, police departments in every corner of the nation say "drugs." They recognize in a way that most citizens do not that the troubles afflicting our cities will not stay there. Ours is an open, mobile society in which bad as well as good can cross borders easily and quickly. There is no "us" and "them" anymore. The problems of one group or one area affect us all.

The concerns raised in this chapter go directly to the heart of quality of life in our country. After three decades of intense government involvement in improving the lives of all Americans, we are arguably no better off than when we started. The percent of people living in poverty has risen back to where it was in the early 1960s, and the number of children in poverty is skyrocketing. Perhaps a million or more people walk the streets with no place to call home; many have severe psychological or medical problems. Crime is increasing; people in neighborhoods around the country are scared. After thirty years and billions of dollars spent in the "war on drugs," our country appears to be the largest drug supermarket in the world. Talk to people from even the smallest towns today about how things have changed and you are apt to hear, "Well, we never *used* to lock the doors around here. . . ."

At the beginning of this chapter, I posed these questions about unattached children: What does it mean to society? And why should you be concerned? The unattached among us are hidden— they have no distinguishing marks, no telltale signs to identify them. Thus, the breadth and depth of the problem is hidden. We are getting the first inklings of the immensity of what faces us in the offices of psychologists, social workers, and government agencies, where professionals are asking, "Where are all these empty, angry people coming from?" It is being reported, in a fragmented way, in our news media. People who read the news with a critical eye are starting to make the connection between rising crime rates among younger and younger children and how we are raising our children. The nation is realizing that the conservative battle cry of "family values," previously used to bludgeon political opponents, probably has more merit than the politicians know.

Unfortunately, as a nation we are still groping in the dark. We continue to attack the symptoms of the problem, not the root causes. And we continue to enable the unattached, allowing them to go on and create a new generation of conscienceless. Unless we change how society deals with seriously disturbed individuals, our schools will be overwhelmed, our jails will be overflowing, and our governments will be bankrupted. It will be a marvel if we don't see a virtual police state in many localities around the country. It will be the only way to deal with the problem.

In the next part of this book, we will begin to study how we have come to this pass as a society. We will investigate exactly what causes children to grow up conscienceless, from drug addiction in the womb to societal influences. Once we have laid the matter bare, we can look at how to combat the problem.

Part 2

THE CREATION OF CONSCIENCELESS CHILDREN

4

THE FIRST YEARS

Since the root cause of consciencelessness in an individual is disruption in the bonding that takes place during gestation, infancy, and early toddlerhood, we must look at how attachment occurs and how the brain develops to understand how we must treat severely disturbed individuals. This understanding will cast light on adult behavior that is seldom visualized as dependent on bonding. However, once we start thinking in terms of attachment and bonding, "normal" behavior, psychopathology, and therapeutic options can all be seen in a more productive way.

How Bonding Occurs

Generally, bonding is possible between individuals—of any age and for good or bad—when one of them is in a position of helplessness and the other is in a position of helpfulness or authority. One person is in pain or agony, either physically or psychologically; he has an overwhelming need that must be met. The other person fulfills this need by giving food, love, care, shelter, and so on. The need is elemental; if it is not fulfilled, the needy one has no hope for the future. The helper rescues the needy one from this bleak situation, and the rescued one attaches to the rescuer both physically and psychically.

The first time in life that this occurs is with the fetus in the womb: everything that the fetus receives—food, stimulation, protection, warmth—comes from her mother. The fetus can hear, too—many parents talk about how their very young infants recognize songs the mothers sang before the children were born.

After birth, the most recognizable situation promoting bonding—and the one that evokes the greatest emotional reaction—is when the child is hungry. The infant does not know the concept "hungry"; she only knows that her body aches for something. She responds in the only way she can, and begins to cry. As her hunger builds, the baby can be said to go through feelings of helplessness, anger, and hopelessness, which together form rage. Since this is a survival issue, her rage reaction is total and oceanic. Screams resound throughout the house.

Enter a parent to rescue her. Talking to the child with a soothing voice, the parent picks up the infant, holds her, caresses her, rocks her, gives her food. While the baby is sucking, she focuses on her parent's face, locking eyes. Her parent smiles at her, and the baby smiles back.

With these few simple steps, parents accomplish a number of things. They satisfy their child's need for food. They give other sensory inputs that the child will forever after associate with love and satisfaction: skin-to-skin touch, soft voice, close eye contact. Think of the rituals of dating in the teen years and beyond, of becoming friends with someone else: "Jason, would you like to go out for dinner?" "Susan, would you and Tom like to come over for some drinks?" What is laid down in infancy carries on for a lifetime.

The reciprocal smile between parent and child is the beginning of a loving bond for the child. The child makes a connection between herself and another being, and she learns that such a connection is good. When the baby smiles, her mother and father smile back and do things that she likes—cooing, cuddling, playing. This loving interaction will stay with the child forever.

As for eye contact, researchers agree that it is an important aspect of the child's early development. At about five days of life, the nursing baby's eyes lock on to her parent; at ten days, the baby tracks her parent's eyes as they move back and forth. Later in life, such eye contact will be equated with high self-concept and truthfulness, two highly prized characteristics in any individual.

By rocking their baby, parents also assure that the baby's brain and nervous system will develop properly. Labyrinthine stimulation—the movement of inner-ear fluid against the tiny hairs there—gives the infant a sense of movement and direction change. This is the same sensation that makes older children and adults scream with excitement when riding million-dollar amusement park roller coasters. What is fun for adults and children is essential for normal neurological development in infancy. Thus, the beauty of a parent absentmindedly bouncing a baby on his or her knee; the parent is not only doing what comes naturally, but is helping to assure the child's normal brain development.

This is of the utmost importance, for both brain and personality are forming together during infancy. During gestation and throughout the first two years of life, the brain is in a sense being "hard-wired"; billions of cells are making trillions of connections. Each cell has its own "address" in the brain, so if connections are made haphazardly, the brain will not function correctly. Studies have shown that these connections can be facilitated by love and affection, and disturbed by abuse and neglect. It is a rare child who will not show learning and cognitive disorders if abused during the time of early brain maturation.

Every day, almost every hour, parents come to the child's aid, and the baby learns to trust her parents. Whether she is hungry, afraid, in pain, lost, frustrated, or just lonely, mother or father can rescue her. The infant learns that she can depend on her parents, that she can trust her parents to take care of her.

This is the basis for bonding for an infant—the closeness of a parent, the satisfaction of needs, the development of trust. Children who make such attachments at a very early age usually go on to trust themselves, to trust the people around them, and to trust humanity in general. These people tend to live their lives in a relaxed manner because they have a positive outlook. They assume that things will turn out well, and are accepting when things go poorly. They assume that the people with whom they come in contact are doing right unless the opposite is proven.

While the infant is developing trust in her parents and then generalizing that trust to other people, she is also developing a conscience, which is actually caring about other people and understanding that one's actions affect others. As discussed in Chapter 1, early in life the child learns that her actions affect how her parents react: when mom is happy, good things happen—I get fed, or cuddled, or smiled on. When mom is angry, bad things happen—she yells at me or even spanks me. The child learns that she has an investment in doing the right things—what her parents tell her to do—in order to keep her parents happy.

As she grows, the child goes through predictable stages in rounding out her conscience. Stage 1 usually falls between the ages of twelve and twenty-seven months. At this time, the child's actions are simple responses to needs or wants: "I want to do it, so I'll do it." There is no thought to consequences, no consideration of danger to self or others, no understanding of others' feelings. As the child pulls tables down or spills paint or plunges her fist into the cake, she begins to learn that if she does something wrong, the result is unpleasant—a scolding or worse. Pretty soon, the child enters Stage 2 (from about age two to three), in which her thinking might be "I would do it, but my parents would yell at me if I did." This causative thinking, although primitive and inaccurate, leads the child into Stage 3 (late in the third year to age five), when her thinking changes to "I would do it, but my parents might find out." Now the child is thinking things through, weighing the risks and benefits of her actions.

At this point, the child is really starting to stretch her physical and mental limits. Her parents typically encourage her with a "Good for you!" or caution her with a "Honey, be careful." The child learns that when she does something thoughtlessly, bad things can happen (she can fall and get hurt); when she thinks about things and accomplishes something, good things happen and other people are happy. This interaction with her parents teaches the child two emotions—guilt and pride—and one important thought pattern—acceptance of responsibility. Again, as with the rocking and feeding that assuaged her hunger pangs, these associations will follow her through her life.

In Stages 2 and 3, the brake on the child's actions is external—fear of what her parents will do. A big step occurs when the child reaches Stage 4 at about six or seven years old. "I would do it, but if my parents found out, they would be upset" might run through the child's mind. The child is now connected to the outside world—how another person feels is important to herself. The kernel of conscience is well developed at the age of five or six when the child begins to want to do the right thing on her own. Finally, by age eleven, the child reaches Stage 5—a fully developed conscience. When presented with the opportunity to do wrong, the child thinks, "I don't feel good about doing something like that."

Now the child appears to have a complete conscience. She is attached to her parents and the world around her. She is no longer concerned only with her wants and needs; she understands that there are larger concerns in the world, such as the good of a group. She is well on her way to becoming a functioning member of society.

How Bonding Is Broken

Luckily, for most American children, the stages of conscience formation are followed without a misstep. However, for hundreds of thousands of other children, the fragile thread that ties the stages together is snapped in infancy and early childhood, and conscience formation and trust in others is broken. The incidence of this all-too-common occurrence in our society is rising with the increasing numbers of children of drug users, teenage mothers, and abusive parents who are not able to provide for their children's needs. These children never learn that other people are important to them, and they never learn to trust other people. They do not attach to a parent or anyone else; they feel no closeness to anyone; they do not bond. If they are seen by a psychologist, they may be diagnosed as having reactive attachment disorder.

As John Robertson found out in the Tavistock Child Development Centre, the chain of development is weaker than most of us think. (See Chapter 1.) At one time it was believed that childhood grief was short-lived; that a young child soon got over the loss of (or abandonment by) a parent. Now we recognize that such a loss affects the youngster for years. As John Bowlby, an associate of Robertson's, discovered, the loss of a parent for even a short time has lasting impact on the child. In the course of studying how children react to losing parents, he followed a two-year-old girl, Laura, who was hospitalized for eight days for surgery. He recounted her loss and her desperate crying for her mother. When the child returned home, she seemed to become her old self. Six months went by. One night, as the family was watching the film of Laura leaving the hospital, Laura became agitated. Screaming, "Where was you all the time, Mommy? Where was you?" she turned angrily away from her mother and ran to her father for comfort.

It takes no great leap of intuition to realize that if there are lasting effects from such a short separation, the effects of long-term loss must be shattering to children. Indeed, it is these children whom Bowlby and other psychiatrists have characterized as unreachable:

> On the immense task set by the treatment of the affectionless and delinquent character, all psychiatrists are agreed. Because of their almost complete inability to make relationships, the psychiatrist is robbed of his principal tool . . . he has yet to learn methods of affecting for the better patients who had no feelings for him at all. . . . The failure in treatment of all those who had suffered rejection or had never had a loving relationship recalls Dr. Goldfarb's remark that he has never seen "even one example of significantly favorable response to treatment by traditional methods of child psychiatry." Another doctor goes so far as to say that "once the defect is created it cannot be corrected," and recommends that methods of care should make no attempt to cure or correct, but should be protective and should aim to foster a dependent relationship."

Perhaps nothing can replace the lost parent. In the 1940s, Renee Spitz studied two groups of children: one group raised from birth in a foundling home where each child was attended by a nurse who was responsible for eight to twelve children, the other group raised in a nursery where each child was cared for by his mother. Both settings offered adequate nutrition and excellent care and housing, but the children coming out of the two were radically different:

> While the children in "Nursery" developed into normal, healthy toddlers, a two-year observation of "Foundling-home" showed that the emotionally starved children never learned to speak, to walk, to feed themselves. With one or two exceptions in a total of ninety-one children, those who survived were human wrecks who behaved in a manner of agitated or apathetic idiots.

Others backed up Spitz's findings. Mussen and Conger wrote in 1956 that infants who had excellent physical care but poor emotional care exhibited persistent language and speech difficulties, behavior problems, overt expression of anxiety (restlessness, hyperactivity, inability to concentrate), aggression (temper tantrums, impudence, destructiveness, antagonism, and cruelty), and emotional impoverishment. Tests revealed that "long after they had been placed with families, institution children were still less mature, less self-controlled, more passive and apathetic, less persistent in goal-directed activities, and less willing to conform to social customs. Most of them did not develop strong or affectionate personal attachments, but remained emotionally cold and isolated, capable of only the most superficial interpersonal relationships."

These scientific studies are important, but it does not take an advanced degree in psychology or years of clinical practice to understand what breaks the formation of conscience in very young children. All we need do is look at what is happening to our young people in our cities and suburbs. Drug and alcohol abuse are rising, as is the number of babies being abused and neglected. A feeling of entitlement seems to be sweeping the country, and people are less inclined to take responsibility for their own actions. Families are being broken up at a terrific rate. Parents are turning over responsibility for their children to surrogates—the schools, baby sitters, television. Random violence not only takes the lives of parents, but threatens the development of whole neighborhoods of children. Poverty and lack of education and job skills are dooming children to repeat the cycle of neglect that they have suffered.

Let us investigate these life challenges from the child's point of view to see how they combine to short-circuit the bonding cycle and create a conscienceless child.

The Path to a Conscienceless Child

There are many life paths that can lead a child to a conscienceless existence, but the most insidious hurdle for any newborn is substance abuse by the mother while the child is yet unborn. Every day in our newspapers we read stories about drug raids, dealers taking over neighborhoods, international drug cartels, and the like. These high-profile cases frequently involve dozens of people, hundreds of millions of dollars, various enforcement agencies, and top-level spokespeople. If it's good news, officials come from everywhere to have their pictures taken and to say a few words about how we are winning the war on drugs. If it's bad news, community leaders come out to castigate the government or the police, presenting the case for how terrible life is under the sway of the druglords.

But who hears about the battles to control substance abuse among mothers and fetuses? This is not the high-tech blitzkrieg of the Gulf War; this is akin to the trench warfare of World War I, in which gains are measured in yards, not miles. The theater for this war is often a large hospital in city or suburb, rich community or poor, to which a young drug addict has come to give birth to her child. Perhaps she has seen a doctor before, perhaps not. Certainly, her diet has been terrible, because her desire to stay high far outweighs her feelings of responsibility toward her child. There are publicly funded programs that could help her clean up and give her child a good start, but she doesn't know about them or forgot about them, and really doesn't care about them. The woman comes to the hospital on her own, or with a family member or a friend—rarely with the father. Perhaps she hasn't even told the father.

The child is born, often very prematurely and seriously underweight—he might weigh only three pounds. Often, there are obvious physical birth defects; more frequently, the defects are subtle.

Because of the premature birth and the in utero stresses, something inside the baby is not right. It might be a malfunctioning valve in the heart, or a ruined kidney, or a breakdown in the brain. Very often, cocaine babies have strokes shortly before birth. Immediately, the child is placed in the neonatal intensive care unit, hooked up to a respirator, an IV, a catheter, and a monitor. There is no chance for the child to lay with the mother, to feel skin against skin, to be fed by someone who loves him. There is only the constantly changing shift of nurses and aides.

The child, like any addict deprived of his substance, must go through withdrawal. This is a terrible thing to watch, as the helpless newborn twitches uncontrollably and cries out in pain. Nothing can stop this pain—neither feeding nor cuddling—so even if the mother could care for the child, there would be next to nothing she could do. Finally, the fits pass, but the residual effects of the cocaine do not. The child cannot make smooth transitions from sleeping to waking. He "startles" awake and starts crying at a feverish pitch. While awake, he isn't alert and responsive—he cries until he is exhausted and falls asleep.

After two months in the hospital, the child is deemed well enough to go home.

Two months old. What milestones have passed in the confines of the pediatric ward with no caring mother or father! The hours of eye contact and smiles that the child has missed. The hundreds of feedings that have been given by tube or by a nurse with fifteen other babies to care for. The cuddling, the finger play, the rocking the child has been denied. All of these things that encourage attachment and normal brain development in infants, and which start them on their way to developing conscience, have been lacking.

What the child has gotten from this period is a feeling of deprivation. And because of the rage, rejection, and depression the child feels, his body produces chemicals that skew the neurological connections that are being made rapidly at the time. This produces lifelong deficits, as the trauma a sapling encounters is reflected in its subsequent growth.

The child comes home, and the mother has made the best

of her situation. Family members have given her presents in the hopes that the young mother will be able to cope. Perhaps the mother, having made a promise to get off drugs for her baby, has managed to keep that promise through all the temptations of these two months, and the first few days go well. The young mother, who might be only fourteen herself, does her level best, but what parenting skills can a child have? How can she know that she has to turn the baby while he is sleeping, sing to him, hold him while she feeds him, smile at him, cover him, check on him in the night? And how can she be expected to know how to care for an already damaged child, or to have the patience that the child needs?

Soon enough, the baby cries and keeps on crying. The mother, having run through her limited repertoire of solutions, snaps. In one terrible scenario, she dunks the baby in a scalding bath because he won't stop wailing. In another, she walks out, leaving the baby alone while she goes out for a break or to get high.

Instead of learning to trust, the child learns that he cannot trust. He is hungry, and no one feeds him. He is bored, and no one plays with him. He cries, and he is told to shut up. The world has no constancy for the child; he receives less attention, less food, less stimulation than he did in the hospital.

Now the child is six months old, and his chance for easy bonding with someone is practically gone. When his mother does try to hold him, he refuses eye contact, his eyes wandering all over the room and never seeming to rest on any one thing for long. He seems all elbows and knees, pushing away from his mother rather than cuddling in. This makes his mother furious and resentful, reinforcing her negative behavior toward him.

At some point, the mother goes back on drugs (if she ever quit). Her life is no better since the baby was born—of course, it's worse. Having a baby doesn't make her special anymore; in fact, the kid is a drag. She can't go out, she can't have parties anymore, she *always* has to be there for the damned child! Not understanding or caring that being responsible for a child is a twenty-four-hour-a-day job, she begins to leave her child alone; at first for a few minutes to score some crack, and then for longer periods. One night, she doesn't come home at all. Neighbors hear the baby crying, the authorities are called, the child is taken to a shelter. There the cigarette burn marks are discovered, and the mother is arrested for abuse, neglect, abandonment, and possession of drugs.

So the child experiences his first loss of family—another break in the attachment cycle. His mother, poor caregiver as she was, is gone, and he is taken to new surroundings. To observers, it seems curious that he doesn't cry when he is taken away to a new home, but there is little reason for him to cry. The child had no attachment to his mother—she was just another in a long string of caretakers. Because of the lack of bonding, he can't discriminate between family and strangers.

If he's very fortunate, he will live with his grandparents or other relatives; otherwise he may be placed in a foster home to await adoption. Whatever the case, the child is likely to experience a long string of failed placements in the next few years.

The damage to the child's personality is usually complete by the second birthday. By that time, parents or guardians have noticed that the child is "difficult." Although he may have caught up to other children in physical size, he is almost certainly behind them in other developmental areas. According to the DSM IV description of reactive attachment disorder, there is "absence of visual tracking and reciprocal play, lack of vocal imitation or playfulness, apathy, little or no spontaneity." He has an extremely short attention span and is easily distractable, and as he grows older, shows no capacity to think ahead or understand cause and effect. As he nears his third birthday, when normal children are well into Stage 2 of conscience formation, he stays stuck in the first stage, continuing to take what he wants, when he wants it, and no parental controls stop him. As we have seen in earlier chapters, you can yell at these children, spank them, even restrain them, but they will not respond with improved behavior.

Since he is now a toddler and has the freedom of his legs, he becomes a terror and has to be watched constantly. This puts an incredible strain on the guardians, who don't know which way to turn. Having raised either natural or other foster children, they can't conceive that their parenting skills could be so useless. No matter what they do, the child only seems to get worse, and as he gets older, he adds more disturbing habits—self-abuse, stealing, hoarding food, messiness, aggression. (See Chapter 1 for a description of these characteristics.)

Now it is too late to change the course of the child's development without massive interaction and expense. He has missed out on the essential learning that well-nourished and cared-for children receive in the first years of life. He has not bonded, so he has no feelings for anyone—he doesn't even care about his own self-preservation. He does not recognize guilt when he does something wrong, nor does he feel pride in doing something right. He doesn't have the ability to take responsibility for his actions. And his chance to learn these things is basically over, since they needed to be learned when his brain was developing so rapidly in his first two years of life. Now the wiring of his brain is essentially complete, and the skewed patterns that he learned will determine his actions into adulthood.

Poor Parenting Exacerbates the Problem

The chronology in the preceding section assumes that the at-risk child's parent is a drug abuser. But unattached children are not produced solely by crack addicts. Although drug abuse by the mother is a common cause of unattachment, it is certainly not the only one. There are any number of social or personal problems that can cause a break between child and parent. For instance, the mother may be physically incapable of caring for the child—perhaps she has to be hospitalized during the child's first year. Perhaps the infant herself is hospitalized and denied the loving contact of her parents. As noted before, a loss of as little as eight days has a lasting effect on the child. Or maybe the mother has a postpartum depression so severe that she doesn't care about her baby—doesn't rock her or hold her or give her eye contact. Perhaps the family is going through some crisis that keeps the parent from giving the child the attention she needs. The child may experience unresolved pain that prevents her from getting relief; thus, despite all her parent's ministrations, she can't take in the bonding behavior. Or the child may have congenital difficulties that make bonding impossible. More likely is the possibility that the child's parents do not know or are not interested in caring for the child, as is so often the case with teenage parents. As we have learned in the last decade, hundreds of thousands of young children are neglected or abused physically, psychologically, and sexually by parents and other guardians.

A break in early bonding bodes ill for children; so also does poor parenting. A child doesn't suddenly go out of control for no reason; usually the way the child was raised is a major factor. And although the popular idea of a dysfunctional family is one in which drugs, alcohol, and abuse are found, such a family can be created just as well by adults who simply do not parent well.

In a sick family, when children go bad the parents tend to blame the children or console themselves with the thought that their children's actions are a result of adolescence. The parents rarely look at their own actions, which more often than not encourage irresponsibility.

Four main dysfunctional behaviors distinquish the dynamics of a sick family. First, the parents try to do good things for the kids, but do not recognize that love and consistent discipline are interrelated. Instead, they equate love with unstinting giving to their children—giving time, toys, attention, protection. They feel that the more the children are given, the more grateful they will be and the more responsible they will become. They put their children ahead of themselves. This shows the kids that their parents don't respect themselves; thus, the children don't respect their parents. If the children make mistakes, the parents don't allow them to suffer the consequences—pain, embarrassment, punishment—so that the children will not repeat their mistakes. The parents protect their children from these perceived dangers. The children grow up hostile to their parents, but dependent on them, because their parents denied them the freedom to suffer.

Second, the parents tend to blame the children for the poor behavior that their own parenting has caused. The more the children misbehave, the more the parents give them. The parents hope the children will appreciate them and behave better, but what they are doing is rewarding bad behavior. As the behavior continues, the parents typically say, "Look what we've done for you! How can you treat us like this?" The parents also rail against the children for not listening to them. The parents tell their children to stay away from drugs, to be nice, to do good, but family dynamics actually discourage the very behavior the parents talk about.

Third, the hostile-dependent children take up all the family resources. Despite all the time and money that parents expend on these kids, nothing improves.

Fourth, as the situation worsens, the parents try harder to make things right. Unfortunately, they use the same techniques that created the mess, escalating the problem. The parents keep on giving, meeting the ever-increasing needs of their children, who become less self-sufficient and more demanding. Generally, this vicious cycle does not have a healthy conclusion. The parents reach a breaking point at which they can give no more. The children, previously resentful that their parents didn't allow them freedom, are now doubly resentful since their parents cut them off. In most families, the generations become estranged for good. In extreme cases, the rageful children physically attack their parents.

Amazingly, human behavior is mirrored in the behavior of other mammals. Breaks in bonding and dysfunctional parenting cause "conscienceless" behavior in mammals other than humans. (In Chapter 7, I will discuss how holding therapy also works with other mammals.) In 1994, in the Planesberg Game Reserve in South Africa, wardens found that someone was killing the beautiful white rhinos there. Each carcass was found with gaping wounds in its back. Officials soon discovered that young bull elephants in the reserve were responsible. However, the only previous recorded incidents of elephants attacking rhinos occurred when the animals met at watering holes and the mother elephants felt threatened. The young bull elephants in Planesberg were going on a rampage *seemingly for no reason!*

In the late 1970s, Planesberg had been a pioneer in taking elephants that would have been killed in other parks as part of regular animal population management programs. More than seventy young elephants were moved to Planesberg along with only two adult females to care for them. Clive Walker, chairman of the Rhino and Elephant Foundation of Africa, claims that the present problem goes back to the childhood trauma suffered by these elephants—watching their parents being slaughtered, then being trucked off to new surroundings—and the subsequent lack of parental authority throughout their formative years. Thus, a seemingly positive program that began with good intentions resulted in mayhem for the clients.

In our society, adolescents run wild, killing for no apparent reason. Like the elephants, they may have suffered in the first year of life when the foundations for conscience—both psychological and neurological—are laid down. As with other infants, their brains were being hard-wired, so to speak, but the connections were made wrong. The roots of causal thinking—the ability to plan ahead, to wait—were stunted. Other people appear to be hurtful, not helpful. The rage that is these children's primary emotion follows them through life.

Now it is possible to see why teaching "values" to school-age children or "giving more" to these children is doomed to failure. We are not dealing with a need for more knowledge, but with a deep-set personality problem, ultimately reflected in brain connections themselves, that is very resistant to change. However, before we can succeed in helping these disturbed individuals, two even more important changes must occur in society: first, in how we deal with the present generation of irresponsible teenagers and adults; and second, in how we care for our youngest Americans.

5

SOCIETY'S ROLE IN THE DEVELOPMENT OF CONSCIENCELESS CHILDREN

In thinking about how society contributes to the development of conscienceless children, I am reminded of what Sergeant Gary Meeker of the Milpitas, California police said about the teenagers who didn't report the murder that their friend bragged about (see Chapter 2): "What the hell has happened to these kids?" Echoing this is the plaintive remark by Larry Jensen, a part-time ranger and guide at Lake Powell, Glen Canyon. Part of his job is to show tourists and boaters Anasazi ruins high in a cave:

> These ruins are a national treasure. In the morning when we first open up we have to clear out feces where people have defecated on floors and walls and, of course, now, there is the reek of urine everywhere. I don't understand why people act like this. They didn't used to act like this. What's going on?

What appears to be going on is that Americans as a people engage in less thoughtful planning, are less intelligent, have less conscience, and are less caring. All of these are basic ego strengths built on genetics, perinatal events, and infantile care. The ramifications of decay in these ego strengths are painfully illustrated by incidents such as the 1991 tragedy at the New York Celebrity Basketball Game, in which eight people were trampled to death. The crowd was unable to handle the simple frustration of being turned away at the door. Pushing to get in, the crowd broke the glass doors, crushing the people in front. As the bodies were being carried out, narcissistic and uncaring children were scrambling for autographs and posing for pictures with their favorite entertainers. The December 30, 1991 *Denver Post* reported the comments of a bystander: "'Trying to get their autographs while people are dying . . . the city is really going to hell. People don't care,' Victor Black, 27, said outside the gym. 'It's a sad reflection on what the city is becoming.'"

Black's concern was right on the mark, but too localized. This kind of behavior is a sad reflection on what the entire country is becoming. In the October 21, 1991 issue of *USA Today,* Carolyn Pesce wrote of life in Houston:

> People here are afraid to go out during the day. Even police officers say they won't go to automatic teller machines when they're unarmed.
>
> The crime wave now hitting the nation's fourth-largest city is affecting everyone: blacks, whites, rich, poor, educated and uneducated. It's the number one reason most people want to leave the city, a *Houston Post* poll shows.
>
> "Houston," says District Attorney John Holmes, Jr., "is being eaten up by crime."
>
> Each headline seems more horrifying than the next: A Ninety-Nine-Year-Old Woman Raped; A Father and Two Young Sons Tied Up at Home and Shot in Their Heads, Execution Style; A Three-Year-Old Caught Stealing Crack Cocaine; An Eleven-Year-Old Abducted and Raped While Walking to School.
>
> "I've seen enough violence to last me a lifetime," says police officer Steve Marino, standing inside a yellow tape marking off a recent murder.

From sea to shining sea, the tide of inhumanity is turning against us.

Children are the real infrastructure of our society—if our youngsters are damaged, society will not survive. And our infrastructure is crumbling.

Informed estimates place the number of children in America

involved in out-of-home placement (foster homes, hospitals, treatment centers, and so on) between 750,000 and 1 million. Fully one-fifth of America's children are being raised in out-of-home placement or in poverty. Close to 500,000 children are born drug-exposed every year. Of the more than 4 million live babies born in the United States each year, 20 percent are born to single mothers, many of whom are teenagers. That's more than 800,000 children a year. Thirty percent of our country's children live in homes with only one parent, and 10 percent of these children have neither parent at home.

Thus, hundreds of thousands of children enter American society each year with two strikes against them. First, their parents or guardians can't or won't care for them, either physically or psychologically. Second, their life situations would make even Horatio Alger quail. Abuse and neglect. Ragged diet. Substandard or no shelter. Poor schools. Little love and no hope.

All too often, society itself issues the third strike for these children.

How the Media Affects Children

To understand how society has exacerbated this crisis of unattached children, we must first look at the messages that our culture gives the young.

A survey done in 1985 by the *Weekly Reader* showed that before fifth grade, the most influential factor in children's attitudes toward drug and alcohol use is the media—TV, movies, and magazines. After fifth grade, the media lose the top spot to the influence of peers, but they still run a close second. (Although the *Weekly Reader* is better known for its short, readable articles that appeal to young kids than for its scientific polling, the survey is significant because it looked at the attitudes of our youngest schoolchildren, a much-overlooked group.)

Since they have so much pull with our youngest citizens, it is essential to see how the media treat drug and alcohol use, sexual activity, violence, and other topics that are so destructive to our young people. The public relations departments swear that the corporations running the media are responsible citizens; that the people in charge of what we watch, listen to, and read are truly concerned about fighting moral decay in our country. They go to great lengths to show that their TV programming is balanced, that they are not promoting antisocial behavior in their movies, and that they are working in the public interest. To back up their claims, they talk about their unbiased newscasts, their "family-oriented" programming, their socially important movies, and other high-sounding projects.

However, at other times these professionals claim that the media are not responsible for society's values; that they simply reflect what is happening in society. When questioned about the propensity of nightly news shows to lead their broadcasts with lurid stories and graphic video of death, rape, and scandal, the answer is typically, "That's what the audience wants to see," or "The competition does it, so we have to do it, too." When discussing violence and sex on TV dramas watched by millions of largely unsupervised children, the response is often, "If the parents don't like it, they should turn it off." If the question of the mores found in the blockbuster hits in our movie theaters is raised, the answer is often, "The public obviously wants to see these movies."

So which point of view are we to believe? Are the media responsible or not responsible? Although this question can be argued ad infinitum, one thing is certain. As long as TV and radio networks, movie studios, and newspapers are commercial ventures, they will ultimately be ruled by the bottom line. Thus, it is almost a certainty that the media will not take the unprofitable route of getting out in front of the curve of public opinion. Leadership is always lonely.

A number of events in the last few years have underscored this. In June 1992, President Bush held a press conference that none of the three major TV networks carried on the grounds that the President would use it for political purposes. Of course, this was during the presidential campaign, and the network executives were probably considering that they would have to give equal time to the other candidates. As it turned out, the press conference was an issue-oriented one, remarkably devoid of the political posturing that normally characterizes appearances by our elected representatives. One of Bush's major topics was the balanced budget amendment, which he was vigorously supporting. Less than a week later, on June 11, Congress voted down that amendment. Most Americans never heard what the President had to say on the matter.

Later that month, the Democratic presidential candidate Bill Clinton had to go on Larry King's talk show on CNN to get his point of view out to the public. This was not the first time a national candidate had done this, as Ross Perot had started his campaign on King's show several months before. But it was significant in that it showed the lack of confidence the candidates had that they could speak to the voters through the traditional news sources. Throughout the presidential campaign, all three major candidates appeared on talk shows or in "soft news" morning shows and drive-time radio slots, capped by Clinton's saxophone-playing appearance on the *Arsenio Hall Show.*

One could argue that this merely marked a change in how the public gets their information about important events, and is a portent of things to come in the interactive media age. But more likely, it indicates the public's short attention span about hard topics such as the complex social, economic, and foreign policy issues that face us. As news shows on the TV networks have lost viewers, they have changed their formats—not to give more in-depth coverage of topics, but to shorten the coverage of major topics and lengthen the coverage of "entertaining" news. Film of public figures actually talking about the issues have been shortened drastically, so that these people now have less than ten seconds to express their facts or opinions, and even then they are at the mercy of the editors who need to make it all fit together on the tube.

What does deserve massive coverage by the media? It appears that the personal peccadillos of public figures are given at least as much front-page attention as are national issues such as health care, the homeless, and the economy. During the confirmation hearings for Clarence Thomas, who was nominated to the Supreme Court by President Bush in 1991, the debate over whether or not Thomas sexually harassed Anita Hill obscured any testimony that Thomas gave about his opinions on abortion, civil rights, minimum sentencing requirements, or other major topics. Halfway through his term, President Clinton was better known for the extramarital affairs that various women alleged he had had with them than for any policy stands he was taking. Any story about the personal life of entertainer Michael Jackson was at the top of the news, as were the break-up of Roseanne and Tom Arnold, which athletes were currently enrolled in substance abuse programs, and which politicians or police officers were being tried for corruption.

The distinguishing characteristic of the front-page stories seems to be their value as spectacles. Opening-story position seems to be reserved for the grabber—the story that will make the reader buy the paper and force the viewer to keep from jumping to another channel. Substantive analysis is generally kept on the inside pages, or is presented on Sunday morning or on late-night interview programs.

The quintessential news story occurred in June 1994, when a white Ford Bronco traveling down a California highway preempted hours of television programming. The car was being driven by Al Cowlings. In the back seat was O. J. Simpson, former football star and media celebrity, owner of the car, and a suspect in the double murder of his ex-wife Nicole and her friend. Simpson, reportedly distraught over the death of his ex-wife and pressured from all sides, was supposedly holding a gun to his own head.

TV news helicopters tracked the car and the pursuing police vehicles for miles, relaying video to all the networks. (The only network that didn't preempt its shows was NBC, which was airing the NBA playoffs at that time. NBC did include the Simpson video in the lower right corner of the TV screen, and switched to live updates when it could.) Cowlings was not speeding and no other motorists were endangered—in fact, it seemed as if the police were merely escorting a dignitary along the road, rather than trying to capture a fugitive. When Simpson arrived at his destination, there were more hours of video featuring the Bronco parked in the driveway, and this continued until falling night made it impossible to see anything. Only much later did Simpson surrender quietly to the authorities.

For hours, all of the major TV news forces were focused on a non-event during which essentially *nothing happened!* Yet the ongoing reports riveted millions of Americans to their screens. What kept them there? The possibility that Simpson—a celebrity, someone we all knew, someone who had been figuratively in our living rooms for years—would blow his brains out. Psychologists and criminal experts with imposing credentials weighed in with their learned opinions. Grim-faced news anchors incessantly repeated the details of the sordid affair, trying desperately to fill time while waiting for a climax. For the American public, thoughts of national health care, ethnic strife in Europe and Africa, landmark peace talks between Israelis and Palestinians, the economy—in fact all the ascendant issues of the day that truly affected our lives—were wiped away. In the following weeks, the Simpson case blanketed the news, threatening to overtake the king of over-exposure, the Buttafuoco-Fisher mess. And the media circus continued into the fall and winter with Simpson's trial.

Trials of mass murderers. Scandals involving public figures, such as the Whitewater investigation. Police action. Shootings. Drugs. Human suffering. These are becoming spectacles that the American public watches as if they were performances in a circus. We ooh and aah or cluck our tongues, but rarely do we think about what should be done about these crises.

The media caters to this lack of critical thought by supposedly "balanced" treatment of the news. For instance, when the case of Rodney King, who was beaten by Los Angeles police after leading them on a high-speed chase, was in the news, reporters benignly referred to King as "the driver of the car." The public was rarely apprised of the facts that King had violated parole, that he was driving drunk during the chase, and that he had threatened the lives of dozens, if not hundreds of people during his spree through the densely populated streets of Los Angeles.

In a follow-up story in the June 9, 1992 issue of *USA Today,* Desda Moss gave some background on King: "He dropped out of high school, married a girl from the neighborhood, got in trouble with the law—he was convicted of robbing a convenience store—and generally led an unremarkable life." Since when is robbing a convenience store an indication of an unremarkable life?

The sad part is that the public reads or listens to this kind of reporting generally without question. Playing out their childhoods in which they sat in front of the TV at three, Americans simply absorb what the media says while real thinking, creating, and doing are lost in adulthood as they were lost in childhood. As people of all ages see more murders, more drug abuse, more family violence, and more corruption on the news shows, they become inured to the seamy underside of human behavior. Instead of repulsive behavior to be avoided, it becomes a common experience, and not such a big deal. When children read about sports millionaires going through drug rehabilitation time and again while paying only minimal retribution, it begins to appear that drug use isn't so bad. And when children see drinking and drugs coupled with glamorous parties and beautiful people, the use of these dangerous substances begins to look like fun.

According to *TV Guide,* television viewers are "exposed to some 9,230 scenes of suggested sexual intercourse or sexual innuendo" in an average year, and "94 percent of the sex on soap operas involves people not married to each other." On television, in the movies, in rock videos, and in romance novels, sex is glamorous, exciting, and spontaneous. The characters act on their impulses, and what results is a beautiful coupling that fades to black.

The amazing thing about media sex is that there is rarely a mention of contraception, no consideration of disease, and almost no one gets pregnant! As one AIDS activist noted about a 1994 film in which Bruce Willis plays a psychiatrist who beds a number of his patients, "He has sex with five different partners in the course of the movie, and not once is a condom shown—not even a wrapper on the bedstand."

And this trend promises to get worse. As more TV channels come on line, competition for the viewers' attention will become greater, which will probably result in more entertaining news shows than ever. More video of blood and gore, more misconduct in high office, more specials on drug dealers, more violence. Dramas will become more explicit, and comedy specials will become raunchier. We now have an all-news channel, an all-comedy channel, an all-cartoon channel, and an all-food channel. The originators of such programming saw an opportunity, and were able to sell the idea to sponsors and cable companies. Perhaps we'll soon have an all-crime channel or an all-domestic abuse channel, too. And as the percentage of two-earner families and single-parent families increases, the children who have power over the remote controls of the land will be supervised even less than they are now. Rare indeed will be the informed discussion that a child has with an adult about what is shown on TV.

Although a direct link between what is shown on TV and movie screens and people's behavior has not been definitively proven, these movies and TV shows do have strong effects on our fantasies, especially those of impressionable teenagers. Spontaneous, beautiful, powerful sex with no consequences is what teenagers (and undoubtedly many adults) would like—they could experience the feelings and emotions of sex, which teenagers are big on, while not being responsible for what happens, which teenagers have problems with. None of the methods of contraception in wide use today in the United States has been proven effective with teenagers as a group, for each method requires something that teenagers seem to be lacking: thoughtful planning. Surveys have shown that, because of a combination of misinformation, myth, inconvenience, and youthful irresponsibility, the majority of teenagers do not use contraception each time they have sex. Many teenagers believe that pregnancy cannot occur the first time someone has sex, and most teenagers are sexually active for a year before seeking birth control help from a professional. As Lisbeth Schorr writes in *Within Our Reach* (1988):

> Many youngsters hesitate to obtain contraceptives because they think it "unromantic" to anticipate a sexual encounter by making preparations for it. As one young teenager explained, "The first time, it was like totally out of the blue. You don't . . . say, 'Well, I'm going to his house, and he's probably going to try to get to bed with me, so I better make sure I'm prepared.' I mean, you don't know it's coming, so how are you to be prepared?"

Schorr also relates that one of every five girls gets pregnant during the first six months of sexual activity, half of all initial premarital teenage pregnancies occur in the first six months of intercourse, and more than one fifth occur in the first month. So although the media moguls may say that what they present to the public does not affect what teenagers do, it certainly isn't helping any.

How Government Entitlements Affect Children

Although TV and the other media have a major role in shaping the attitudes and behavior of our children, governmental policies have an even earlier effect on conscienceless children. There are many ways that the government interferes with the proper raising of children, all of them well-intentioned. These generally result from the welfare-state philosophy that some of the populace cannot be responsible for themselves, and so the government must care for them. What started out as an economic rescue plan during the Great Depression has become an ongoing bureaucratic monster that has changed every citizen's relationship to the government. Instead of getting the government off the backs of the people, we need to get the people off the back of the government.

The attitude that "the government will help" is so pervasive that it is difficult to decide where to begin. For almost any social problem, there is a government agency that will take responsibility for it. This is why government seems to have grown far beyond our ability to control it—the American people have turned over their responsibilities to the government. Rather than making the sacrifices in life-style necessary to be responsible for what were once considered personal matters—caring for an aged parent, riding herd on our children, driving safely, keeping our greed from running away with our common sense—we have effectively asked the government to attend to them for us.

It should not be surprising that the way the government deals with conscienceless children and the parents who produce them is to assume all responsibility for them. Social workers and psychologists check on the children and the mothers. Welfare departments give them a monthly stipend, and food stamps are available, too. Schools provide special education classes for the children. The government pays for medical care, also.

Essentially, the government keeps those people who need its help in a dependency state, never allowing them to grow into adulthood. These people are not required to feel the consequences of their actions, the way other adults must. Thus, they don't have to grow up—they can continue their self-destructive, antisocial habits.

The government provides food, shelter, and clothing, but generally requires little in return. Although there is plenty of talk about getting people off the relief rolls, little is done about it. A few states have "workfare" programs—those who get aid must do some work for it—but these are mere stop-gaps. Most of the work is menial, and provides people with neither skills nor ambition to find work in the private sector. There are few job-training programs, and those that are available are underfunded for the task at hand.

The overriding mentality of human services departments is one of entitlement. People are entitled to health care, shelter, clothing, food. But since the government tells these people that they are *entitled* to these things, the people come to feel that they *deserve* these things just because they are alive. That means that these people owe nothing to the government (and indirectly to the greater society) in return—no change in attitudes or behavior, no social responsibility.

Bad Governing Is Like Bad Parenting

The fact that America has so many disorganized, neglectful, and abusive parents has not happened by accident. The agony being suffered by our country is analogous to the agony in a dysfunctional family, in which kids "go bad" in adolescence. Of course, children don't hit adolescence and suddenly become rebellious. Their behavior depends upon the way they were raised from infancy.

In Chapter 4, I described how bad parenting contributes to the development of severely disturbed, hostile-dependent children. This same vicious cycle characterizes the policies of American government toward its citizens. In fact, the similarities between the dysfunctional nuclear family and the dysfunctional national family are striking.

Both the family and the national government are hierarchical structures. A healthy family is ruled by two parents who have different ideas, but who work together. The nation is mainly ruled by two powers—the President (executive branch) and Congress. The population, like the children in a family, ask to be heard and try to influence decisions, but it is the President and Congress who are ultimately responsible for setting policy. Like the parents of a family, the government is responsible for providing an environment in which its children can pursue life, liberty, and happiness. It must set policies that will produce functioning, responsible citizens so that the nation will maintain itself.

Now, let's see how well the government provides this environment.

When average Americans look at the finances of the country, they see a budget process that would be the ruination of any family. All knowledgeable citizens recognize that when responsible families run out of money, they either stop spending or go out and raise more money by working. But when the government runs out of money, it either borrows cash or prints new money. The result is that government decisions to spend more outnumber decisions to cut spending by one hundred to one.

Less obvious to citizens is that the social programs of American government, although well-intentioned, are direct causes of the social problems the country now suffers. Most of us don't notice the rise of problems such as teen violence, young mothers, welfare dependence, graffiti, disdain for authority, and irresponsibility amongst the general public that plague the country. Rather, we usually awake one morning and "discover" the issues full-blown on the morning news programs. We clamor for government to "do something" about the problems; our parents in Washington pass laws and appropriate money. The problems don't go away, and so we clamor for the parents to "do more." The parents pass more laws and earmark more money, the problems grow larger, and the hostile-dependent cycle escalates. In most cases, the government continues to give even though it is bent ever lower under increasing entitlements. But sometimes the parents reach their breaking point on an issue and cut off funding. Then whichever dependent group that has been receiving all the money and attention (state and local governments, neighborhood groups, schools, road departments—the list seems endless) flies into a rage. We need this money! We are owed this money! How dare you parents not give it to us! Give us the money or we'll attack (not vote for) you!

This is exactly the route that a dysfunctional family—with overprotective parents and hostile-dependent, delinquent children—takes to self-destruction.

Large segments of the American population are now hostile-dependent. The rules governing who qualifies to receive government help mandate that these individuals remain fragmented and unable to help themselves. A 1992 article by Gary Bauer commented on this:

> Millions of [people] "choose" single motherhood only because government makes it look like a good deal. Government offers the unmarried mother an attractive contractual arrangement: the equivalent of somewhere between $8,500 and $15,000 per year in combined welfare benefits on the condition that the young woman *not work for pay, and not marry an employed male.*

What the government offers her is a classic contract. In consideration of the government's offer of a package of benefits, the mother agrees not to engage in the activities that are crucial to the formation of a decent society. Government has bargained for social breakdown, and it has gotten it. (*Washington Watch,* June 1992)

In Hennepin County, Minnesota, welfare workers estimate that the average mother receiving aid gets $20,000 a year in welfare benefits, housing subsidies, and food stamps. It would be economic suicide to give up these benefits and go to work for minimum wage. And there is currently no limit to how long citizens can stay on the welfare rolls. In fact, in a June 1994 speech, Senator Daniel Moynihan, chairman of the Senate Finance Committee, postulated that welfare should *never* be cut off for any family. He was opposing the idea that recipients should be allowed two years on welfare and two more years on workfare. And most in Congress oppose limiting welfare payments to mothers who continue to have children.

The government, as any dysfunctional parents do, has led the way for its children's irresponsibility. Instead of leaving the children open to the consequences of their irresponsible actions, government policies shield citizens from the necessary agony that promotes growth and maturity and contribute to their lack of responsibility. Consider these examples:

In 1993, a group of overworked Humbolt County, California, social workers showed me a fake certificate they had made up expressing their feelings:

Why work for a living when you can come to Humbolt, California and live for free?
$400 per month living expenses
Free board
Free room
Free birth costs for all children
Free health and death benefits
Remember—all you have to do is *not* work!

An angry social worker in Minneapolis recounted this tale to me: "A welfare mother recently self-righteously told me, 'I can't believe you went back to work part-time when your baby is only sixteen months old. I'd never do that!' Boy, was I mad. I thought, 'Sure, I'm going back to work because I'm paying for all the babies that you're staying home with!' Somehow, the torch is going out on my flaming liberalism."

At a workshop in the Pacific Northwest, I heard an even more pathetic story from a Washington State social worker. She was talking to a young man who was proud to have gotten off of welfare. "How did you do it?" the social worker asked.

"I do professional fathering," he replied. When the surprised social worker asked what he meant, he said, "Well, a lot of these women want to have children so that they can get more welfare money. But the husbands and the men always hassle them. I get them pregnant, I don't hassle them, they pay me, and I'm history."

In Minnesota recently, a welfare mother with six children was given a home by the Department of Social Services. The Department found that this was a much cheaper solution than trying to rent her an apartment large enough for her family.

This topsy-turvy situation is not limited to families on the welfare rolls. Able-bodied men and women with all sorts of skills have no qualms about taking government handouts. An ex-Navy pilot related this story:

> After thirteen years with the Navy, I was ready for a vacation. I was ready to hit the slopes and ski my brains out. The beauty of it was, I found I could have a *paid* vacation. Working certainly would have put a cramp in my post-Navy style of life! Every week I had to go down to the unemployment office, and I would dutifully ask if they had work. Of course, they had some jobs, but none in my specialty. I would ask them what they had in the way of employment for a person who was experienced in a single-seat jet. It turned out that they didn't have a lot. Of course, I had to fill out these forms about looking for work, so I would talk to the pilots who flew into the ski area and ask them how the weather was when they flew in. They were my "employment contacts." Frankly the whole unemployment thing was a joke.

A bright, motivated school psychologist whom I know told a similar story that also illustrates the hostile-dependency that government programs engender. Funding cutbacks in her school system had caused her to be fired from her job. She called me on a case for consultation, as she saw private patients. Then, before hanging up, she said, "As you know, I've been dropped by the system. Actually, I'm enjoying my vacation. It's great not to have to go to work every day, but to qualify for my unemployment, I have to make two contacts a week for a job. Can I use this phone call as one of my contacts? Isn't the government dumb?" Even she was being driven to bite the hand that was unwisely feeding her.

A lawyer talked about his baptism of fire with Colorado State Unemployment:

> Christina was my first secretary. She worked for me when I first got out of law school and we got along fabulously together. She was genuinely a hard worker and very efficient. I was very liberal with her hours and she would sometimes come in late and leave early. When I had an occasional noon meeting, I felt good about asking Chris to take notes. After she had worked in the office for six months, I called her in one noon to take shorthand notes during a meeting and was flabbergasted by her refusal to take notes. I just couldn't understand it. When she first refused, I thought she was kidding. I said, "Chris, I'm not kidding. Come on in. I need you at this meeting." She looked at me and said, "Well, I'm not going to take notes. This is my lunch hour, and if you don't like it, fire me."
>
> I was so young and naive that I simply didn't get the picture. So I said, "Chris, come on now. You know you are forever taking sick leave and I give you lots of time off and pay you for it anyway." She again said, "Fire me." So I said, stupidly, "Okay, Chris, you're fired."
>
> She had worked for me just long enough to qualify for unemployment insurance. She would not have qualified if she had quit. It was important for her that I fire her. My monthly unemployment insurance payments shot through the roof. They are based on whether or not an employer has ever had claims. As a young and naive person, I fought this with the unemployment board. I didn't realize then that the board, regardless of the merits of the case, was on the side of the employee receiving unemployment

benefits. After all, they are in charge of distributing the money. It's their job that is also on the line.

The result of all this entitlement is that Americans from all walks of life are learning that they need never suffer the consequences for their behavior. If someone falls on the ice, it is the neighbor's fault for not shoveling the walk well enough. If someone spills coffee from a takeout container in her lap while driving, it is the restaurant's fault for serving its coffee too hot. If someone has a swimming pool in the back yard and neighborhood kids climb over the fence and drown in the pool, it is the pool owner's fault for having an "attractive nuisance." If a person burglarizes a building and, while escaping over the roof, falls through a skylight, it is the building owner's fault for not keeping the roof safe. Why is America such a litigious society? It's not because we have too many lawyers. Since we have demanded that our government overprotect us, we have become a nation of victims. In America today, one can declaim "I hurt myself, and it's your fault," and be believed.

The Negative Impact of Child-Protective Agencies

While government policies add to the number of irresponsible people in society, government child-protective services add to the burden of those trying to work with the products of these policies—the severely disturbed children of these poor parents. An ever-increasing number of mothers who are children themselves (psychologically and chronologically) are reproducing. They are unable to care for themselves, unsure of their children's paternity, and have often been abandoned by the fathers. Those young mothers who were the subject of childhood abuse continue the generational cycle, and neglect and abuse their children. Rarely does a week pass without the news media reporting an infant left to die ignominiously in a dumpster, on the roof of a building, or in a public bathroom.

Public outrage forces overburdened child-protective services to crack down on abuse. Child-protective teams review their case-loads, a majority of which are disturbed children living in institutions or foster homes, and promulgate more rules limiting discipline methods. The result—increasing numbers of disturbed children who, by mandate, must be treated with progressively less-effective techniques.

This means that the people who bear the brunt of governmental intrusion are not the abusive birth mothers and fathers. The birth parents may be in jail, although it is more likely that they are free on the street, continuing their life-style. Instead, it is the foster parents and institutional workers who have to deal with the victims of abuse who are hobbled by these regulations. It can be dangerous caring for unattached adolescents and teenagers—what these children will do to others is often beyond the belief of people who deal with normal or slightly disturbed children. Restraints of some sort are often required for these kids, from simple holding to safe mechanical devices that are used in hospitals across the country. However, the ability of these caring workers to reach disturbed children is hampered by rules that often confuse the necessity of strong methods (disturbing the disturbed) with the abuse that originally caused the childrens' problems. The paradox is that these regulations increasingly close down treatment options for these children.

For instance, one method used to calm an out-of-control child is to place her in a well-controlled quiet room. The child quiets herself without hurting herself or others. However, in many states, such an innocuous treament is prohibited today. Of course, when the child commits a serious crime outside the treatment setting, it is against the law *not* to lock her up.

Examples of such overly restrictive regulations abound. In 1985, Forest Heights Lodge (a facility for disturbed children) and the Association of Foster Parents had to battle the Colorado Department of Social Services and psychiatrists from a local, well-known child abuse center to obtain the right for foster parents simply to swat difficult children on the rear!

In another case in Colorado, an obstinate child in Denver

refused to put on her shoes for school. Her mother, seeking to avoid a terrible (but child-desired) confrontation, responded, "Well, honey, I would do it differently, but if that's your thing, go for it!" She allowed the child to go to school shoeless. The outcome for the child was positive: she never again disputed the need to wear shoes. However, that day in school, she told officials a sad story: "We don't have enough money to buy shoes." Her mother was reported for child abuse. It was only with great difficulty and after much investigation by child-protective services (and perhaps because of a TV news special that focused on the case as an example of parents allowing children to experience the consequences of their own poor judgments) that she was able to clear herself.

The manipulative nature of most unattached children makes things worse for therapeutic foster parents who have to deal with government bureaucrats. Very often, it takes lengthy experience with a child to recognize what he is doing. And observing a single child's behavior over a long period is something that no overburdened government agency can do.

Tom was a twelve-year-old who was treated at Evergreen and then placed in one of our better therapeutic homes with a very loving and giving family. However, the boy was a perfect "victim/victimizer." (When children are both victims and victimizers, they lay the foundation for an inability to give to others while demanding others to give to them. In adulthood, this is one of the hallmarks of narcissistic and borderline personality disorders.) While victimizing other children and even adults with his angry, noncompliant, destructive behavior, he complained bitterly that people picked on him and that he never received his fair share of anything—particularly food and attention.

Tom had nothing good to say about his family to school officials. As is so often the case, the officials believed Tom's sob stories, even though he was victimizing other children and teachers at school. The school, having severe concerns over the quality of his foster care, called me, and I visited the school hoping to help them realize how Tom was manipulating them.

As I was speaking with the principal, trying to help her understand Tom's conning, convincing nature, an angry social worker burst into the office, seething with indignation. "It's happening right now!" he shouted. "The kid's in the lunchroom and his parents sent no money and he has no lunch. He has to beg the other kids for something to eat!"

Fighting an urge to pump my fist into the air and shout, "Yes!" I followed the social worker to the lunchroom. Tom, wearing a face full of longing and desperation, was indeed mooching off the other children. When he saw me, he was stunned. This was the last thing he expected.

I walked right over to him and said sternly, "Okay, Tom, game's up! Give me the straight story right now." I wasn't sure what Tom would do or say, but since he knew that he couldn't con me, I expected him to say something. Surprisingly, he didn't say a word. Instead, he reached under his seat, pulled out a very full bag, and slammed it on the table. "What's that?" asked the confused social worker. "My lunch," answered Tom. Dumbfounded, the principal asked, "Then why were you mooching off the other kids?" Glancing at me, Tom answered truthfully, "I didn't want anyone to know I had a lunch because I wanted everyone to feel sorry for me."

This quickly straightened out Tom's situation, but for each such incident, there are many more in which the foster parents must go through close investigation and repeated home visits before child-protective services agree that they are doing their jobs well. And in too many cases, additional restrictions are placed on the foster parents that make their work harder.

Bob and Kathy Lay are outstanding therapeutic parents living near Denver. They were helping to care for a victim/victimizing child who was admitted to the program from out of state after sodomizing and cruelly treating other children. He had previously turned in other foster parents to his school for abuse, and he did so with the Lays. School officials investigated his charges against the Lays and judged them unfounded, for they recognized that the boy was a chronic liar. The boy then complained to neighbors, who called the county protective services.

The agency investigated the home. Although Bob and Kathy had previously served as knowledgeable instructors in Pennsylvania for other therapeutic parents, the county here ruled that the methods they used were unacceptable. They set new limits for the Lays and the program that they worked with. The directive from the State of Colorado read as follows:

> Only when the child is out of control to the extent that he/she is actually displaying behavior that is a danger to him/herself or others, should restraint methods be used. Further, until restraint methods are taught to the foster parents, children should not be restrained by them. If a child is a danger to him/herself or others and the foster parent cannot handle the child, the therapist should be notified to handle the child or the police should be called.

Ironically, many disturbed children have tough times at night, when no therapist is available for an immediate home visit. Following this directive means that the therapeutic family would have to put up with the abuse, which is not helpful for the child, or call the police. Perhaps the child will get mild treatment from the police. But what is more likely with an out-of-control youngster is that he will be restrained with more force than the foster parents would use, handcuffed, and very possibly locked up in a cell.

Discouraged, the Lays noted, "This really says that [the boy] can scream abuse at us, kick the wall, throw things in the house, and there is nothing physical we can do to control him. That is all the child understands at this point. Now he knows that if we hold him, he can complain to the child abuse authorities." These loving, successful foster parents had no choice but to institutionalize the boy, who continued his downward progress with unabated destructive behavior. (The Lays felt that the boy could have been turned around with only another year in a highly structured, highly nurturing environment.)

Colorado Social Services did not stop there. It also found in talking to the Lays' other foster children that some did not like to be cuddled at night or have their feet rubbed prior to bedtime— "It hurts," these children complained. (All loving and controlling interaction "hurts" unattached children.) Therefore, the state set even more limits on the Lays: "The team [Colorado Institutional Abuse Team] members expressed concern that each child should have the right to refuse foot rubs or cuddling if the child wished to do so."

Bob Lay lamented, "Is there any hope? These are the people who are supposed to be understanding and advising families treating seriously disturbed children and they are telling parents they can't hug the seriously disturbed child if the child does not want it! It is as if a child were constantly running into the street, and the parents were told they can't hold him back if the child doesn't want it! Physically or psychologically, the child is going to end up dead. I guess it wouldn't matter so much if these people weren't the 'experts' with the power to tell the rest of us how to treat! Of course, the real losers are the children and society, which will have to deal with these kids in nontherapeutic settings—the courts and the jails."

Colorado is not the only state in which therapists and parents who practice intrusive techniques are confronted with skeptical and unbending bureaucracies. Joyce, the administrator of a California residential treatment program for adolescent boys, wrote to me, alarmed that decisions concerning treatment are now made by state licensing personnel rather than therapists and staff at the residence, limiting treatment options. One of the regulations propounded by the licensing bureau concerned a child exhibiting escalating out-of-control behavior. If a staff member laid hands on the child to guide or push him out of an area (say, away from other children), and the child turned and attacked the staff member, the incident would be considered "staff provocation." Any restraint needed after that would not be authorized or legitimized because the staff "provoked" it.

Joyce ruefully noted a conversation with an employee of the licensing bureau: "I asked the state licensing personnel if they were saying that there could be no options for helping a child control his behavior between verbal interaction and full restraint. The bureaucrat answered, 'I can't tell you how to run your program, but I can tell you the regulations.' Although the bureau would not be specific, the program was denied the use of holding sessions, a guiding arm around the shoulder, and even a hug that might elicit a negative response because these simple, effective interactions might cause a youngster to lash out and subsequently require restraint."

Joyce pointed out the paradoxical results of the misguided regulations: "When a child is angry, a gentle hand on the shoulder guiding the child away from the area often *prevents* the need for full restraint. With these new regulations, restraint will be used more frequently! These regulations have obviously been drafted by someone who has never worked with disturbed children."

Although Joyce was railing against an injustice that occurred to her program and others in California, she put her finger on a major problem when bureaucrats oversee foster homes and institutions that deal with severely disturbed children. The people who promulgate these rules generally have no experience with the population they are trying to "protect." The agency heads frequently get their jobs through political patronage, so their qualifications for the position may simply be that they campaigned for the winning candidate. The decisions that these people make are just as likely to turn on political considerations (what will keep their patrons in office) as on what is best for disturbed children. The civil servants who handle the day-to-day paperwork of the agency receive little special training in anything other than the agency's directives. Thus, their knowledge and what they find acceptable is restricted to the agency's manuals and memos. The social workers and psychologists directly employed by the agency are generally overburdened with cases. There are so many forms for them to fill out that they have little time to spend observing the children and the programs. Consequently, from top to bottom in these agencies, it is easier to follow what the supervisor says to do, not what someone in the field is proving works with real children.

It is also safer for bureaucrats to do what is popular rather than what is good for the kids. The agencies that regulate foster care listen closely to the winds of public opinion, even though the public is almost completely uninformed about what it takes to treat severely disturbed children. Child abuse by daycare workers and teachers is top-of-the-news material, and the unthinking public then suspects all caregivers. This puts pressure on child protective agencies to be overprotective. Another anecdote that Joyce recounted to me concerned what happened after a child was supposedly injured (broken rib) while a therapist was holding him in what is called the "basket restraint." This is a very safe restraint in which the worker or therapist sits behind a child. The child's arms are crossed over his chest, the worker holds his wrists, and the weight of the therapist is never placed on the child. "As for the broken rib that allegedly occurred," Joyce told me, "that can happen with *any* restraint. It is actually *less* likely to occur with a basket restraint." But in spite of the dozens of years that this restraint has been used, and the thousands of children it has been used with, it is now neither taught nor condoned in California because it was used inappropriately in one case. This is like banning the use of all automobiles in California because a careless driver had a wreck.

"Adolescents at Austin Center Abused, Report Says." This stark headline from the *Minneapolis Star Tribune* in January 1990 spelled the end of an old and effective Minneapolis treatment center. I received a copy of the article from an outstanding Minnesota therapist in private practice. Although she was not connected with the center, she had seen many extremely difficult children reached there following years of fruitless placement elsewhere. Her terse note on the corner of the page showed her sentiments: "Another great treatment center bites the dust."

The article reported that "Hennepin County officials said some of their clients feared for their safety, while Mower County officials reported physical restrictions lasting for hours and a 'reform school' atmosphere." The article detailed a county report that included, among other things, the following recommendations:

> Assurance that clients and guardians are fully informed of their rights, including the right to refuse aspects of treatment.

Modification of restrictive policies, including limiting physical holding of clients to fifteen minutes.

The Austin Center dealt with very disturbed adolescents and
teenagers. Assuring these clients the right to refuse aspects of treatment is analogous to allowing a two-year-old to refuse to go to
her room when her parents tell her to do so. And after more than
a quarter-century working with unattached children, I know that a
solidly difficult child doesn't come close to thinking the holder is
serious about treatment after only fifteen minutes of holding.
Sometimes it takes an hour or more just to get through to the child
that the holder is in control. Only then can any meaningful therapy
begin. By ensuring that the center did not have a reform school
atmosphere, the government agencies involved ensured a reform
school *reality* in the future for many of these children.

Another organization that has come under governmental scrutiny
recently is the Straight Treatment Program, which operates residential programs for drug-addicted adolescents and young adults
in several states. The program uses highly confrontive techniques,
and clients are referred to it only when other treatments have
failed. Although the treatment is not explicitly conceptualized as
attachment therapy as I will discuss in later chapters, clients are
pushed to rage, are made to feel helpless and hopeless, and are then
shown love by the group—all characteristics of the first-year-of-life
bonding experiences. Like all such programs, it is controversial,
and any public discussion of it is polarized between vocal support-
ers and vociferous opponents. It is not supported by the psychiatric
establishment, and those opposed to the program are mainly concerned about its controlling or possibly abusive aspects.

An article by Skip Hollandsworth in the June 1990 issue of
Texas Monthly explored this program in a fairly objective manner. Hollandsworth reported that a Texas gubernatorial candidate
chose the Straight program to help his own son, and urged the
state to spend at least "$50 million for adolescent-treatment cen-
ters based on Straight principles." Hollandsworth also quoted Dr.

Ian MacDonald, former director of the Drug Abuse Policy Office at the White House, as saying, "[Straight's] structure can deal with the most severe kids in our society, forcing them to change, giving them discipline."

This is a beautiful, observant comment by someone who is not directly involved in intrusive therapy. Predictably, however, the psychiatric community as a whole is not so enchanted with Straight. The program has been characterized as "fiercely controlling," and a rival traditional hospital spokesman said, "By the time a kid gets out of the program, he really has trouble thinking for himself." Without cynicism, I answer this criticism with two questions: Was the kid truly "thinking for himself" before he got into the program? And why such a concern for a child's thinking skills when the child is an out-of-control, self-destructive, violent, drug abuser whose next "treatment center" is likely to be jail? Thinking skills can be taught later. As Ann Petito, past director of the Dallas Straight program, noted in Hollandsworth's article, "In treatment like this, we're dealing with little animals. People forget that these kids are druggies. They cannot maintain any self-control. It's our job to get out their anger and remold their lives." These antisocial kids are not going to change just because society would like them to. They must be forced to look at themselves and to see the damage and pain they are causing themselves in order for them to want to change.

In spite of Straight's overall success with their clients, the program was investigated by the Texas Commission on Alcohol and Drug Abuse after complaints from some parents. One host-home father allegedly tied a child up to keep him from fighting. In another case, a child was allegedly not given medical treatment after his nose was broken. There were stories of "kids being forced to urinate in plastic containers and having to sleep five to a room in a host home." Hollandsworth reported that the Texas Commission required that Straight not use towels and sanitary napkins to restrain kids who were acting out, among other restrictions.

Other actions were taken against Straight centers in other

states. In Virginia in 1983, a center was ordered to pay $220,000 in damages to a young man who claimed that the center illegally held him against his will. Lawsuits were filed against a Straight center in Cincinnati on behalf of clients who claimed they were painfully restrained or imprisoned in small time-out rooms for hours at a time.

On the surface, these charges against the Straight program seem to have merit. According to the interpretation our courts and legislatures have given the Constitution, it's not right for people to be restrained against their will. People shouldn't be subjected to pain if they don't like it. And the prevailing attitude in the country today is that people should have medical treatment if they desire it.

However, we must look at these charges in the context of who is involved. The Straight program deals with drug abusers. In general, drug addicts don't care about anybody or anything; all they care about is getting high. People who have to handle these cases— nurses in hospitals, administrators of rehab centers, police—know that addicts are as manipulative as they come. They will say anything to get you to do what they want you to do. In addition, the worst ones will lie, steal, and even kill for their habits. So if one of them says a therapist "hurt" her, or that she was "imprisoned," a grain of salt is certainly a necessity. As I mentioned before, all controlling interaction "hurts" unattached children.

Along with the skepticism reserved for testimony from such individuals must go a larger perspective. If the addict experiences some pain when restrained with a towel, it is certainly less than the pain she will feel if she were to be arrested and handcuffed. The same goes for the child who is angry about being held against his will in treatment. Would he be less angry if he were turned loose from therapy untreated, to continue his destructive behavior and be incarcerated later in the county jail? Hospitals and treatment centers do not hold clients against their will without reason; in general, hospitalization or treatment against the client's will is attempted only when the client has a history of very poor and self-destructive choices. These people are angry, resentful, uncooperative, and often violent, and most have amply demonstrated self-destructiveness and danger to their family and others.

The Texas Department of Mental Health and Mental Retardation (DMHMR) oversees the operation of psychiatric hospitals in that state. The regulations it has promulgated concerning treatment of clients are not the most onerous ever seen in the country; rather, they are symptomatic of how government bureaucracies are hobbling treatment of severely disturbed children.

The DMHMR mandated the following rules in 1992:

> The behavioral and privilege status of children cannot be posted in the hallways or common areas, as this is "demeaning" to the patients.
> Adolescents must have access to telephones where they can talk in private.
> Visiting by parents and friends cannot be restricted.
> A notice stating that children have the right to report concerns about treatment must be conspicuously posted in all units. [The required notice contains a telephone number of a government hotline children or adolescents can call if they do not like their treatment.]

The reaction of the professionals in charge of the children was dismay, shock, and outrage. It also changed nothing. "Boy, it's 'drug city' time around here," said a therapist in one hospital. "These kids are going to be *dealing* from the units. There's no way to stop it when calls can't be monitored and any friends or family can visit. With rules like these, treatment stops.

"I don't know what gets into these government bureaucrats! All I can figure out is that they never worked in an effective treatment program and know little about disturbed adolescents. All across our state in regular classrooms, teachers check off the kids' behavioral status on the bulletin boards, and level systems are clearly displayed. The kids need this! No one thinks that those checkmarks are 'demeaning' in the classrooms, and now we can't post status in a psychiatric hospital. . . . The kids hate it. They used to be able to be encouraging to their friends: 'Hey, Mark, get off of Level 2 so you can come on the trip with us.' Now all that is gone, and peer pressure is being reduced to seeing who can smuggle in the most drugs."

As for calling a hotline to complain about treatment, if treatment is to be effective for young delinquents, there *should* be things about it that the adolescents definitely do not like. Most of these children are absolutely anti-authority. To encourage them to call a hotline to report disagreements with treatment massively undermines that treatment. Imagine if parents were required to post a similar sign in their homes for their children: "If you don't like how your parents are treating you, call. . . ."

It is as if, in a schizophrenic way, government places progressively stricter regulations on what it can control to make up for being barely able to touch far more important elements—such as birth parents who abuse and neglect their children in the home. Those who must follow government regulations are easy targets for harassment through strict limits. Although the government cannot seem to reverse the increase in child abuse and neglect that produces angry, unattached, dangerous children, it does seem to be doing all it can to restrict therapeutic professionals who are trying to fix these broken children. And as the next chapter details, the psychiatric community is doing precious little to help.

6

THE THERAPIST'S ROLE

Our government bureaucracy, with its well-intentioned but misguided attempt to "help" everyone, is responsible for many of the thousands of disturbed children our society produces every year. Unfortunately, official psychiatry, which should be trying to combat governmental policies that exacerbate psychological epidemics, is of little help either. A typical statement is the following one given in May 1990 by the president of the American Psychiatric Association. After noting the significant rise in teens killing others, she said:

> The literature in this area presents widely varying views on juvenile murderers, and case literature has not yielded a unified perspective. While some in the field have held that these youths are simply cold-blooded murderers, others take the more sympathetic view that they are the products of their environments.
>
> This second hypothesis may more often be closer to the truth. Although there is no typical profile of the juvenile murderer, most have been found to share at least one factor in their backgrounds: They have been subjected to some kind of physical and/or sexual abuse; in short, they are already psychiatric casualties before they pull a trigger or lift a fist.

This sounds like a well-considered, evenhanded presentation. However, what she and much of the psychological establishment ignores is that juvenile murderers are often both cold-blooded *and* products of their environment; the either-or logic that this speaker used simply clouds the discussion. Sympathy has nothing to do with the issue. The question is how to reach these juveniles so that we can stop them from murdering, stop them from attacking others, stop them from having and abusing their own children and starting another generation on the same path.

Helping Professions or "Hindering" Professions?

It is my contention that character-disturbed children can be reached only by applying nontraditional intrusive techniques. Only after these children have recreated the first-year-of-life bonding cycle and formed an attachment to other people can they be treated with traditional therapy. In other words, therapists can't build therapeutic relationships with these children using traditional techniques because these children cannot relate to others on any basis.

Sadly for these children, the psychological establishment doesn't recognize this. The professional community doesn't quite know how to respond to intrusive therapy. Although the confrontive techniques that I teach have been around for a long time (for example, Anne Sullivan used them with Helen Keller before World War I), many people still feel that they are new, weird, harmful, ineffective, or dangerous. Niko and Elizabeth Tinbergen, therapists who used these techniques with autistic children, wrote in their 1983 book, *Autistic Children: New Hope for a Cure,* that this perception is especially ingrained in psychiatrists, psychologists, and other established therapists who have been trained in solid traditional techniques—good techniques that work with most children and adults most of the time.

However, there is a fast-growing body of children with whom these traditional techniques do not work. Tennessee therapist Sharon Gary, who uses intrusive therapy, recalls an example from her early years in the field:

> During my training, my professor was working with a seven- or eight-year-old kid who was running around the playroom. There was a toy phone available, and the professor picked it up, and for minutes on the phone said, "Calling Bobby, calling Bobby . . . Bobby, will you please pick up the phone." It was as if my professor thought something great was really happening while the kid ran around paying no attention whatsoever. I

remember, even as a student, being suspicious that this play therapy session really was not therapeutic.

I recall that during my own psychiatric residency, I "invited"
clients to work on their problems. But so many disturbed adolescents and adults said, in essence, "Screw your invitation," that I
started getting disconcerted. Everything that I had been taught
would work—interpretation, reality therapy, understanding, positive regard—wasn't working!

It took me some time before I found out why these people were
rejecting the invitation. Some of these individuals did not have a
core—in popular psychology, they had no "inner child." They
couldn't form attachments to other people, and when things went
wrong, it was always someone else's problem.

Others of these individuals did have a core, but they had experienced so much loss and pain starting early in their lives that the
core was crusted over as a defense against further pain. The crust
is lighter and easier to get through under certain conditions:

The child is younger.
The child once had someone to whom he was close.
The child's loss was not multiple.
The child has dealt with some feelings.
The abuse and neglect were not severe.
The child is not physically impaired.

If these conditions prevail, the crust may be slowly melted away by
giving the child unqualified positive regard, or chipped away by
forced holding and snuggling. However, when the child is older, the
crust is usually much stronger. This child may have never known
her parents, may have a long history of neglect, may have been
shunted from one foster home to another. In such cases, the crust
must be shattered by very intrusive recreation of the bonding cycle.
Once heavily confrontive techniques clear the crust away, traditional techniques can be used to work through the underlying
problems.

However, the bulk of therapists are locked into using techniques that are unproductive with seriously disturbed children. They start off using traditional, nonconfrontive techniques that simply bounce off these children's crusts. The average therapist gives far too much respect and tacit approval to neurotic or disturbed needs that are the result of childhood trauma. This mistaken, yet conventional, doctrine decrees the following:

> Abused children have problems with punishment; therefore, punitive measures should never be used.
>
> Sexually abused children may hate to be touched or lovingly held by a therapist of the same sex as the abuser; therefore, this shouldn't be done.
>
> Children from dysfunctional families have been heavily hassled; therefore, they shouldn't be hassled.
>
> Children who have suffered loss will be harmed immeasurably if left by their parents; therefore, they should never be left by their parents.

The traditionalist logic behind this can be stated, "You can treat very disturbed children, but only in a way *they* feel good about." This is absurd, for it saddles therapists with techniques that are known to be ineffective. As one therapist told me, "At least we know we're not doing any harm." But knowing we're not doing any harm doesn't justify not doing any good. All too often, children are treated over and over with the same fruitless techniques, and at a cost to society that increases with each passing year.

Confusing Pain and Abuse

People who have seen well-conducted confrontive sessions in their entirety are invariably favorably impressed, as are professionals who are in the trenches with very disturbed children. This group is receptive to these techniques because they have seen how ineffective other forms of therapy are for children who are candidates for confrontive techniques. On the other hand, those who have not seen the therapy for themselves, but who have heard about it from others or have viewed sections of videotapes of the therapy (sometimes on news programs) without seeing the results almost uniformly have severe reservations if not outright hostility to such therapy. And good therapists who have gotten positive results from most children with traditional techniques are predisposed, understandably, to distrust those who use confrontive techniques.

What critics in the field concentrate on is the supposed abuse that they perceive during confrontive sessions. This is how one Denver psychiatrist reacted after viewing a tape of therapy:

> The practitioners appear to be taking a sadistic sort of pleasure from their maltreatment of the child. They call him names, ridicule and berate him, direct profanity toward him, and require him to direct profanity toward them in return. They require intense and unrelenting physical contact which is in itself overstimulating and could easily be construed by the child in sexualized terms. In addition, they frequently "knuckle" the ribs of the child in a way which appears quite aggressive, and appears to be perceived by the child as aversive and both physically and mentally painful.
>
> In short, the "therapy" appears to indicate the belief that the end justifies the means; hence, it is acceptable to strip a child of his basic rights as a human being of treatment in a caring and respectful manner, and that it is also acceptable to exploit the small stature and weakness of the child relative to that of an adult in a physically abusive fashion so long as it is aimed at ridding the child of his "inner anger" (which most likely derives from a past history of abuse much like that which is now billed as "therapy").

This angry response comes from a physician who saw only part of a therapy session with a homicidal boy. It is honest and perceptive, *but it is by no means the complete story.* The physician may not have known that this child was removed from his home after he made serious, repeated death threats against his siblings, and that he raped his little sister on numerous occasions. The physician may not have known that this boy threatened his crippled younger brother with a kitchen knife, and that he had a long history of being unresponsive to usual therapeutic techniques. The physician doesn't mention in his review of the tape the loving, rocking, sobbing, and cuddling-in that took place after the child had finally expressed his rage. And the physician may not have known that, while undergoing this therapy, the boy was behaving more appropriately at home and at school than ever before.

In the last sentence of this doctor's evaluation is a thinly veiled accusation that intrusive techniques are abusive. This is an important point to consider. Intrusive techniques do cause discomfort in the clients, and clients do perceive that they are "painful." Is this abuse, though? First, look at the clients. Unattached children invariably say that any controlling touch "hurts" them; they perceive pain in any sort of contact that they themselves do not control. And these children are expert manipulators; therefore, the source of the complaints must be considered when evaluating their validity. Second, look at the definition of *abuse*. The best definition that I have heard is that abuse is physical or psychological pain caused by the wrong person, acting in the wrong way, at the wrong time, for the wrong reason, with a negative outcome. *Helping* these children involves causing them psychological or physical discomfort for the right reason, at the right time, to obtain a positive outcome.

Unfortunately, the psychological profession tends to focus on the discomfort or pain itself, and calls that abuse, without looking at other variables. Pushing a person to rage is not something our culture teaches is a good thing; most people want to be calm and friendly. But suffering is part of almost any truly corrective emotional experience. Shedding layers of emotional scars is neither easy nor comfortable for the afflicted person, and when it is done in a rush, as when intrusive techniques are used, it is extremely difficult for untrained individuals to watch.

As a result, detractors concentrate on the heavily confrontive techniques. In professional circles, those who employ intrusive techniques when absolutely necessary are branded as using them all the time, just as a physician who is willing to use electroshock therapy (which can be helpful with some intractable depressions) becomes known as "the shock doc." The media generally feeds this, as pictures of intrusive techniques have much higher shock value than do pictures of play therapy or music therapy.

Ignored is the fact that intrusive therapists freely admit that these techniques are unnecessary with most clients, and that when they are necessary, they serve only to open the client to love and attachment to others. They are the best and quickest way to purposefully reach unbonded children, character-disturbed individuals, and neurotics who hide life-threatening conflicts and self-destructiveness with massive denial. When the client is open, traditional techniques are used long-term for good and lasting results.

Lack of Support for Therapy That Works

When confrontive techniques work with a previously unreachable child, there is usually only grudging acceptance rather than support from the professional community. As a result, there may be little follow-up available for children who need additional help. The following experience, related to me by a mother I met when I was conducting a workshop, is repeated in case after case. Years previously, her daughter Wendy had undergone confrontive techniques as a young adolescent with a competent therapy group. I know several of the therapists who had been involved in her treatment, and they are outstanding professionals:

> We moved here from [the state where the therapy had been carried out]. With all Wendy's losses, I am sure the move was hard for her. And she regressed some. Wendy had been helped so much. I just took her into our local therapist to be fine-tuned, but it has gone the opposite way. He had heard of your holding techniques and said he didn't believe in them. Now we are back to square one and she is screaming at me and Ed while hating herself! Now she says she was just "play-acting" at being loving and all the gains she made in therapy were a con! And I know that's not true. She did well for years, then met some friends here and backslid. But I honestly think the therapist is undermining all the good changes she made because he doesn't agree with the therapy. The saddest thing of all is that he thinks he is helping!

You might ask why this mother didn't just walk out of the therapist's office and find another professional. Sometimes, this is not possible. In small towns, or in areas far from population centers, alternative therapies are not always available. Some towns may have only one therapist or center, and sometimes these centers have to follow the philosophy laid down by an inflexible bureaucracy. There are insurance considerations as well. The family may get its health care through a managed-care group with which their employer has contracted. That group may not include physicians who believe in intrusive techniques, so payment for any such treatments would have to come out of the parents' own pockets. Getting a private bureaucracy to change its ways is like getting the government to move. How can one family fight that?

I would love to end this chapter on a positive note—something like, "Despite these problems, things are getting better." I can't do that.

Things are not getting better.

Children are becoming sicker and more difficult to reach, and there seems to be an inability on the part of American psychological professionals to understand that the needs of solidly disturbed children differ from those of overindulged or anxious children. The underlying therapeutic message is that gentle love is enough for all of America's unhappy children. However, severely disturbed children come from backgrounds of abuse, neglect, multiple moves and losses, and problems that originate in infancy. These children need a different kind of love—the type that forces them to love others.

It is ironic that at a time when therapists show great concern about the use of highly confrontive techniques, the states of Colorado and Virginia are working with delinquent juveniles in what can only be called boot camps, complete with disrespectful, insulting "drill sergeants" and demeaning tasks imposed for infractions. These are being administered through the penal systems of those states, perhaps because the psychological community is not yet ready to accept attachment and bonding techniques. The programs have very low profiles, as must be the case in this age of litigation. I can see that if information leaks out on the methods necessary to reach these severely disturbed youths, these programs will probably be shut down quickly.

The process of educating professionals to the advantages of using intrusive techniques is slow—by and large, these techniques are not taught in medical schools, and most physicians still see them as possibly dangerous methods used only by some charismatic practitioners on the fringe of the field. Some insurance companies, faced with the possibility of fighting off lawsuits from disgruntled parents or clients, are withdrawing or restricting insurance for centers that use the techniques.

In court cases and in legislative chambers, the testimony of unattached children and professionals untrained in intrusive techniques is given greater credence than that of trained therapeutic professionals. These manipulative children know which buttons to push to make outsiders and government agencies do what they want. (I have many tapes of children admitting lies that they told about therapy to parents, police, and government and school officials.) This results in government agencies passing increasingly punitive rules restricting treatment options for severely disturbed children. And the professional advice that helps shape these rules usually comes from therapists who have no training in intrusive techniques and who very often have never dealt with unattached children.

Perhaps the only way professionals can learn how to deal with the unattached is through firsthand experience. Letter after letter comes to me detailing how unwary professionals misunderstand how manipulative unattached children are. Usually, these letters are from parents of conscienceless children, but the following letter is from Troy, a thoughtful professional who "felt sorry" for a waif-like adolescent we will call Roy, who claimed that his family "didn't understand him." Troy had Roy moved to his own home in an effort to help him, but Roy merely ripped him off materially and emotionally. When Roy entered therapy with another professional, Troy found himself being blamed for Roy's problems.

Troy first wrote to me in the hope that I might be able to help, but I had to reply that Roy was too old for confrontive therapy unless he himself felt the need and initiated it. Although I could do little, Troy was impressed because I was the first person who seemed to understand his situation. His reply is so typical of those parents or caring professionals who learn the hard way: by becoming involved with a severely disturbed teenager. The signs and symptoms are all here: the boy is a con artist, and helping professionals are sucked in by his act; therapy, though good and expensive, doesn't help; those who befriend the child feel frightened and violated by his rage:

I thought I'd drop a quick note to let you know what transpired with Roy and I since you have so kindly taken an interest.

In September or October his counselor phoned and requested that I reenter treatment/counseling sessions with Roy. She said she had come to realize that excluding me was probably not for the best since they would only have Roy for a comparatively short time before I may have to deal with him again. So, reluctantly, I nervously attended a meeting with him and her after not having had any contact for something like nine weeks. Roy, in his own subtle way, and using the communication we know from each other, cut me down, berated me, and basically seemed to enjoy humiliating me while using the power he drew from having "*his* counselor" on his side. When he left, I was pretty devastated and even more so when his counselor said, "I think that went extremely well." She was totally oblivious to the recurring statement from Roy that "Now that I have reestablished contact with my *real* family, I don't need or want you around." I left basically knowing I was about to become the bad guy and scapegoat for all his problems. Two weeks later, fully intent on saying goodbye, I met with them again. As we sat down, Roy started crying . . . much to his counselor's surprise. When she asked what was wrong, Roy said, "Troy's about to say goodbye . . . I feel it." Well, before I could say anything, he begged, pleaded, and cried for forty-five minutes, telling me he needed me and was sorry he said all he did since he really didn't mean what he said about wanting me gone. The poor counselor, who never thought he had any feelings for me, was completely taken in, not recognizing what I thought was probably a con. Rather than fall back into a routine of immediately accepting him back, I told him I would be in touch (and now I'm *very* glad

I handled it that way). Due to scheduling problems, I was unable to meet with him for a few weeks, but I sent him a letter detailing my feelings and my concerns, and letting him know that if he wanted my support, he would have to put forth the effort to keep me informed and keep in contact with me. After a month, with no contact, calls, etc., whatsoever from him, I found out that the residential center had begun giving Roy four-hour passes. He was using them to contact old friends and some old drug contacts, but never once made an effort to contact me. So, I contacted his counselor and found out that he told her this about me: "Troy will never leave. Anytime I want him there he will be there, and I don't need to hassle with contacting him. The people I want to see right now are my friends. Troy will come around soon enough." After that, I simply wrote Roy a note severing all ties with him. I now honestly feel that his crying episode was nothing more than another manipulative ploy, and a con with tears, which is exactly what I told him.

So, I have not seen, heard from, or had contact with Roy for thirteen weeks now. I intend to keep it this way, forever if I have to. I really felt that until he realized that I wasn't there and did walk from him, he would continue to feel like he could use and assault me and the friendship. In addition, it is fairly clear to me based on the people he is choosing to contact on his passes that he will either drop out of the program, or shortly after completing it will return to the drug abuse. Worse, the people at the center don't see it! That will only accelerate his antisocial personality disorder, I think, and make him much more violent (probably toward me again).

The last I heard, he has done as I predicted and has made me the bad guy. I was told in no uncertain terms by his family that Roy's drug use, social problems, and distancing from them were all my doing and thank God they were clued in by Roy on how hurtful I was to him! Roy told me about the same things about his family when I took custody of him. So anyway, as hard and painful as it is, I am trying to go on with my life and put Roy in the past. My only fear is that he will someday retaliate violently against me.

I cannot begin to tell you how many people, both parents and professionals, have related similar stories to me.

Unless we can change the prevailing attitude among government regulators and the professional community that pain and discomfort equals abuse, that simple love and understanding are what all troubled children need to become functioning citizens, and that disturbed people can only be treated gently because of past abuse, there can be little hope that American society will be released from the cycle of increasing crime and increasing justice system costs. Therapists will label more children as unreachable, the state will build more prisons, juvenile homes, and hospitals, but we shall never see the end of it. For these unreachable, unattached adolescents and adults will continue to wreak havoc on the streets, will continue to have new unattached children, and will continue to degrade us all until we all end up living in our own private jails.

Part 3

REAL TREATMENT FOR CONSCIENCELESS CHILDREN

7

THERAPY CAN WORK

Despite the dismal record that traditional modes of therapy have had with the unattached, there is an approach that provides hope for these children. This is intrusive or confrontive therapy, and it is the only approach that has proven effective.

Helping Children *Get* Better, Not Just *Feel* Better

Intrusive therapy involves physical holding and sometimes verbally provocative techniques that bring on expressions and feelings of loss, pain, rage, helplessness, and finally hopelessness—the process through which a person must go to form attachment. It forces psychological engagement when an individual would rather withdraw or passively or actively control the situation. The therapist makes the client confront the anger that is trapped inside, rather than nibbling around the edges of it.

The intrusive techniques cannot be adequately understood from simply reading about them. Learning intrusive techniques can only take place through mentoring. It takes many months of frontline experience with a qualified therapist for a newcomer to use the techniques effectively.

In Chapter 1, I introduced the concept of reciprocity as it applies to an infant—the reciprocal smile plays a major role in the child's initial bonding. Bonding with others in intrusive therapy sessions takes place partly through the emphasis that the therapist places on reciprocal responses, and each session ideally ends with a reciprocal smile. It takes energy, knowledge, and time to go through a process that leads a pouting, negative, angry child to

109

become someone who relates quickly, easily, and with a smile. This is the reason that transcripts of intrusive therapy sessions seem so repetitive—the therapist is working to obtain the right verbal response (quick, loud, snappy) from the child before expecting to obtain the right behavioral response:

Therapist: Got it?

Patient: Uh-huh.

Therapist: "Uh-huh!" I don't want an "uh-huh!" Got it?!

Patient: *(Slowly)* Got it.

Therapist: I don't want a slow "got it," I want a quick "got it." Got it?

Patient: Got it!

Therapist: Super! That sounded great! Now I want you to get that cup and bring it here. Got it?

Patient: Got it!

Therapist: Fast or slow?

Patient: Fast!

Therapist: Right! Thanks! Go!

Disturbed children have poor reciprocity. This is often what parents mean when they complain, "This child doesn't give." What they actually mean is, "This child doesn't give *back*," for these children do give, but only on their own terms. Sometimes parents of attachment-disordered children make seemingly nonspecific, yet evidently very painful, complaints, for it is hard for the parents to nail down the exact reasons that they are unhappy. At times the child is loving and giving; sometimes she is able to do her chores appropriately. Overall, however, the child does not respond appropriately. (Responding to someone is reciprocity.) Here is what an adoptive father said about his daughter:

> It is hard to describe sometimes what goes wrong. When my wife and I are excited about something, Janice isn't. There may be times when she's telling a joke that we *all* laugh at, but that's rare.
>
> I guess, mainly, we attempt to laugh at her jokes, but she has

a hard time laughing at ours. Generally, when we are excited and up, Janice is two-thirds morose or pouting for no good reason. On the other hand, she gets excited about things that we don't. She might be talking about what a hunk some boy is, and obviously and without conflict can hardly wait to jump his bones. It's hard to get excited envisioning that. She's all excited about getting a car, and she has horrible coordination. When and if she gets a license, she'll be a menace on the highway. We can't share her excitement about that. She gets excited about the possibility of attending a rock concert when she has saved no money for it. She has no idea how to get there and back, except Mom and Dad are somehow expected to come through and drive her. It's hard to get excited about that. Looking at it honestly, the times that we all share the same happy response is when we're giving her a present.

Pushing Severely Disturbed Children to Bond

Since the severely disturbed children who are candidates for intrusive therapy have never developed basic trust, this therapy helps them form it by purposely recapitulating the first-year-of-life experiences. This is not easy for lay people and even professionals to watch, for what the practitioner is doing is actually pushing (provoking) the client to feel helpless and hopeless, like a baby, by holding the client and making him uncomfortable. The result is that the client goes into a rage. However, this rage is not the simple screaming of an infant—the child yells, strikes out, tries to bite, sulks, curses, threatens, struggles, and kicks before finally submitting to the therapist's authority. Through this experience, the client learns that he can allow someone else to control him without getting hurt, which is often the opposite of what the child learned early in life. After this, the child can work through the rage in an atmosphere of love, leading to attachment and bonding.

With a younger child this rage can often be accomplished by simple holding in the adult's lap long enough for the child to go through the bonding process. With an older child, or with a child whose defense mechanisms are stronger, more than simple holding is required, as the rage trapped in such a client is less accessible. To provoke a response, the therapist may have to confront the child verbally as well. This combination of verbal and physical confrontation may be disturbing and even frightening, but it works. As with the younger child, the older client experiences helplessness, hopelessness, and rage, capitulates, receives acceptance and love from the therapist, and begins to bond.

This therapy is called by various names around the world—containment and trust, circle of inclusion, trust and attachment development, and holding therapy—and some practitioners claim that what they do is actually different from what everyone else using these techniques does. (This is the Madison Avenue approach—"Ours is Newer! Better! Different!") In all cases, though, the activity centering around holding therapy is based on a recognition of the interwoven nature of the following steps in bonding for the client:

The safe expression of rage, and a safe way of working
    through it
Relinquishing control
Developing trust
Working through loss and separation
Building attachment and bonding

Although the exact techniques used to achieve this may vary from therapist to therapist, the essential goal is the same. For instance, all twelve-step programs emphasize the essential truth that control must be relinquished as basic trust is recognized, accepted, and internalized. With adults, intrusive therapies are used in reality attack groups and in certain drug or substance abuse rehabilitation centers. And echoes of these concepts have been popularized in sexual therapy under the "joy of surrender" rubric.

Outward Bound makes extensive use of this concept. Years ago, as a consultant to the program, I saw severely disturbed children after they had faced a safe but fearful experience in a raft or on a rope on the side of a cliff. They were forced to relinquish control and depend on others. Only then could they bond to their leader. Listen to the experience one "river rat" has had with these kids (and I have heard similar testimony from many other leaders):

> On the first day, there is nothing but trouble from the kids. They don't want to get up; they need to be poured from their sleeping bags. They moan about the food and won't help fix it.
>
> One day on the river changes all that! After I've yelled "back paddle," "paddle right," and "paddle left" for a day, they honestly believe I've saved their asses from every hole on the river, and maybe I have. By the next morning, it's "How can I help you with breakfast, Jean?" It's a complete transformation.

Before talking of pushing children to health, let me reemphasize that cooperation rather than confrontation works with most clients most of the time. Given time, average clients will come to understand their problems, and will work through them bit by bit. However, invitations to cooperate are not useful with the conscienceless children who face therapists today. The longer the child is allowed to keep control, the more the child's heart is encrusted with impenetrable defensive layers. These layers block the painful feelings of loss, sorrow, and bereavement that the child must feel in order to bond, until the child is finally beyond help.

Critics of holding therapy have said, "Why push so hard? Take it slower; instead of forcing out a pot-full of rage, dip it out with a teaspoon. Either method will eventually get to the sorrow, emptiness, and loss, which are the real issues."

Perhaps the teaspoon method will eventually work. But many of these kids don't have much time. A year can make a lasting difference! Many of these kids wreck more than one foster home in that period. While the therapist is dutifully chipping away at the defense layers, the child can be stealing, assaulting people, smoking crack, or worse. As one therapist lamented about a teenaged client, "I was afraid her uterus would expand before her brain." Although these kids' minds may not be mature, their bodies certainly are, and they have a propensity to have, and later destroy, their own babies.

Recently, a Colorado convenience store was robbed. This is such a common experience nowadays that it has become fodder for late-night talk show monologues. If you look at the robbery from the point of view of the criminal, the act has a sort of perverted sense to it—he was low on cash, he wanted some, he had the means to get it (a gun), and he took it. But he then forced everyone in the store, adults and kids alike, to lie face down on the floor, and then *shot them one by one.* An army of therapists with traditional teaspoons could never help this type of severely disturbed individual in time to prevent him from committing other such attacks.

Opening Up the Severely Disturbed

Intrusive techniques do not cure by themselves. They do, however, open the individual's heart to love and positive relationships. They help children respond and bond quickly, so successful therapy outcomes are much more likely. The client accepts and wants change, based on his identification with the confrontive person. Only then is it possible to establish a therapeutic alliance; only then can traditional methods be used. Thus, to the charge that the changes caused by intrusive techniques do not last, the response is, "Of course!" The changes are locked in with essential follow-up and follow-through over time. Great therapists and great techniques will influence the amount of change, but the time it takes the client to assimilate that change is a biological given that can't be speeded up.

To get the client opened up, the therapist must first not validate the client's neurotic or disturbed needs resulting from childhood trauma. Children by their actions say, "Considering all I've been through, you don't dare touch me (talk to me, look at me, etc.) like that! I have my needs and you had better respect them." Adults will come right out and say this, in one way or another. The average therapist will agree with the client's assertion, back down from challenging the individual, and effectively relinquish control of the therapy to the client!

What the bulk of professionals must realize is that when needs are based on dysfunctional backgrounds, it is better not to validate them. Far too many therapists are horror-struck at the idea of a male holding an out-of-control, rageful, previously abused girl. But here are my notes on what happened the first time I saw a young girl who had been sexually abused at her preschool three years earlier, and had been going to a traditional therapist ever since:

> I first saw Joyce in a private conference room at Denver International Airport. When I entered the room, her therapist of three years sat beside the desk that Joyce hid beneath. "She always acts like this, and often is in too much pain to talk with me," he explained. It was obvious that for three years he had respected Joyce's need for her space while attempting to build a therapeutic relationship that simply wasn't there. I pulled Joyce out from under the desk, saying, "Okay, kiddo, let's have some fun." While her therapist at first watched in horror, I bounced Joyce on her back on the sofa. She started laughing. By and by I had a conversation with her about her preschool experiences which she talked about easily. "This is the most she's talked in three years!" exclaimed the startled therapist.

What the therapeutic community must do is wake up and realize that if a dysfunctional need or response is to be changed, it must be worked through. Therapists aren't in business to help people *get over* their feelings—friends and well-meaning neighbors do that. The result is that the feeling is rationalized and walled up, and another layer is built between the person and his feelings. The feeling doesn't disappear; the person just can't access it. If the person can't access the feeling, the feeling can't be resolved.

This is what happens to empty, conscienceless individuals. Their pain, sorrow, or loss was so great early in life that they walled it up in order to survive. They don't like experiencing their feelings when another person assumes control. Thus, when working with the conscienceless, provoking may often mean interacting with nearly the same level of intrusiveness that brought about the feelings in the first place. This is not easy on the patient, but it is the therapist's job to disturb the disturbed.

Holding Disturbed Individuals

I emphasize the need for touch, usually dispensed as holding, when working with severely disturbed children. However, touch by itself is not helpful—when it is given and who controls it decides its effectiveness. Disturbed children often insist on touch and even provoke it as long as it is carried out on their terms. This manipulative behavior only serves to enforce their control of the situation, and allows no opportunity to build trust. For instance, Donna, an eleven-year-old in residential treatment, had developed a number of ways to control how and when she was touched, according to her caseworker:

> One of her main problems in the cottage is her relentless attempt at seeking the attention of all child-care workers. Earlier, this was often achieved by behaving inappropriately and usually ended up in very negative ways; i.e., being dragged off to the quiet room kicking and screaming. Now she continues to bug us at every turn with unimportant questions, aches and pains, and so on.

At this point, the caseworker showed me a small plastic bottle with a weird collection of bits of styrofoam, plastic shavings, lint, and pieces of pencil lead. Donna reportedly would put these objects in her eyes and then come out running, her eyes swollen and red, complaining of "something in my eye." She also poked small holes in her abdomen with the tip of a crochet hook, which was discovered when she complained of a skin rash. Such attention-getting devices actually reflected Donna's need to be touched and cared for, but on her terms.

Sadly, touch-deprived kids are in a bind. Although they need more physical contact, touch, and holding than the average healthy child, they themselves deflect others' attempts to touch them. First, they may be most unlovable, and an untrained, exasperated worker's reaction will often be, "Who wants to hold a kid like that?" A fair reaction, but unproductive. Second, they don't easily accept touch and love when they are offered. A young child will likely struggle away, shouting, "Don't touch me!" The response of an older individual might be, "What are you, a homo?" These individuals view the touch they need so badly as a potential means of control. A simple hug means terrifying containment. If they are held by a trained therapist, on the therapist's terms, they will usually go into a rage.

What comes to my mind when I see this happening is a cornered cat arching its back to appear ferocious and antagonistic. When faced with such an animal, even the largest dog will back off to a safer distance. Our usual reaction is to stay away—most of us feel that it's not worth the scratches to try to get close to such an animal. But someone who works with animals knows better. When the cat is first picked up, it will go into a greater fury, clawing and biting to try to break free. However, if the handler continues to lovingly contain the cat, while talking softly to it, it will settle down and begin to accept the love and petting. Rageful children react likewise to the loving, therapeutic holding that I will describe.

The calming effect of loving, tender holding may be seen in other mammals. Roger Payne, who has studied the behavior of whales for many years, wrote the following in a March 1976 *National Geographic* article:

> The mother whale simply endures the hijinks of an infant as if her peaceful good nature were an endless resource from which she, and the calf, can draw. I have watched many a calf boisterously playing about its resting mother for hours at a time, sliding off her flukes, wriggling up onto her back, covering her blowhole with its tail, breaching against her repeatedly, butting into her flank, all without perceptible reaction from the mother. When finally she does respond to the torment, it may be only to roll onto her back and embrace the infant in her arm-like flippers, holding it until it calms down.

An excellent approximation of the treatment needed to reach today's delinquent children can be found in the way that animal trainers "gentle" wild horses. Although many therapists may resent comparing children to horses, we can learn a great deal about humans by studying how other mammals respond to responsible and caring authority. Very often I have seen out-of-control toddlers who, I am sure, would be reached more quickly by a loving animal trainer than by parents who plead ineffectively for the children to stop misbehaving.

Here is what R. M. Hayes says about gentling a wild horse in the book *Horse Breaking*. First the trainer ties one of the horse's hind legs to its tail, and then loops the rope around the horse's neck. The horse's own struggles against the rope force him to roll over on his side:

> No attempt should be made to throw the animal forcibly down; for the effect we would aim at is that to be produced by his giving in to power which he finds irresistible. Hence, the more he fights and pits the strength of his muscles against the action of the mechanical appliances, the better will be the result of our victory.
>
> I have never seen in many scores of cases any injury result from it. The horse may now be kept, say ten minutes on the ground with his head pulled around to his side and gentled. When gentling the horse on the ground, the breaker should remain on [the horse's] back . . . so as to keep out of reach of his heels. The gentling is performed by passing the hand over various parts of the body, gently rubbing, kneading, or bending them as required to make the horse relax his muscles. . . . The object of the gentling is to show the horse that he need fear nothing from the touch of man, and that he must submit to it. To carry out the latter part of this condition we may, if the horse shows fight while gentling him, pull his head sharply around to his side by the cord so as to punish him; and when he gives in, we may, as a reward, relax the tension.
>
> If the animal goes down without a struggle and sulks on the ground, he should be forced to "show fight" by keeping him in the constrained position until he has got rid, by ineffectual struggling, of most of his "temper." When a horse begins to groan and to considerably moderate the violence of his struggles, we may feel confident that the sulk has been taken out of him, more or less, and that he is fit to be allowed to get on to his feet again. If error happens to be made with respect to the amount of the effect produced, it should be on the side of leniency rather than on the side of severity; for the operation can always be repeated and more time given on the next occasion. Whatever punishment we employ should never be pushed beyond the point necessary to

gain the required object, which, in this case, is the attainment of love and authority over the horse.

What a beautiful expression of the art of bonding! The client (horse) is held (restrained) and begins to struggle. If the client resists passively, the therapist (trainer) provokes the rage. The therapist continues to hold the client, while talking to him gently and stroking him. The client feels rage, then helplessness, and finally hopelessness, giving in to the therapist and accepting his love and authority.

Famous Examples of Intrusive Therapy

There are many examples of the effectiveness of intrusive techniques with humans. Since the founding of Alcoholics Anonymous in 1935, the bonding cycle of induced helplessness, hopelessness, and rescue has been talked about at most AA meetings. And reading the Bible, both the New and the Old Testaments, shows that God used intrusive techniques himself. The clearest example of this occurs in Psalm 107 of the *Book of Common Prayer,* where God handles manic-depressive, addictive, eating-disordered, and character-disturbed individuals with bonding. Today, His actions would certainly result in charges being leveled by child-protective services:

> Some sat in darkness and deep gloom, bound fast in misery and iron;
> Because they rebelled against the words of God and despised the counsel of the Most High.
> So He humbled their spirits with hard labor; they stumbled and there was none to help.
> Then they cried to the Lord in their trouble, and He delivered them from their distress.
> He led them out of darkness and gloom and broke their bonds asunder. . . .
> Some were fools and took to rebellious ways; they were afflicted because of their sins.
> They abhorred all manner of food and drew near to death's door.

> Then they cried to the Lord in their trouble and He delivered
> them from their distress.

The cycle of provocation, rage, helplessness, hopelessness, and
bonding is clear.

Perhaps the most popularized use of intrusive techniques in our
time is the story of Anne Sullivan and Helen Keller. As a toddler,
Keller was a classic unattached child, although such a diagnosis
was unknown at that time. We all know of the climactic scene from
Keller's *The Story of My Life* when Sullivan tried to gain some
authority over the animal-like Keller in the dining room. During
much of that scene, Sullivan held Keller in her chair, forcibly made
her use utensils to eat, and refused to let Keller control the situation. At one point, Keller punched Sullivan in the jaw, but Sullivan
got up and continued to force Keller to submit to her authority.

This was not the only control battle the two had. Rather, it was
one of the first of many, and for a long time these battles became
worse. Sullivan was allowed to separate Keller from her parents,
whose influence was counterproductive, and the two lived for a
while in a small house on the Keller estate. Helen Waite described
what happened in her book *Valiant Companions:*

> The little house might be a small paradise, but its two occu-
> pants were in no heavenly state of mind, not for the first couple
> of days at least. Separated from her family and familiar sur-
> roundings, Helen fell into a paroxysm of combined terror and
> anger and expressed it in the only way she knew, by kicking and
> screaming. Annie stood by helpless and leadenhearted. When
> supper was brought, Helen grew calmer and brighter and ate
> heartily, and then played with her dolls; when Annie indicated
> it was bedtime, she allowed herself to be undressed and tucked in
> readily enough. But when she felt Annie get in beside her, it was
> another matter. Helen jumped out the other side. Annie picked
> her up and put her back. Helen rolled out again. The ordeal
> lasted for two hours.
>
> "I've never seen such strength and endurance in a child,"
> Annie wrote to Mrs. Hopkins, "but fortunately for us both, I am
> a little stronger."
>
> Eventually, Helen surrendered and lay on the edge of the

bed, a sobbing curled-up little girl, and Annie lay on her side of the bed, weary in both mind and body, and filled with tormenting doubts.

Poor little girl, it wasn't her fault she was so locked from all human communication and understanding! Annie suddenly remembered what Dr. Howe had said about Laura Bridgeman: ". . . She was like a person alone and helpless in a deep, dark, still pit, and I was letting down a cord and dangling it about in hopes that she might find it, and seize it by chance, and be drawn up into the light of day and human society."

How soon would Helen find the cord that Annie was trying to let down to her?

In the morning Captain Keller looked through the window on his way to his newspaper office, and Annie realized all too well that no father could consider what he saw encouraging. It was mid-morning, and Helen was sitting in the middle of the floor, a bundle of misery, with her clothes scattered about her, having fought off all Annie's attempts to dress her. Whatever he was thinking, the father concealed it from Annie, and only greeted her with Southern courtesy, but her heart sank as she saw the haggard look on his face as he turned away.

After the battles, the confrontations, and the capitulation that is present in every holding, the light finally dawned for Keller. Waite wrote of this, and quoted from Sullivan's own correspondence:

> How and when the thing happened no one who was concerned ever knew, but suddenly it dawned upon Helen's dark little mind that this person with her was no ogre who had snatched her away from her family for some cruel purpose, but someone whose touch was gentle and friendly, who knew more things even than her mother, and who wanted to show her how to do them. Here was someone to be trusted, depended upon—and more—to be obeyed.

> Under Annie's guidance she made an apron for her doll, and it was a good apron. She learned to crochet, and when she'd made a chain long enough to reach across the room she chuckled and held it lovingly against her cheek. And Annie could write excitedly to Mrs. Hopkins:

> My heart is singing for joy this morning! The light of

understanding has shown upon my little pupil, and behold all things are changed!

The wild little creature of two weeks ago has been transformed into a gentle child. She is sitting beside me as I write, serene and happy, crocheting a long red chain of Scotch wool. . . . She lets me kiss her now, and when she is in a particularly gentle mood, she will sit in my lap. . . . The great step—the step that counts—has been taken. The little savage has learned her first lesson in obedience. Already people remark the difference in Helen. Her father looks in on us morning and evening, and sees her contentedly stringing her beads and sewing, and exclaims, "How quiet she is!" When I first came her movements were so insistent that one always felt there was something unnatural and weird about her.

The little wild animal was transformed into a gentle child in only two weeks because of almost continuous strong confrontive therapy. The therapy was used to take control in order to build basic trust and attachment. Today, such a child as Keller would be removed from the foster home and placed in residential treatment, for no parent would be allowed to take the measures necessary for cure. Besides hospitalization, the child would probably be placed on drugs and restraints, and would most likely spend years oscillating between passive-aggressive refusals, overt rebellion, and trips to the isolation room. And any teacher or therapist handling the matter as Sullivan did would be at serious risk for abuse charges.

Intrusive techniques have been toyed with reluctantly or enthusiastically, stumbled onto, or used thoughtfully for years. These techniques have had strong proponents, some of whom have been fairly charismatic individuals who, when using this treatment, appear to achieve astonishingly quick results with very difficult clients.

The intrusive techniques all have a number of goals that are sometimes separate, sometimes interdependent: to force attention; to force interaction; to force acceptance of the therapist's reality; to force compliance; to force responsiveness and (after capitulation) a reciprocal loving response.

Intrusive techniques have generally been shunned by the traditional professional community and by the bureaucrats who run government social service departments. The main criticisms that I have heard from detractors commonly take one of the following forms:

"That doesn't always work."
"In the wrong hands, that can be harmful!"
"I wouldn't want something like that done to me."
"The end does not justify the means."

Despite the outcry against intrusive techniques, the children who have been helped by them and their parents almost universally praise them. Whereas others can evaluate holding therapy from a theoretical standpoint only, the parents who have gone through it with their children under the guidance of a trained therapist know how it works, understand its limitations, and testify to its results.

Professionals who advocate intrusive techniques do not ignore the concerns voiced by detractors. But they do not let themselves be blocked by what are in reality tangential matters. They know that this therapy will not work for 100 percent of unattached children, but they also know that there is no therapy that guarantees success. They agree that untrained individuals practicing this therapy can cause harm, but this is true of any treatment.

As for whether the techniques are abhorrent, long experience with them proves that they are not. Perhaps it takes a strong-minded therapist to follow through on this sort of treatment, especially with severely disturbed children. Such a therapist knows that the rage of these children is necessary, but ultimately ephemeral. It will blow away, and then the children will be able to bond and work through their feelings.

In essence, the end *does* justify the means. The purpose of intrusive techniques is not to denigrate or degrade, which is the purpose of abuse. The purpose is to open up severely disturbed individuals so that less-confrontive techniques can work; this makes confrontive therapy a beginning rather than an end. In most instances, those who are treated with intrusive therapy are not sal-vageable any other way. Without this therapy, the true end for these disturbed people would be self-destruction, antisocial behav-ior, or jail. And what justifies those ends?

When to Use Intrusive Techniques

What factors indicate the use of intrusive techniques? In Chapter 2, I listed the characteristics common to unattached children. These include the following:

Self-abuse
Cruelty to animals
Cruelty to other children
Lack of affection toward caretakers
Superficial friendliness toward strangers
Speech problems
Thought problems, especially with cause-and-effect thinking
Hording or gorging food
Severe control battles at home and in school
Lying in the face of the truth
Lack of long-term friends

Although many children with different diagnoses have some of these symptoms, children who cannot bond generally have most of them. As you can imagine, confrontive techniques can be used with children who have varying diagnoses, and they are certainly the treatment of choice for children with severe attachment problems.

After the diagnosis of attachment disorder is ascertained, there are certain other indications that intrusive techniques will be useful:

The client is in heavy denial and is threatening his own health or life.
The client has not responded to other, more traditional methods used by a competent therapist.

The client has a history of infantile or toddler problems.

Gaining Therapeutic Contract

The first thing a therapist will do to lay the groundwork for successful holding sessions is to gain a good therapy contract with the client. This contract specifies the therapist's expectations for the sessions, and empowers the patient by allowing him to participate in the therapy. A good contract details the expectations of both therapist and client; uses language and explanations that the client (or client's family) understands; includes confirmation of the understanding, either written or on tape; and encourages discussion of both benefits and complications.

Getting the therapy contract finalized can involve some complicated "negotiations," especially with adolescents who are adept at blocking emotions and manipulating other people. But this is a critical process—without a realistic contract, success is impossible. There are normally five distinct steps in the process, which is intended to lead the client to recognize that the problem exists within himself and that he does want to work on it.

The first step centers on the question, "Are you happy?" or in more therapeutic jargon, "Do you want to change things outside or inside yourself?" Obviously, if a person says he is happy with a situation, he will entertain no ideas about changing. The initial confrontation between therapist and client often occurs right here, as the therapist begins to establish a therapeutic relationship according to his rules rather than the client's.

Severely disturbed children, especially those who have been hospitalized, usually answer the question "Are you happy?" with "Shit, no! I'm not happy. I'm not happy being here!" It turns out that the adolescent is unhappy with his living quarters or his parents or his teachers or his therapist or anything else—*except his own behavior.* The severely disturbed never see the problems as resulting from what they themselves do. At this point, the therapist might use some rough humor so the client will understand that the therapist knows this answer is simply rationalization. (The language the therapist uses matches that used by the patient.) So the therapist might reply, "I get the drift Howard. You just happened to run into two different sets of fucking parents, a fucking judge, and a fucking probation officer, and now you're stuck in a fucking hospital talking to another fucking therapist. No wonder you're angry! You've been around too much sex." Inevitably, the adolescent at least smiles at this old joke, laughing as his rationalization is made explicit.

Continuing in this light vein, the therapist might say, "Gee, Howard, with all these problems around you, you really need a sociologist. I only help people when they think there is some problem inside them." This begins step two in the contract process—the client must admit that he is responsible for his own unhappiness. Unless the client recognizes the problem inside himself, there can be no change—just like with an alcoholic. If the adolescent won't agree to this, he might as well be put on medication or put away so that society (and the adolescent) can be protected. The client doesn't have to agree that he is totally responsible for his unhappiness—*partially* responsible is enough.

When the client admits his unhappiness is partly his own doing, the therapist takes hold of the door the client has cracked open and pushes: "Well, do you want to work on that part?" This is step three. The adolescent doesn't want to remain unhappy, and the therapist is offering some hope. The client doesn't know how this will work out, nor does he understand that he will be submitting to the therapist's will. At this point, he probably believes he can manipulate this therapist like he did the others. No matter.

The therapist continues to push on the door: "Do you want to work hard on that part?" Step four involves real commitment on the adolescent's part. The therapist challenges the client with the statement that real desire is shown by action, not by mere talk. Many people talk about changing themselves, but many people die unhappy with themselves. Can the adolescent measure up? Now the therapist holds out hope: "Everyone has a right to die unhappy. But in your case, Howard, I think you might be a person who will become unhappy being unhappy. You might be one of the few who really do want to work on it.

"If you are going to change your part, you're going to have to work extremely hard—in fact, harder than you've ever worked before. You're a smart guy, and if this job were easy, you would have already done it. But it's not easy. Are you sure you can be strong enough to succeed?"

When the client agrees that he can do this, the door is wide open. However, the therapist keeps pushing, for the next question is the toughest: "Do you want to work hard *my way*?" Step five—now the client has to agree to submit to the therapist's authority, to follow the plan that the therapist lays out. In bearing, being, and manner, the therapist relates the following: "Howard, not only are you going to have to work hard, but you are going to have to do things in a very special way—my way. That's because you've been doing things your way for your entire life, and look at where that has gotten you.

"Now *my* way may be using paradoxical techniques. It could be that doing it my way looks to you like you're doing it your way. I'll tell you to do it the wrong way, which is not really my way. You'll rebel against what I tell you to do and do it your way, which will be the right way. Or you might find yourself sitting in the lap of therapists like you never got to do when you were little, and expressing your hopelessness, helplessness, and rage, and working those feelings through to a successful conclusion."

Intrusive Techniques

When the contract is complete, attachment therapy can begin. Since children with attachment disorders generally have problems with closeness, especially when they do not control it, this therapy is often carried out in the holding position. Typically, the therapist will sit on the floor and hold the patient in his lap. The patient will generally take a reclining position, face up, so that the therapist is looking down on the patient. This reinforces the idea that the therapist is in charge.

How intrusive the holder (therapist or trained parent) must be depends on the child—the rule of thumb is to use as little confrontation as possible. Although there are no strict boundaries between levels of intrusiveness, three categories can be noted: going with the child's emotions, amplifying the emotions, and pushing for (or leading) emotions.

The first category involves the lowest level of intrusion. Because most attachment-disordered children do not like to be cuddled, they become angry from simple holding. Their emotions naturally flow from rage to helplessness to acceptance to reciprocity and trust. The holder merely has to not let go when the child demands it, and then let the process take its course, perhaps facilitating movement from one stage to the next. (Often, parents can be coached through this while they are holding the child.)

The second category is used when the client is talking about his emotions, but is not really feeling them. The adolescent is probably afraid of the depth of these emotions, and so shuts down when he reaches a safe level of expression. However, feeling emotions to their fullest and having those emotions accepted is what builds trust. It is up to the therapist to amplify the emotions so that the client can feel them.

The simplest way to amplify anger is for the holder to ask the child to repeat an angry statement louder. The holder may also become loud, but only in proportion to the client's intensity. Sorrow and loss can be amplified by "super-empathy": when the child relates a sad happening, the holder says, "Oh, I am *so* sorry that happened to you. I bet you felt real sad. Breathe deep, and let it out. It's okay to cry." This often results in the child sobbing while the holder cuddles him. (The therapist generally models this level for the parents, instructing them how to show correct emotions for the child.)

Special preparation is needed to use the third level of intrusion. Pushing for particular emotions with older children involves verbal and (sometimes) physical techniques that can be easily overdone. The holder may make provocative comments, deride or scoff at what the child says, use paradoxical techniques, and occasionally make the child physically uncomfortable. These techniques must be used knowledgeably and purposefully, and the holder must be conscious not only of what the child is doing and saying, but of what he himself is doing and feeling. The holder must push the child to the emotion the child is hiding from, which may not necessarily be the emotion the holder feels is important.

These stronger methods can be extremely helpful in certain cases; they can also be controversial and legally dangerous. People who are not involved in this sort of therapy easily misunderstand what is going on. Because the most controlling children are generally the most manipulative, the holder might be open to charges of abuse once the child gets done distorting what has happened to the police or child-protective services. If outsiders were to view a video of a therapist using highly intrusive techniques without being familiar with the client or the rest of the treatment, they could easily imagine the therapy is abusive. Such misinformed opinions do not take into account the entire healing process. By the same token, a video of open-heart surgery would cause equal concern if it implied the patient would be left in the mid-surgery condition. This would be a terrible misuse of the power of the film-maker, as heart patients receive meticulous follow-up care. So do holding patients.

An Example of Contracting and Holding: Charlie

To illustrate how contracting and holding progress, let's look at the case of Charlie, an obese and angry fourteen-year-old who is still encopretic. Abused by his father and rejected by his mother, he had extensive unsuccessful outpatient therapy and was hospitalized for several months. A negative, passive-resistant boy, he couldn't express his emotions directly or verbally. He hid feces, denying a psychological problem and maintaining that his problem was medical. Nevertheless, he filled his pants when angry over not being given a pass, when told he was on restriction, or when being requested to go to an activity he did not enjoy. Although he was not totally lacking in attachment, he had disordered attachment, strong denial, and intimacy problems, and he was filled with rage.

Unable to express or even recognize his feelings of anger and depression about his abuse and rejection, he shellacked his soft, pudgy, almost effeminate personality with a tough-guy veneer.

Here's how our first meeting went. I began contracting with Charlie with these sorts of questions and statements: "Why am I seeing you? . . . I understand you have led a shitty life. . . . Do you make your statements through your mouth or with your lower end? . . . I guess if I had lived your life, I'd feel pretty crappy, too. . . . What a common problem you have! . . . How good are you at expressing 'shit' through your mouth? . . . What a bummer to keep your thoughtful mouth closed, and just leak things through your anus. . . . I saw you in team [therapy] yesterday, and you have great comments for other kids. You're pretty bright! I guess you've just been giving yourself shit. . . . So you're saying you would like to work on your feelings now?"

As you can see, the confrontation started early. The language I used was related to the information I had about the boy's history. I have found this to be effective almost universally. If the client is a pilot, I talk about not flying straight outside the cockpit; with a painter, I might say he is just doing touch-ups rather than a complete job. This directed language hits home with clients. One of the notes in Charlie's chart was that his grandparents had returned him at age nine for psychiatric hospitalization. During our contracting session, I said, "Charlie, the bummer of it is, you impress me as a kid whose own grandparents couldn't stand him." Charlie's eyes opened wide and he replied, "How'd you know that?" Years later he told me that it was at that point he knew I had his number and that I cared, and it was only then that he wanted to *really* work.

When Charlie said he wanted to work on his feelings *now,* I sat down on the mat on the floor and held him in my lap. Since Charlie could not express his emotions by himself, I started with moderate intrusion. We talked about his situation, and I amplified his feelings of loss and sorrow: "So, you never had a father to talk to? How sad. *(Slight tears from Charlie.)* . . . Gee, he beat you all around your stomach? . . . So, your mom got so tired of the shit, she just said, 'Forget it'? . . . So, you're saying that when you are mad, you say, 'I just have to not think about it'? What a bummer. *(Patting his stomach)* And all those feelings get stuck down there."

Charlie was not a hardened psychopath, so I lovingly and gently explored the situation while holding him in my lap. When this led to tears and emotion, I showed him that I accepted them, and we worked through them. I allowed Charlie to feel sad with me, to express his emotion, without negative feedback. This helped to build Charlie's trust in me. There was no reason to push Charlie roughly into anger, for rage can be more lightly obtained later, after the sorrow or depression is partially resolved.

Charlie handled all of his emotions at this point with a brave smile. When we talked of subjects he would rather have avoided, he made light of his abuse and lost eye contact.

When Charlie told me that he wanted to work *hard* on his feelings, I said, "Now? Are you sure?" When he replied "Yes," I held him tightly, shook his head hard, and began with a strong "I can be a real son of a bitch" routine: "So, you probably thought you could get your shit together by sitting down and talking, huh? Well, guess again! *(Charlie stiffens up.)* . . . Good! Just lie there, Charlie. How do you feel about me? Good—just lie there and struggle, but don't say anything about how you feel. Great! That's the story of your life!" At this point, my holding was making Charlie feel helpless; no matter how he struggled, I countered him and held him close.

The holding session now moved into its middle stages. During this time, reciprocity occurs in the expression of anger as past and present feelings are explored. To help Charlie get into his emotions, I put pressure across his rib cage, and the results were howls of protest. (He complained that this was where his dad had beaten him for years.) I knew that my pressure was not hurtful to him, and so I continued it and hassled him with new vigor: "Great! Just keep struggling, Charlie. . . . This is the story of your life. . . . Why don't you just poop in your pants right now. That's how you handle your feelings. . . . Oh, great. You're feeling confused. Well, let's get unconfused. . . . How are you feeling about me right now? *("You're an asshole!")* Asshole! That is a *thought*. You're thinking that I'm an asshole is not a real feeling! *("Okay, I'm feeling that you're an asshole!")* Oh, give me more shit." Charlie was now approaching hopelessness, as he was realizing that he was not going to get relief on his terms. Only by capitulating, by handing over all control to me, by bonding, would he be able to get free of my hold.

During this part of the session, Charlie said that he hated me, hated his dad, and hated taking orders in the hospital—this from a boy who had been unable to verbalize his feelings. His ability to access and talk about this deep emotion came from the heightened intrusiveness I used; it would not have come from simple holding or amplifying.

The end stages of this session involved getting a reciprocal smile from Charlie and ensuring the session ended on a positive note. As we did in contracting, Charlie and I just talked to each other. He was sobbing, our eye contact was close and loving, and Charlie was emotionally open: "How do you think you did today in dealing directly with your emotions? . . . Did they come out of the upper end or out of the lower end? . . . What kind of grade would you give yourself? . . . Is this the best you have ever done? . . . How are you feeling about me now? *("I still hate your ass!")* My ass! Oh no, anything but that! Don't hate my ass. Hate my toes, hate my face, but don't hate my ass! *(A burst of laughter, which Charlie tried to hide but then openly enjoyed.)* Which reminds me, whose ass have you been hating? *("Don't try to use that psychological stuff on me!")* I love to use this psychological stuff because you're a kid who's smart enough to understand it. *(Smile.)*"

The session ended with a genuine hug between us and a "Thanks, Dr. Cline."

Charlie was by no means "cured" after the session outlined above, but he had attached. We now had a basis for a therapeutic relationship, so there was now the *possibility* that he could be cured. Without the holding, amplifying, and pushing, that potential would never have existed.

Usually a relatively short period is devoted to holding and confronting in relation to the client's total therapy; some clients may require only one session to get moving along the road to health, while others might need weeks of heavy confrontation. In extreme cases, holding can continue for a year or more, with the techniques becoming progressively milder. The therapy can be physically exhausting, especially when the client is a large teenager who is severely disturbed. In fact, in most cases involving older patients, I always like to have another trained adult (either another therapist or a parent) help with the holding, for with such a client there is always the risk of physical attack.

My rule of thumb is that if the therapist cannot hold the client with one arm while keeping the other arm free to control the child's head and prevent biting, help is required. I remember the reaction of one young therapist who, early in her training, had a rough session with a child: "Foster, this is hard work! You didn't tell me I would need three arms and an iron bra!"

Holding with an Older Child: Ann

The following excerpts from a transcript of a session with Ann, a fifteen-year-old girl, and her mother, Mary, demonstrate that intrusive methods can be used effectively with conflicted individuals as well as those with reactive attachment disorder. (Appendix A presents other transcripts that demonstrate how confrontive therapy produces breakthroughs for previously unreachable children.) This is a long passage, and if it is your first experience with a session of intrusive therapy, stay with it until the end. You may feel uncomfortable as you follow the action, but the outcome of the session is amazing!

Ann was certainly an attached child, but she could not focus on the real issues—her feelings about herself and her father. She was frightened of the intense rage she felt toward him. Burdened with guilt, Ann expressed her intense feelings, too painful to recognize, as self-destructive suicidal behavior. She projected rage and anger onto her mother while denying the trauma bond with her father.

Ann was referred to me for a one-session consultation by a

clinical psychologist after she had walked out on one of their sessions. This was not an uncommon occurrence for her, as she had walked out on sessions with other psychiatrists. A total of five therapists had tried and failed to reach her in the preceding four years. She shunned her mother, took drugs, refused to attend school, and threatened to commit suicide.

What caused Ann to become suddenly rejecting and angry in the sixth grade? Several years before, Ann's mother had remarried. Her stepfather, an executive with a large company, had forced Ann to have sex with him, and threatened that he would commit suicide if Ann ever told anyone about it.

Ann told. He killed himself.

Filled with guilt, loss, and anger, Ann went downhill. Feeling responsible for his death, she unconsciously felt that she deserved to die and was bringing this on with her self-destructive behavior.

The only way to reach Ann was to break through her terrible wall of denial and introjected anger. Because of her record with therapy, it was clear that variations on the "let's sit down and talk it over" approach had not worked. She needed heavy confrontation and a definite push to look at herself and her feelings. And there was little time. Her mother did not have the money or the insurance for private hospitalization, and treatment would not be possible in a state institution, where Ann could legally be held for only a short time. She would manipulate the staff and convincingly deny suicidal thoughts, and the physicians would be forced to discharge her.

It is a common therapeutic direction that children of incest cannot be held or restrained by a male therapist. This old dictum is incorrect in some cases, for it robs affected children, who feel guilty, dirty, and untouchable, of a corrective emotional experience. Frequently, children need correct touch to resolve old feelings. As I have discussed, it is necessary to respect individuals, not the neurotic needs based on their past dysfunctional interactions.

When I told Mary how the session would go and warned her about what Ann would experience, she responded, "How much worse can it get? She's already thinking of suicide. You do whatever you think is best, and I'll understand." Such support was essential for the success of the session, for I needed Mary's help after we reached the point where Ann was honest and angry with me and needed to work things through with her mother. Mary would watch the session from behind a one-way mirror with the sound piped in, and come in when I said, "She should be joining us now." Then Ann came into the therapy room.

Cline: Come in. . . . So you're unhappy with psychiatrists, or how do feel about shrinks in general?

Ann: They're screwed.

Cline: Is that right? What does "they're screwed" mean?

Ann: They're stupid!

Cline: Is that right? How do you make that determination?

Ann: They just are. They talk about things that are none of their business.

Cline: How about Dr. Grunfeld [the referring psychologist]?

Ann: I don't know. I only talked to him once and he started talking to other people.

Cline: You what?

Ann: I only talked to him for about twenty minutes.

Cline: Why was that? Because he wouldn't talk to you any longer?

Ann: I don't know the reason.

Cline: Because you wouldn't talk to him?

Ann: No, I talked to him. I only talked to him about twenty minutes, then we quit talking.

Cline: Why? Was that his idea to quit talking or your idea?

Ann: *(Put out)* Yeah, it was his idea to quit talking.

Cline: *(Pushing and talking loudly)* Do you really believe that? Is that really straight? I mean, you honestly, really, deep down in your soul believe that it was his idea to quit talking? I mean, have you twisted it around in your head that much?

Ann: *(Showing surprise at the strength of early confrontation)* Yes, it was his idea to quit talking! There was nothing to talk about! There's really nothing to talk about. Why don't you just get off my case?

Cline: Why should I get off your case? You know, you have quite a case to be on.

Ann: I don't care.

Cline: You keep screwing it all up.

Ann: I don't care.

Cline: You don't care?

Ann: No.

Cline: I thought perhaps you do care. I thought you might be unhappy being unhappy. I mean, some people like being . . .

Ann: *(Mumbles)* I don't like being unhappy.

Cline: Huh? You *are* unhappy being unhappy?

Ann: Yeah. This doesn't make me happy talking to a bunch of shrinks. Not going to do any good anyhow.

Cline: Is that right? Is that like you want to make that a promise or is that like a statement?

Ann: It's a statement.

Cline: Is that a statement? It's not . . .

Ann: *(Mumbles)* If I want to do somethin', I'll do it.

Cline: Hmm?

Ann: *(Challenging and rebellious)* If I want to do something enough, I'll do it!

Cline: Oh, well, right. If you want to shoot yourself, right? Run away, go ahead. Act like a shit? Yeah. Anything you want to do, you can do, Ann. For sure, for sure you can do it that way. But what good does it do you? Hmm?

Ann: *(Tearing up)* Nothing. If it makes me feel good . . . if I want to do something, I'll do it.

Cline: Well, what about if you want to do something that's bad for you? Does that make you feel good?

Ann: Like what?

From the child's concerned tone of voice, it was obvious that she thought I was talking about her relationship with her stepfather. It might have been better for me to respond, "You know darn well what! You tell me!" This could possibly have led to a fruitful discussion about the relationship. Or, Ann might have closed down, as she had with her other therapists.

Cline: Scream at your mother, act like . . . act crappy, lie, take pot, tell her to fuck off, use foul language, leave around her, act like you hate her. Do you end up feeling good about yourself when you do those things?

When a person is displaying two-year-old negativism, I may use anal terms. This is effective, because it shows the client that I know that she knows exactly what she is up to.

Ann: No.
Cline: Huh?
Ann: No.
Cline: I know you don't.
Ann: She's the one that brings it on. I don't get mad at her. She's a bitch . . .
Cline: *(Interrupting)* She brings it on?
Ann: Um-hmm.
Cline: Oh, look at me and tell me your mother brings it on. Does your mother . . .
Ann: My mother brings it on.
Cline: Brings it on. Is that a fact?
Ann: Yes.
Cline: How does she bring it on?
Ann: Just by stupid things.
Cline: Like what?
Ann: Like tonight. She's being a bitch.

Cline: Bringing you here?

Ann: No. Just being a bitch. *(Mumbles)*

Cline: What?

Ann: Been a bitch all week.

Cline: You know what I think? I think that every time you think you're a bitch, or you think you're sick, then you say to your mother, "You're sick." You project it onto her. Every time you hate yourself, you end up saying, "I hate other people. I hate Josh [former therapist]. I hate my mother. I hate Tim [stepfather]. I hate . . . when you're just hating yourself, and so you act hateful. That's what I think. I think every time you end up hating yourself, then you say you hate other people.

Ann: So?!

Cline: And I think it makes you really unhappy.

Ann: Yeah? What can you do about it!

Cline: Well, would you like to do something about it?

Ann: *(Determined)* No! I want to go home.

Cline: *(Understanding—Ann has been pushed far enough at this point.)* Do you really?

Ann: Yes.

Cline: *(Understanding)* Do you want to live at home or do you want to get away from me, and home's a nice place to be?

Ann: I want to go home . . . so I can go out . . . do something.

Cline: Play foosball? Have another attack?

Ann: Uh-uh. I want to go out.

Cline: Um-hmm. Sounds like a real happy life, one happy life.

Ann: It's not too bad.

Cline: Um-hmm. Go home, have a flashback, act crazy, space out. You'd prefer to act crazy.

Ann: I don't act crazy!

Cline: You do act crazy.

Ann: So what! It's none of your business.

Cline: *(Sarcastically)* Isn't it, really?

Ann: No.

Cline: Whose business do you think it is, Ann?

Ann: It's my business.

Cline: Are you handling it very well, Ann?

Ann: *(Mumbles)* I handle it. I don't care.

Cline: Hmm?

Ann: *(Very antagonistic)* I don't care!

Cline: I say you do care!

Ann: *(Almost hopeful)* What can you do about it if I don't want to do anything about it?

Here, Ann was wondering if I could continue to be in charge of her in spite of her resistance and self-destructive maneuvering. She was really saying, "Can you help me to help myself in spite of myself?" I answered her metaphorically by taking control of a little piece of obnoxious behavior—telling her to spit out her gum, and then throwing it away. She had been sitting there snapping the gum and looking generally disinterested and put out. By throwing away the gum, I was saying directly to her unconscious, "I can take control of your actions and I know what to do with them."

Cline: Right! Spit your gum out. It looks awful with you sitting there chewing it. I will throw it away. I mean, for somebody fourteen . . . are you fourteen or thirteen?

Ann: *(Put out)* Fifteen.

Cline: You're fifteen?

Ann: *(Sighs)* Yes.

Cline: Is that really straight?

Speculating that a child is younger and then showing surprise at her actual age when she has been acting much younger is often a more effective lead-in than the overt question, "How old are you acting?" or "Sometimes you feel or wish you were younger?"

Ann: Yes.

Cline: Do you think you act it?

Ann: Yes.

Cline: Do you really?

Ann: *(Softly)* Yes.

Cline: I don't think that you act it very well. I think you act about . . . a lot younger. But you know the nice thing, Ann, is that according to your mom, she loved you a lot and you loved her a lot until you were . . . until the things started going wrong about Tim. Then, because you felt so crappy inside, you started saying, "I hate you, mother!" A little teeny girl standing outside by the garage saying, "I hate you, I hate you." So you hate yourself. Why put it on her, then feel worse, then get into a vicious circle?

Ann: *(Challenging)* Well, if she'd let me live my own life, she wouldn't have to bother with it, would she?

Cline: Well, why don't you think she wants you to live your own life?

Ann: I dunno.

Cline: Well, guess.

Ann: She says I'm going in the wrong direction.

Cline: Right. Why does she care!

Ann: And she should be pretty damn proud of me. I haven't even gotten high for a week.

Cline: Is that right? *(Laughing)* Well, good . . . pretty good, Ann. Pretty good for you, huh? No high all week?

Ann: Yeah.

Cline: You mean no drug ingestion all week?

Ann: Yeah.

Cline: Well, fantastic! Shake! *(Shaking hands)* Really good. No high all week. Why does she care whether you go the wrong way?

Ann: I don't know. Because I'm a baby. I don't know.

Cline: *(Persistent)* No, why does she care?

Ann:	*(Feeling too guilty to simply say, "She loves me.")* I don't know.
Cline:	How do you think your mother feels about you right now, if you're really straight about it?
Ann:	Right now she probably hates my guts.
Cline:	Does she tell you that she hates your guts? I mean, does she come right out to you and say to you, "Ann, damn it, the way you're acting, I hate your guts." Does she say that?
Ann:	No.
Cline:	Why doesn't she?
Ann:	*(Mumbles)* She acts it.
Cline:	Oh, she acts like it?
Ann:	Yes.

What I was about to say was directed to Mary, who was listening behind the one-way mirror. She needed to know that she was going to have to come through as strong and firm. This would help relieve Ann's guilt. Up to this point, Mary had generally tried to be understanding and to just "take it" when Ann acted out. Trying to be nice only increased Ann's guilt and heightened her projected anger.

Cline:	Well, would you rather she say it or would you rather that she act it out?
Ann:	I'd rather she say it.
Cline:	You'd rather she say it! Could you handle it? If she said, "Ann, I hate your guts the way you've been acting," could you handle it, or would you run away and not be able to handle it?
Ann:	I'd be able to handle it and say, "It's your problem."
Cline:	You would! Really, the way you've been acting, you'd say it was her problem that she hated you?
Ann:	Yes.
Cline:	How do you think you feel about yourself, Ann? Do you think you really feel good, or not so good, or how do you think you feel about yourself inside?

Ann: So-so.
Cline: What's "so-so" mean, Ann?
Ann: So-so.
Cline: What's "so-so" mean?
Ann: I dunno.
Cline: What's "so-so" mean?
Ann: I like myself. I don't like myself. I dunno.
Cline: I say you do know. I say you don't want to look at
        that.
Ann: I don't even want to talk to you.
Cline: I bet you don't. You know why you don't want to
        talk to me?
Ann: Why?
Cline: Because I don't think you feel very good about
        yourself and you don't even want to look at that.
        You want to stay away from it. So, instead of say-
        ing, "I don't want to look at myself," you say, "I
        don't want to talk to you." Just like you say to
        your mother when you hate yourself. You say, "I
        hate you, mother." Why are you crying right now?
        Why do you have tears?
Ann: I dunno.
Cline: You do know why, I think, Ann.
Ann: Why?
Cline: Because I think you know I'm right.
Ann: No.
Cline: That's why you have tears. Well, I told your mom
        to wait a few minutes and then join us. *(Looking
        at watch)* She should be joining us now.

When Mary walked into the room, Ann got up and tried to
leave. I told Mary to take Ann's wrists and hold them, as I was
doing.

Cline: Mary, hold her wrists.
Mary: Look at me, Ann.

Ann: No!

Cline: No, you can't make her look at you because she's pulling a Tim. See, he's not looking at anybody either right now.

Mary: Where'd he end up, Annie?

Cline: Yeah, where'd he end up?

Ann: *(Struggling to free herself)* Leave me alone!!

Cline: Hold her really tight, Mary. Good.

Mary: *(Sarcastically)* Is this a flashback, Annie?

Cline: Yeah, it is a flashback. Sounds like a flashback. Maybe she's going to have a bad flashback. Maybe it's an epileptic attack. You never can tell. It's really hard when someone touches you and cares about you, isn't it, Annie? Huh? Such a bad girl doesn't deserve it.

Ann: Leave me alone! I hate you all!

Cline: Do you hate us all? Why don't you just say it, then. You know, that's one thing about you, Mary—you never say it. See, Annie's growing up just like you. Do you hate us right now, Ann?

Ann: Yes.

Cline: Well, why don't you say it?

Ann: Just said it.

Cline: *(Stronger)* Why don't you act it out, Ann? *(Ann struggles.)* Say it again, Ann. Get it out of your system.

Ann: *(Screaming)* NO!

Cline: Good! That was fantastic.

Ann: *(Screaming)* Leave me alone!

Cline: Hold her tight, Mary. You're bigger than she is.

Ann: *(Struggling with all her might and screaming)* LEAVE ME ALONE!

Cline: Oh, leave me alone. Keep screaming it. You know what? You can't stand your mother touching you, can you? You don't deserve it, do you? Isn't that the way you feel inside, Ann?

Ann: No!

Cline: "I don't deserve for her to touch me." *(To Mary)* Gee, she's sweet. She's been really sweet the last week?

Mary: A real doll. A living doll.

Cline: I bet she is a living doll.

Mary: Do you hate me, Ann?

Ann: Yes!

Mary: I hate you, too, for the way you act.

Cline: Good. Say it to her loud. Say, "I hate you, too." Say it really loud to her face.

Mary: I just *hate* you for the way you act!

Cline: Yeah.

Mary: Do you like the way you are?

Ann: Yes.

Cline: She must love it.

Mary: I don't like the way you are!

Ann: Good! It's your problem, isn't it?

Cline: Is it really? *(To Mary)* You're not going to keep living with it. It's not going to be your problem for long, is it, Mary?

Mary: Not for long, Ann. *(The struggle gets intense again.)*

Cline: Hold her good, Mary.

Ann: Let go of me! *(Ann struggles so much that she can't be held in her chair.)*

Cline: Let's get her right down on the floor and you hold her there.

Ann: No!! *(Struggle to hold Ann on the floor)* Leave me alone! *(More struggling)* Get off of me!

Cline: Okay. All right. *(To Mary)* Now look at her and tell her what she's been like living with. Hold that arm right there.

Mary: You know what you've been like? You're a bitch!

Ann: *(Wails for the first time)* Leave me alone.

Mary: I don't like living with you the way you are! You understand?

Ann: Leave me alone!

Mary: I'm not going to live with you the way you are anymore.

Cline: Good for you. Fantastic! It's not much fun to live with her when she's acting like a bitch, right? And tell her that's how she makes you feel a lot of the time.

Mary: You make me feel like I killed him! *(Ann still struggles.)*

Cline: Tell her that again.

Mary: You hear me? You make me feel like I killed him.

Ann: *(This is the breaking point.)* Leave me alone! I hate you. I hate you! I hate you!!

Cline: You don't like looking at that, do you?

Ann: *(Begins hysterics)* Leave me alone!

Cline: Yeah—pull a Tim now. Why don't you space out and pull a Tim. He's being left alone. Just space out, Ann—go ahead and space out. Poor old Tim.

Ann: *(Scratching and screaming)* Leave me alone!

Cline: Good hysterical attack! Do it again! Say, "Leave me alone!"

Ann: No.

Cline: Yeah, come on, Ann!

Ann: Leave me alone!

Cline: Get it out!

Ann: *(Breathing hard)* Leave me alone!

Cline: *(To Mary)* Do you know why she wants you to feel like you killed him? Because she feels like it. So she feels a lot of anger. She feels shitty so she tries to make you feel shitty. She feels like she killed Tim, so she tries to make you feel like you killed him. She feels lousy about herself, so she tries to get you to feel lousy about yourself. It's really too bad when she's not straight, isn't it?

Mary: It's ugly, Ann.

Cline: It's really ugly. She could be kind of a pretty girl, right? Instead, she acts pretty ugly, right, Mary? Is this a pretty good attempt at pulling a Tim right now? Eyes closed, not looking at you. Trying to tune out. You're pulling a real good Tim, Ann.

Mary: Yeah, just like he did, Ann.

Cline: It is? He did? Just like this?

Mary: For all of two years, that's just what he did. She looks like him.

Cline: Is she looking like him right now?

Mary: I couldn't talk to him either, you know?

Cline: Same exact way, huh?

Ann: Let go of me.

Cline: She probably liked him a lot and that's why she's ending up so much like him.

Mary: That right, Ann?

Cline: Yeah. See, she doesn't want to admit that she liked him a lot because it makes her feel too guilty. You know, she thinks it's all his doing.

The remainder of the session, about fifteen minutes, was similar to what you have read so far. Ann expressed more of her hate and rage, and did some crying. I forced her to look at the fact that she felt as if she had killed her father, but assured her that anyone, under those circumstances, might feel the same way. I tried to be as understanding as I was confrontive. When Ann left, she was in a "mostly mollified" mood. She answered with monosyllables and was slightly unfriendly to me.

During the next week, I thought of Ann several times, and wondered how things were going with Mary. Then one day as I was passing through the waiting room at Evergreen Consultants, a lovely young woman greeted me with, "Hi, Dr. Cline." She looked vaguely familiar. Only when Dr. Grunfeld called me into his office to let me know how things had gone with Ann did I realize that the young woman was Ann! She had been so pleasant that she was unrecognizable.

The following was recorded in Dr. Grunfeld's office:

Cline: All right, Mary. What was Ann doing on the way home [from the session]?

Mary: Well, on the way down the mountain, she was dead quiet and I was sure she was thinking, "I'll pack my clothes and see how far I can get." But by the time we got home, it was, "Mother, may I," and "Yes, Mother," and "No, Mother." It's been that way all week.

Cline: So, it's been a really good week?

Mary: Yeah, I think she really needed that [therapy session].

Grunfeld: Also, I have on tape something that I think is neat. I asked her how things were going, and she said, "Well, they're going a lot better with Mom." "Why do you suppose that is?" "I don't know." "Do you suppose that your visit with Dr. Cline had anything to do with it?" "No-o-o." *(Laughter)* "I'll bet it did. Do you want to see Dr. Cline again?" "No-o-o." "What if it helps you?" "Well, I guess." I'm certain she realized that is what she needed.

Mary: She got a telephone call that night, after we got home, from a boy who was in the hospital. He's still there. And he kept threatening to run away and he was gonna commit suicide and told her he ate half a box of detergent and all this. Well, he didn't. You know, it's one of those things. And I should have taped it because she gave him your whole number—"Why you stupid, immature. . . ." *(Laughter)* I could hear her on the phone in the next room, so I know you got through.

Cline: Mary, you know you really came through strong. I was very happy with the way you came through to her. I mean you took her hair and put her down—"This is the way I feel." Nothing else would have quite gotten through to her at that time.

Mary: Yeah . . . I did ask her if she had her traveling shoes on, because at home she put her climbing boots on. She said she didn't want to leave. And she told me coming up the mountain that she was afraid they would put her in a reformatory at court, and I said, "Do you think you need to be in a reformatory?" She said, "No." I said, "I think they'd like to have you home better, but we'll need to work this thing out."

After talking with Mary and finding out that her relationship with Ann was good and on an entirely different footing from the previous week, I saw Ann. She was not the same girl. She sparkled, joking and laughing with me easily. I talked with her about boyfriends and how school was, and related to her as one would relate to any fifteen-year-old.

Ann's therapy was far from over. Her deep-seated problems and guilt still needed to be worked through with her regular therapist, and Dr. Grunfeld continued to see Ann and her mother. But the intrusive techniques that we used in that one session broke through to Ann so that she was amenable to more conventional techniques. In her follow-up sessions, she was no longer closed and defiant, and she was open to talking about and resolving her own feelings.

Follow-Up on Forty-Seven Intrusive Therapy Cases

Although holding, confrontive, and intrusive therapy have been carried out for many years, good controlled studies are almost impossible to obtain. In 1991, the Attachment Center at Evergreen began working with the University of Colorado at Denver Center for Applied Psychology to document and follow-up on the cases of forty-seven clients treated from 1983 to 1991. In each of these cases, the child was unable to remain in foster homes or in hospitals while traditional therapeutic methods were attempted. In fact, the average child accepted for treatment in Evergreen has been in five prior placements.

Follow-up of these forty-seven cases shows the following:

Thirty-five children were returned home or adopted into families. Only two children were so disruptive that they needed to be removed from their therapeutic foster homes because their behavior could not be controlled. Only four children left the program prematurely.

Of the thirty-five children who returned home, nine did not continue in their homes. Of these nine, one child lived in the home for four years. Another was doing well in the Job Corps after initial home difficulties, and now gets along with his parents extremely well. Seven children needed further placement.

Twenty-one children were known to be doing well at home. Three were in college, and one was living outside the home because of special education needs.

Although follow-up is continuing with this group, these results are outstanding. Few programs that work with children have such an admirable eight-year record. A number of the children in this study have told their stories on *Donahue, Oprah Winfrey, Straight Talk, Seattle Today,* and other radio and television programs. They are proud of the significant changes in their lives, and they repeatedly state with conviction that had they not been treated, they would have followed a self-destructive path that would probably have led to suicide, homicide, or incarceration for lesser crimes.

Long-Term Success Stories

This book could be filled with successful case histories; in fact, a book of such histories would make fascinating reading. I present the following three histories because of the length of time of follow-up, and because they reflect typical changes experienced by children who go through bonding therapy.

Brenda is a striking woman in her early thirties. In her recent interview with therapist Connell Watkins, she laughed easily and spoke animatedly. Seventeen years ago, this woman was an angry, acting-out adolescent who had spent more than a year at the Colorado State Hospital in Pueblo. She came to Evergreen on solid doses of psychotropic medication. Since she had been unable to stay in a number of good foster homes, it was with some reluctance that we took on this fifteen-year-old. Her first therapy session lasted an entire day, during which Brenda expressed her anger as she never had before—hitting out, kicking, and spitting in the therapists' faces.

During this follow-up interview, a mature Brenda explained that she had suffered emotional and physical abuse as a child, was put into an orphanage, and was adopted when she was two years old. Brenda recalled abusive behavior by her adoptive parents, too; for instance, her mother put a bee down her shirt when Brenda was misbehaving. From ages ten to twelve, Brenda was hospitalized at a private psychiatric hospital in Colorado Springs, where she was medicated with Thorazine, Mellaril, and Dexedrine. From there, she was discharged to the Colorado State Hospital. There, on no medication, she was constantly raging, and remembers spending long periods in isolation.

> Brenda: Yeah, I dropped out of school. I never—I had learning problems, but they weren't from not being able to learn . . . they were from not wanting to be there. I mean, I've learned a lot since I dropped out of school. I read all the time. I learn well. But [in school] I had no motivation. I didn't want to live, I didn't want to go on. I wanted to die. I remember feeling that many times, or that I wished I hadn't been born. . . .

Watkins: During your period in the Youth Behavior Program [at Evergreen] some very controversial therapy was done with you in hopes that it would help you to connect and care. Do you remember what that was?

Brenda: Yeah. . . . It was called Z therapy then; I guess they call it rage therapy now. And at the time, it just seemed really awful. It was hard. Ohh, . . . I remember the very first session. . . . I remember the anger coming out. I remember spitting in my therapist's face. Just like in *The Exorcist,* you know? Just totally uncontrollable. And I told myself before the session, "I'm not going to let him make me go off." I honestly believe that if I wouldn't have had it done . . . I knew that I was angry. Looking back on it now, I know that if I would not have had it done I probably would have either killed someone or killed myself, because I had no love. I couldn't love. I could only hate, because if I loved, then I became vulnerable to be hurt, and I didn't want to love.

Watkins: To love was to lose control.

Brenda: Exactly. And to let other people hurt me. So I didn't want to do that. I know that I could have shot somebody, without a second of hesitation.

Watkins: So you see the holding therapy as helping you to get some of that out?

Brenda: Oh, yeah, a lot of it. I don't think that I could live my life in a normal fashion today if I would have not had it. There's no way I'd survive without it. I'd be in jail for killing. I know I'd kill somebody . . . That kind of anger is unexplainable; it's so strong that it's hard to explain to someone who hasn't had it. It is literally like a demon possessing your body, and you can't control it. And when it gets out, it gets better.

Watkins: I bet that first session was a very long session.

Brenda: I don't remember. I just remember them saying the rottenest things to me.

Watkins: You know they were making you do it their way?

Brenda: Yeah, oh yeah. . . . I had to do a lot of things I really didn't want to do.

Watkins: So in the process of their taking control, physically and emotionally, and having you do things on their terms, you got in touch with the rage, and the rage did come out.

Brenda: It saved my life.

Watkins: Did it? Do you really think the therapy ended on a good note? We talk about the confrontation, and it was really tough. Do you remember feeling any love?

Brenda: Oh yeah. There was love there. I didn't want it, but there was always love there. . . . It's still hard. I mean, I'm not perfectly, 100 percent on the button. No, I probably won't ever be, but that's okay, because I'm a lot better off than I was, and I'm able to give myself to my husband—we've been married for ten years—and I have a three-year-old daughter who I'm able to express my love to.

Today, a girl like Brenda was at fifteen would be ineligible for therapy. Because of the amount of confrontation needed to reach older adolescents, they are no longer accepted into the program. The risks are too great. Brenda would have been lost.

When Chris was four years old, he was diagnosed as schizophrenic. When I first saw Chris at age three, he had a vocabulary of less than a dozen nearly incomprehensible words. Living with him was almost impossible. When he wasn't dragging his mother around by the hand, making high-pitched squealing sounds, he was twisting the knobs on the television or flipping the light switch on and off as fast as he could. He "roamed" rooms, avoiding objects and people without really looking at them. He ran in circles and had no self-help skills.

What mattered most was to have Chris emit an emotion, any emotion, as a response to another person. It was unimportant *how* he related; that he related *at all* was what counted. He was treated in intensive holding sessions lasting up to three hours. Although he flailed and struggled, his therapist, Laurie Smith, was relentless. Holding Chris's eyes open, she forced eye contact, and stroked his face and gave him unwanted kisses in the midst of his wails. Spontaneous eye contact was best when Chris was terrified, which was the only emotion in which he recognized others. Being swung in a circle or being held upside down terrified Chris, and he would then reach out for his therapist.

Smith would take Chris to her home on weekends to give Chris's mother some relief from his constant dragging and roaming. During that time, Smith would noisily roughhouse with Chris and make him relate. One useful aid was the vacuum cleaner, which Smith used to suck on Chris's stomach or blow warm air into his face. Chris howled in terror, but he concentrated on the vacuum or on Smith's eyes, and he related.

As for his time at home, we gave his mother special instructions. Many parents try to give their special-needs children 100 percent of their attention 100 percent of the time, and they quickly wear out. We told his mother to give Chris 100 percent attention for only about half an hour a day, and to force Chris to attend to her during that time. She responded to all self-destructive behavior with a smack on the rear, and when Chris squealed, she forced him to squeal louder with eye contact. When he tried to drag her around, she held him and forced eye contact. For the rest of the time, she simply had to exist with Chris the best she could.

Eventually, less traumatic means were needed to get Chris's full attention. It was a wondrous day when Chris responded to a simple shout of, "Look at me!" It was a joyless response at first, but gradually came the first hints of a reciprocal smile, the first baby gurgles, the first real sobs after wailing. After three months came definite snuggling in, hugs, and the first authentic glimmerings of true attachment.

Chris was treated with progressively less-intrusive holdings for about eighteen months, and he became progressively positive, reciprocal, responsive, and attached.

When I held this interview with Chris and his mother, Chris was thirteen and attending a regular eighth-grade class at a Denver junior high school. He had tested out of special education classes in fourth grade. He is now in college.

Cline: How old was Chris when you felt there might be some problems?

Mother: He was two years old. . . . He wasn't talking, and he wasn't even trying to talk. He said maybe one or two words, but wasn't trying to talk like the other kids did at the same age.

Cline: And you had two older sons, so you knew what was within usual limits and what was outside usual limits.

Mother: Yes. . . . I asked a few doctors around and they said, "Well, why don't you just hang in there? He's just slow in getting started." And then, you know, I waited a little longer and it still wasn't getting any better and he wasn't playing the way other kids his age were playing and he wasn't doing what other kids were doing. He would sit there, and he would . . . I think he broke every knob in the house because he'd keep spinning them—on the television, the dishwasher, whatever. He wouldn't play with other kids, he wouldn't talk, and he never made eye contact. . . . When I went to get professional help, they acted like it wasn't that big a deal—"It'll get better as time goes on." But it wasn't getting better. And then I went to a seminar that you gave at the hospital. You gave a talk on the therapy, and

I had thought that maybe that would be an answer. Dr. B happened to go to the same talk, and I called him when I left there and he had thought maybe that would be an answer. Because at that point—Chris was three—he was thinking there was something a little bit wrong.

Cline: When I first saw Chris at three, he basically just ran around with a high-pitched voice and turned the light switches off and on. You weren't in control at all, and he wasn't responsive to you. Like, you'd grab his hand and he'd pull away and just want to run someplace. And his vocabulary at that time was about four or five words.

Mother: And I had been taking him to speech therapy, thinking maybe that would help. But it wasn't helping. What they were teaching him, basically, was turning on and off the lights, getting a word along with an action.

Cline: Now, the beauty of this situation is that we're about to see a really fine young man here, who is in seventh grade, and in all regular classes— no special-education classes. Where are you going to school now, Chris?

Chris: East Arvada Junior High School.

Cline: And how do you find the work?

Chris: The work is pretty easy. It isn't so hard anymore.

The rest of the session involved testing Chris and talking with him about his peer relationships, which were still difficult at this time. He remarked that the other kids acted like he was a "real dork." I reminded Chris that he had gotten off to a slightly slow start, and that he would more than catch up. Chris's comment was, "Yeah, just because you're a little different doesn't mean you're stupid!"

Dana is a big kid. In 1988, when I did this interview with him, his adoptive father, Reed, and his therapist, Conrad Boeding, he was fourteen, stood about six feet tall, and weighed well over two hundred pounds. He had the typical history of severely disturbed children, with nine different placements before he was five years old. His father disappeared after he was born, and he was abused by his birth mother.

At school he was a bully and showed no interest in learning. He was eventually expelled, and at the time he was first seen at Evergreen at age fourteen, he was not doing well with home education, either. He was adopted at age ten, and his adoptive parents found him to be unloving and defensive. One month after beginning treatment in highly confrontive holding sessions, he was saying that he wanted to return to school. This interview was recorded soon after he went through the holdings.

Cline: Dana, how long ago were you in treatment—when did you finish?

Dana: The week before last week.

Cline: So you started treatment about a month ago. Would that be fair to say?

Dana: Yeah.

Cline: Okay. Now, this is the first time I've met you. I haven't talked to Conrad, your therapist, about this at all, but as I understand it you had some lie-down sessions and went through some really tough times, and probably some kicking, too. There are some psychiatrists who are concerned about holding a kid down and having him kick and go through all that, and they wonder how that can help. I thought that since I'm doing this psych evaluation for you today for school, and since you're good enough to be interviewed, that you could say what you went through and what you experienced, and how it helped you or how it didn't help you, and what you liked about it and what you didn't like, the whole works.

Dana: Okay.

Cline: So you had two weeks of intensive treatment?

Dana: Right.

Cline: And do you think it helped you or do you think it didn't help you?

Dana: It helped me.

Cline: How did it help you?

Dana: I got all my anger and scaredness out of me. Well, not all of it, but the part that I could get out.

Cline: Before we started the tape, you mentioned that the therapy "made you a new person." How did you mean that?

Dana: Oh, it made me a better-loving kid, and I figured that my parents loved me now, and so I'm not trying to be a tough-butt anymore.

Cline: Is that right? Did you try to be a tough-butt before?

Dana: Yeah.

Cline: How did you try to be a tough-butt?

Dana: I tried proving to the world that no one could mess with me.

Cline: Um-hmm. What would you do differently now, or how are you different?

Dana: I tell people when I feel emotion coming on. I don't express my anger by bullying kids. I flop down and do push-ups. I get a pillow and scream into it until I feel that I'm relieved of the anger.

Cline: Do you think of the therapy as having helped you a whole lot, or some, or a little bit? On a scale of zero to 100, how much do you think it helped you?

Dana: About a 95.

Cline: Really! Have you had any therapy before?

Dana: Oh yeah, with George K.

Cline: How much therapy?

Dana: Two and a half years.

Cline: What kind of therapy was that?

Dana: It was sit down and talk, and then go home.

Cline: Do you feel like that helped you quite a bit too, or not as much, or more, or what's your thought on that?

Dana: I don't think it helped at all.

Cline: Maybe you could explain what lie-down sessions are like. What did you think going into this? Were you scared or not scared, or were you just mad . . .

Dana: It was really scary at first, because I didn't know what was going to happen to me. It didn't hurt at all, it was really comfortable—I didn't hurt anyone and no one hurt me.

Cline: Did you get a lot of your anger out?

Dana: Yeah, I got a lot out.

Cline: How?

Dana: They get you really mad and you scream, but sometimes most kids, I would say, use their body at first, but they teach you to say it with your mouth.

Cline: How did they get you to scream? Did they give you a poke in the ribs, or did they just say "Scream louder," or did they just shake your head a little bit, or what did they do?

Dana: If you don't get mad, they keep you in there as long as they want. There's no time set on there.

Cline: I suppose. Do they say all nice things to you, or are some of the things hard to hear?

Dana: The say really rude things to you.

Cline: *(Laughing)* Really rude things? What kind of rude things?

Dana: Like, "You're just a pile of poop."

Cline: Really sort of demeaning things to a certain extent. But then that really gets you mad?

Dana: Yeah. And then at the end, after you get mad, they give you hugs, and put love into your heart. So, you really do feel like you went through a good workout, and then you're really tired afterwards.

Cline: Let me ask your dad, Reed, a few questions. Now, you've been around Dana for, what, a couple of weeks since this was over?

Reed: Yeah.

Cline: How did you hear about this, and what did you think about it as a parent? How did things work out?

Reed: My wife read about it first in a book called *High Risk*. And when we read about it we recognized Dana from a lot of the stuff that was in the book about when they were talking about symptoms and the way people behave, and since nothing else was working, we thought this would be our best shot at getting Dana well. And so we tried for it and we were real glad you guys worked with him, being as old as he is.

Cline: Yes, sometimes with a fourteen-year-old the clinic might say he is too old. Do you notice any difference in him, or not . . . You're laughing. What . . .

Reed: Yeah, a lot of difference. The general expression in his face is more relaxed. The look in his eyes is different, the way he walks around, mannerisms that he uses are different, better. When you hug him, he's not a cardboard character anymore. He expresses himself like he never could before. I don't know if he *could* express himself before. He didn't, but he does now, and that's really good. He's more interested in better kinds of things. He's not interested in being a . . . what do you call it . . . a hoodlum, a juvenile delinquent; he's more interested in playing music and in school. He's more interested in being a regular person.

Reed: You adopted Dana when he was ten, and so you've had him for four years, right? What were those four years like? Were they easy or hard for you and your wife, or what? You're laughing again.

Reed: *(He and Dana are laughing together.)* They were hard, really hard.

Cline: How were they hard?

Reed: Well, Dana . . . every limit that was ever there, he wanted to push it down, everyday, every minute. If he wasn't in control, then he was going to fight to be in control of everything, no matter how much he lost in the fight or how bad the outcome was. Sometimes it seemed like all he wanted to do was to make us abandon him, and that was really hard on us.

Cline: I bet it was. To go through four years of that was probably a lot of hell for you and your wife, and of course for Dana, too. But you were really feeling it, right?

Reed: Yeah. That was really hard for Dana, too, I think.

Cline: Well, thank you so much. Conrad, can you think of anything else?

Boeding: The reason we chose to take this case.

Cline: Yes, explain why we took a fourteen-year-old.

Boeding: Basically because I found the family to be very intact, and both mom and dad were highly motivated to get this done. And after interviewing Dana, it was obvious that he was motivated to get his life turned around. He was frustrated that that hadn't been able to happen for him. And although Dana is fourteen, because of the psychological difficulties in his young life he had many developmental lags, and we thought that he was still emotionally pliable and had some flexibility. That, coupled with the motivation and the healthy parents, made us believe this would be a case we could make a difference on.

Dana and his parents continued more traditional therapy with Boeding, and Dana went back to regular school. Six years later, he is a high school graduate and can relate to other people as, like his father said, a regular person.

8

PARENTS CAN COPE

Parents of truly difficult children come from all walks of life. They might be wealthy, well-educated, and socially prominent, or living on the margins of society. Very often they are adoptive or foster parents, to whom the children came with a history of troubles. They might be birth parents of children who have become character disturbed, even though other of their children are fine. And they might be birth parents whose poor parenting abilities have produced hostile-dependent children, but who want to change. The laments that I hear are remarkably similar from parent to parent. "My child is out of control, and nothing I do seems to help." "We've been to five therapists in the last three years, and they've all thrown up their hands." "I can't get her to look at me, let alone listen to me." "Unless we watch him constantly, he wrecks the house." "These last four years have been hell. We can't go on living like this."

The message of this book is that parents *don't* have to go on like this. With the help of a competent therapist, parents can change the way their problem children act (and how they themselves act), and create a future full of hope for their children and themselves.

Involving Parents in Holding

Chapter 7 described the goals of holding therapy, gave some idea of what the holder does, and showed how children react to holding. Most of the cases discussed there involved therapists as holders, but for those children who are living at home—natural, foster, or adoptive—the parents will be the primary holders. This is only practical, since troubles can occur anytime for these children, and a competent therapist is not always available to contain the child and work through the acute problem. As for ongoing sessions to strengthen bonding, participation by the parents is highly valued, since they are the people with whom the child needs to bond. Therefore, much of the work I do is teaching parents holding and bonding techniques, and how to parent with love and logic.

When parents first come to me or to Evergreen, it is usually through referral from other therapists or because they read about intrusive techniques. Most have been through a number of traditional therapists who have talked, played, and drawn with these kids for hours with no results. Very often, they come to us as a last hope—the child is one step away from either institutionalization or the streets. Although they know that confrontive therapy is extraordinary, they really can't conceive of how intense it is, the fierceness of the anger that will ensue, or the physical demands on the client and holder.

Parents are often scared to hold their children in therapy, for fear that they will hurt them, or that they will cause them irreparable psychic harm with such a confrontation. Working through strong emotions is hard for everyone. Thus, they are normally content at the beginning to let the therapist do it all.

Of course, this is not what is best for the child, so as soon as possible, I involve the parents in the holding, first modeling what to do and then coaching the parents while they hold. This literally hands-on teaching shows the parents that both they and their children can survive a session with each other while working through extremely tough, exhausting issues.

Parents Sometimes Need Holding Themselves

In some cases, it pays to hold the parents before holding the child! A great number of children with reactive attachment disorder are living with unhappy, dysfunctional parents who lack good parenting techniques, which, if not the primary cause of unattachment, have contributed mightily to it. These parents may want to be effective parents, but their own dysfunctional backgrounds may be getting in their way. Not surprisingly, the conditions indicating parent holding are quite similar to those indicating child holding:

The child is unloving, controlling, and rejecting, and has self-destructive habits and behaviors.

The parents were raised in dysfunctional families; for example, the grandparents were alcoholics, or were verbally or physically abusive.

The parents realize they have made mistakes in raising their child and want to change, but find change difficult.

The parents and child have previously engaged in fruitless, traditional family therapy or individual therapy.

These parents often benefit more from *experiencing* good parenting techniques rather than from merely listening to someone talk about them, for being a good parent is as much an attitude and self-image issue as it is what tools or techniques a person uses. It is difficult enough for someone to teach another person an attitude, and expecting an individual with a dysfunctional background to change his attitude after a few discussion sessions is akin to expecting a teenager to be a good driver without intensive behind-the-wheel training.

As one parent told me, "I just can't learn how to be a good parent by watching June Cleaver on TV or having good parenting principles explained to me. I know what to do, but when I do it, it turns out wrong." Another parent had a more wrenching revelation while watching a therapist with her child from behind a one-way window at Evergreen. As the therapist holding her child worked through the child's rage and obtained happy compliance, the mother began to sob quietly. A therapist who was sitting with her asked, "Is it hard for you to watch your child going through this?" Her spontaneous answer was, "No, no. I realize Roger is so lucky to have this experience. But the one who really needs it is me!"

Generally, parents from dysfunctional backgrounds have trouble with power, control, and intimacy. They feel guilty about controlling their own children, and are unable to lovingly discipline with firmness. They confuse "meaning business" with "being mean." Because of a background filled with hassles, they allow and unconsciously encourage their children to hassle them, but then don't know how to control the situation or their own emotions. In situation after situation, mothers who related unhappily with their parents raise children who are noncompliant and disrespectful.

Such parents have trouble seeing themselves as important, so they allow their children to mistreat them and act disrespectfully. They are afraid of their own anger, so they have trouble showing firm limits. They are afraid of loss, so they handle their rejection of the child's actions poorly, confusing that with rejection of the child. They end up trying to discipline their children with statements that are actually requests for compliance: "Am I going to have to . . . ?" "Are you going to make me . . . ?" "Do I need to . . . ?" With these questions, parents unconsciously surrender control, even though they think they are attempting to control their children. The chaos resulting from these mixed signals causes the situation to escalate until the parents feel they must react with anger or force, which these parents have difficulty controlling.

A holding session helps them sort out these issues, both for themselves and as they apply to their children. A perfect example is that of Chris, whose eight-year-old daughter Roz was hospitalized because she was violently acting out and ignoring all controls on her behavior. In her own childhood, Chris had suffered physical and sexual abuse from her alcoholic father. When she was first held by a male therapist, she immediately began to tear up. She felt scared and powerless, recreating her feelings from childhood, when her father beat her with a stick. The therapist agreed that she was helpless and powerless, but showed her that she could feel loved at the same time. She did not have to equate powerlessness with terror and pain, and she did not have to be afraid to use her power with her daughter! After her holding session, Chris remarked:

I never knew, I never realized . . . It was beyond my wildest dreams, that I could feel comfortable and loved in a situation where I had no power. And it was so surprisingly reassuring to me when the therapist easily accepted his position of power, had no trouble with it, expected me to comply, was exceedingly firm and obviously cared about me no matter what. No wonder Roz acts out. I had never separated power and over-control, or discipline and punitiveness. I confused firmness with being overly strict. I had no concept of the difference between meaning business and getting angry. I just had to *feel* the difference.

Therapists who hold adults must have an awareness of their own feelings, sexual and otherwise, as well as of the feelings of their clients. Clients live up to therapists' expectations. If therapists expect that such feelings will not come up—that they are irrelevant to the process—most clients easily and quickly meet those expectations. On the other hand, when therapists expect their patients to have difficulty with touch, then the patients will have no end of trouble. Such overly concerned therapists unfortunately live in a world in which adult patients cannot be touched.

Therapists must also recognize their level of expertise—whether or not they can control the adult and bring him through the bonding process. There must be enough time to work through what is brought out in the session. And in today's litigious times, it is necessary to have another individual present or to videotape the session.

There are stages in holding a parent, just as with a child. (See the example of Howard in Chapter 7.) After good contract is obtained, the parent is seated comfortably in the therapist's lap, in a reclining position, and the session begins.

In the first stage, the therapist establishes empathy with the parent. The therapist might start out with a request like, "So tell me about your dad," or whatever is relevant to the parent's history. As the parent talks about his relationship with his parent, the therapist responds with, "That must have been tough on you." "I understand how easy it is for you to get upset." "That must have been really tough for a little kid." Holding a parent is perfect for this, as the closer the parent is to the therapist, physically and psychologically, the better he will be able to "lock into" the therapist's understanding and acceptance of childhood difficulties.

In stage two, the parent is brought to tears. The deep empathy of stage one usually leads the parent to tear up. At this point, the therapist might ask, "If tears could talk, what would yours be saying?" "Way down inside, what are your feelings right now?" After the parent tearfully relates feelings and facts about childhood grief, the therapist hugs him. Parents who never experienced hugs in childhood sometimes need to be encouraged and instructed on how to do this right—"I want your nose right in my neck, right where little kids snuggle in." "I'd like a little tighter hug on my back, please . . . Thank you." From this stage, the parent learns that when his children are upset, he doesn't need to *do* anything, he just needs to *be* with them.

After the parent experiences loving acceptance of his pain and anguish, he feels safe to express the deeper layers of hate or rage that may lie beneath the sorrow. During this third stage, the therapist amplifies the parent's emotions. After ending the hug, the therapist may ask, "So how else besides 'sad' were you feeling?" or "I bet you have other feelings besides 'sad.'" The parent might softly say, "I felt angry, too."

This is only *talking* about the feeling, which doesn't help. The therapist must get the dysfunctional parent to *feel, express,* and *resolve* the anger. The therapist might ask the parent to repeat a meaningful statement louder, until the parent is expressing the rage. In addition, the therapist might put pressure on certain muscles so that the parent feels slight discomfort. This often works wonders in helping a client release anger.

During this stage, the therapist models easy acceptance of anger. The parent sees that anger is not taken personally—it is simply accepted and worked through.

In stage four, as the holding session ends, the parent may be allowed to sit up to signify equality in the relationship with the holder. In this position, the therapist and parent work on processing the feelings that were expressed intellectually and setting goals for new behavior. The therapist might say something like, "How has this anger affected your relationship with your child (spouse, etc.)?" "That was a great job of expressing yourself. I loved it! I bet you'll love it when your child feels this safe in *your* arms." The parent now knows how it feels to be lovingly controlled, to have feelings accepted, and to have limits expressed. The jumble of feelings from a dysfunctional childhood have been separated and dealt with, and the parent is beginning to work through them. After the experience and modeling, the parent can more easily act appropriately with his child, and he can be coached in holding the child.

How to Be Great Parents

Whether dealing with severely disturbed or normal children, parents need to follow certain guidelines in order to raise successful children. First, good parents *show* their children how to live their lives; they don't say one thing and model another. They worry about how they handle their own lives so that they set a good model for their children, for they know that their children will follow their example.

Second, good parents set high expectations for their children. They let the kids know that what they think is important. This doesn't mean that the parents will operate the way the children want them to; that would produce chaos in the family. But it does show the children that they are worth a lot to their parents. In addition, good parents give their children appropriate chores to do, and expect the chores to be done well. They do not accept excuses for poor or incomplete work, as this gets the children comfortable with meeting lower expectations.

Third, great parents understand that each of their children has different capabilities and interests. These parents strive to give their children the opportunity to try many activities, and to find what is right for them. However, because one child excels in music doesn't mean that any of the others will. And none of the children may like what the parents like. No matter—these parents love their children equally.

Fourth, healthy parents teach children to accept consequences for poor actions and rewards for good ones. And they do this not by talking about "taking responsibility." (In homes where responsibility is talked about a great deal, there is almost always massive irresponsibility.) They provide consequences and rewards as they are merited. Instead of yelling at a child for poor behavior and then cleaning up the mess the child has caused (the "rant, rave, and rescue" method), great parents will explain to the child how his actions caused the problem and that he will have to live with the repercussions. This doesn't limit the child's choices—it lets him know that some of the choices are bad for him. Great parents know that it is only by giving their children the right to fail that they can be given the choice to succeed.

By giving consequences and rewards, great parents help to establish a cycle that is essential to the development of responsible behavior in their children:

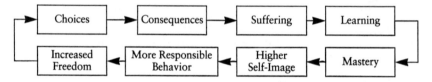

Fifth, functional parents do not try to enforce the unenforceable. Here are three rules that great parents try to live by:

Avoid control battles.
If you must have a control battle, choose the issue carefully.
Parents can win control battles.

In order to follow these rules, there are many other rules that great parents *don't* make: for instance, "Don't take drugs. Don't play with those kids. Don't smoke. Don't drink." These rules are unenforceable; in fact, most self-destructive behavior cannot be controlled by anyone except the individual involved. Instead of ranting at their children about the dangers of drugs, healthy parents say something like this: "Honey, there are drugs everywhere. I'm sure that if you wanted to use them, you could find them. I hope you don't. Drugs could certainly mess up your mind, but you know what I've always said, 'Every child of mine has the right to choose to screw up her life.' I sure hope you won't screw up your life, but if you do, don't come to us expecting to be rescued."

Working Through Feelings

It isn't easy working through a seriously disturbed child's feelings. In fact, even parents who have lived through terrible times with their children are surprised by the violent rage that their children express in holding sessions. It is shocking to see the strength and determination in these little bodies, and an onlooker might wonder if all the sweat and labor is worth it. Even those of us who are intimately involved with the therapy might wonder at times, especially with a deeply disturbed child who may take months to reach. But the alternative—not reaching the child—is much worse than any relatively short-term physical and mental exhaustion.

To illustrate the sort of work it sometimes takes to get through to a young child, we'll look at a case that the great therapist Milton Erickson handled about forty years ago. (The excerpts that follow are from the book *Uncommon Therapy,* written by Jay Haley, an outstanding therapist himself.) Erickson was responsible for illuminating techniques that brightened and enlivened American therapy. The case is one of confrontive therapy with an out-of-control eight-year-old boy, and it is pertinent in two ways: it shows what holding can be like, and it details the important contribution of the loving parent to the therapy.

> A twenty-seven-year-old mother began to encounter serious difficulty with her eight-year-old son, who was becoming progressively more defiant and seemed to find a new way to defy her each day. The mother had divorced her husband two years previously, for adequate reasons recognized by all concerned. In addition to her son, she had two daughters, aged nine and six. After some months of occasional dating with men in the hope of marriage, she found that her son had become rebellious and an unexpected problem. The older daughter had joined him briefly in this rebelliousness. The mother was able to correct the daugh-

ter by her customary measures of discipline through anger, shouting, scolding, threatening, and then an angry spanking followed
by an intelligent, reasonable, objective discussion with the girl.

The good ending is important. This comes close to being a one-
minute scolding, an intrusive technique that will be discussed later
in this chapter.

This had, in the past, always been effective with the children.

However, her son, Joe, refused to respond to her usual measures, even when she added repeated spankings, deprivations,
tears, and the enlistment of her family's assistance. Joe merely
stated, quite happily and cheerfully, that he planned to do whatever he pleased and nothing, just nothing, could stop him.

The son's behavior spread to the school and to the neighborhood, and literally nothing was safe from his depredations.
School property was destroyed, teachers defied, schoolmates
assaulted; neighbors' windows were broken and their flower
beds destroyed. The neighbors and teachers, endeavoring to take
a hand in the matter, succeeded in intimidating the child but
nothing more. Finally, the boy began destroying things of value
in the home, especially after the mother was asleep at night, and
then he would infuriate her by bold-faced denying guilt the next
morning.

This final mischief led the mother to bring the boy in for
treatment. As the mother told her story, Joe listened with a
broad, triumphant smile. When she had finished, he boastfully
declared that I could not do anything to stop him, and he was
going to go right on doing as he pleased. I assured him, gravely
and earnestly, that it was unnecessary for me to do anything to
change his behavior because he was a good, big, strong boy and
very smart and he would have to change his behavior all by himself. I assured him that his mother would do just enough to give
him a chance to change his behavior "all by himself." Joe
received this statement in an incredulous, sneering manner. I said
that his mother would be told some simple little things that she
could do so that he himself could change his behavior, and sent
him out of the office. I also challenged him in a most kind fashion to try to figure out what those simple little things might be.
This served to puzzle him into quiet reflective behavior while he
awaited his mother.

Alone with the mother, I discussed a child's demand for a world in which he could be certain that there was someone stronger and more powerful than he. To date, her son had demonstrated with increasing desperation that the world was so insecure that the only strong person in it was himself, a little eight-year-old boy.

Then I gave the mother painstakingly clear instructions for her activities for the next two days. As they left the office later, the boy challengingly asked if I had recommended spankings. I assured him that no measure would be taken except to give him full opportunity to change his own behavior; no one else would change it. This reply perplexed him. On the way home his mother administered severe corporal punishment to compel him to let her drive the automobile safely. This misconduct had been anticipated; the mother had been advised to deal summarily with it and without argument. The evening was spent in the usual fashion by letting the boy watch television as he wished.

It is essential that parents and professionals work together as a team. If strong methods are required, the professionals must back up the judgment of well-trained therapeutic parents.

The following morning the grandparents arrived and picked up the two daughters. Joe, who had plans to go swimming, demanded his breakfast. He was most puzzled when he observed his mother carry into the living room some wrapped sandwiches, fruit, a thermos bottle of fruit juice and one of coffee, and some towels. She put all these items securely on a heavy couch with the telephone and some books. Joe demanded that she prepare his breakfast without delay, threatening physical destruction of the first thing he could lay his hands on if she did not hurry. His mother merely smiled at him, seized him, threw him quickly to the floor on his stomach, and sat her full weight upon him. When he yelled at her to get off, she said she had already eaten breakfast and she had nothing to do except to try to think about ways to change his behavior. However, she pointed out that she was certain she did not know any way. Therefore, it would be all up to him.

The boy struggled furiously against the odds of his mother's weight, strength, and watchful dexterity. He yelled, screamed, shouted profanity and obscenities, sobbed, and finally promised piteously always to be a good boy. His mother answered that the promise did not mean anything because she had not yet figured out how to change his behavior. This evoked another fit of rage from him, which finally ceased and was followed by his urgent plea to go to the bathroom. His mother explained gently that she had not finished her thinking; she offered him a towel to mop up so he would not get too wet. This elicited another wild bit of struggling that soon exhausted him. His mother took advantage of the quiet to make a telephone call to her mother. While Joe listened, she explained casually that she had not yet reached any conclusion in her thinking and she really believed that any change in behavior would have to come from Joe. Her son greeted this remark with as loud a scream as he could muster. His mother commented into the telephone that Joe was too busy screaming to think about changing his behavior, and she put the mouthpiece down to Joe's mouth so that he could scream into it.

Joe lapsed into sullen silence, broken by sudden surges of violent effort, screams, demands, and sobbing, interrupted by piteous pleas. To all of this his mother gave the same mild, pat answers. As time passed, the mother poured herself coffee and fruit juice, ate sandwiches, and read a book. Shortly before noon the boy politely told her he really did need to go to the bathroom. She confessed a similar need. She explained that it would be possible if he would agree to return, resume his position on the floor, and let her sit down comfortably upon him. After some tears he consented. He fulfilled his promise, but almost immediately launched into renewed violent activity to dislodge her. Each near success led to further effort, which exhausted him still more. While he rested, she ate fruit and drank coffee, made a casual telephone call, and read a book.

After over five hours Joe surrendered by stating simply and abjectly that he would do anything and everything she told him to do. His mother replied just as simply and earnestly that her thinking had been in vain; she just did not know what to tell him to do. He burst into tears at this but shortly, sobbing, he told her he knew what to do. She replied mildly that she was very glad of this, but she did not think he had had enough time to think long enough about it. Perhaps another hour or so of thinking might help. Joe silently awaited the passing of an hour while his mother sat reading quietly. When over an hour had passed, she commented on the time but expressed her wish to finish the chapter. Joe sighed shudderingly and sobbed softly to himself while his mother finished her reading.

With the chapter finally finished, the mother got up and so did Joe. He timidly asked for something to eat. His mother explained in laborious detail that it was too late for lunch, that breakfast was always eaten before lunch, and that it was too late to serve breakfast. She suggested instead that he have a drink of ice water and a comfortable rest in bed for the remainder of the afternoon.

This six-hour session would be illegal in some states. If the child were a disturbed foster child, almost certainly there would be repercussions. If neighbors reported the wailing, cursing, and "piteous cries," child care professionals would likely remove the child from the home. In Colorado recently, foster parents were told they could hold or restrain their child only if he directly attacked them. In some states, it is illegal for parents to even demand their child skip a meal as a consequence for negative acting out.

Joe fell asleep quickly but awakened to the aroma of well-liked foods. His sisters had returned, and he tried to join them at the table for the evening meal. His mother explained, gravely, simply, and in lucid detail that it was customary first to eat breakfast and then lunch and then dinner. Unfortunately, he had missed his breakfast, therefore he had to miss his lunch. Now he would have to miss his dinner, but fortunately he could begin a new day the next morning. Joe returned to his bedroom and cried himself to sleep. The mother slept lightly that night, but Joe did not arise until she was well along with breakfast preparation.

Joe entered the kitchen with his sisters for breakfast and sat down happily while his mother served his sisters with pancakes and sausages. At Joe's place was a large bowl. His mother explained that she had cooked him an extra-special breakfast of oatmeal, a food not too well liked by him. Tears came to his eyes, but he thanked her for the serving as was the family custom, and he ate voraciously. His mother explained that she had cooked an extra supply so that he could have a second helping. She also cheerfully expressed the hope that enough would be left over to meet his needs for lunch. Joe ate manfully to prevent that possibility, but his mother had cooked a remarkably large supply. After breakfast, Joe set about cleaning up his room without any instruction. This done, he asked his mother if he could call upon the neighbors. She had no idea what this portended but gave permission. From behind the window curtains she watched him while he went next door and rang the bell. When the door opened, he apparently spoke to the neighbor briefly and then went on up the street. As she later learned, just as systematically as he had terrorized the neighborhood, he canvassed it to offer his apologies and to promise that he would come back to make amends as fast as he could. Joe returned for lunch, ate buttered cold thick-sliced oatmeal, helped voluntarily to dry the dishes, and spent the afternoon and evening with his schoolbooks while his sisters watched television. The evening meal was ample but consisted of leftovers, which Joe ate quietly without comment. At bedtime Joe went to bed voluntarily while his sisters awaited their mother's usual insistence.

Some professionals construe as overly harsh giving a disturbed foster child oatmeal for two meals in a row.

> The next day Joe went to school, where he made his apologies and promises. These were accepted warily. That evening he became involved in a typical childish quarrel with his older sister, who shrieked for her mother. As the mother entered the room, Joe began to tremble visibly. Both children were told to sit down, and the sister was asked to state her case first. When it became his turn to speak, Joe said he agreed with his sister. His mother then explained to Joe that she expected him to be a normal eight-year-old boy and to get into ordinary trouble like all regular eight-year-old boys. Then she pointed out to both of them that their quarrel was lacking in merit and was properly to be abandoned. Both children acquiesced.

A simple six-hour holding session and tight follow-up was enough to make enormous changes in Joe because he had been previously bonded to his mother. He was covering the grief from the loss of his father, and perceived a potential loss of his mother to suitors, and so covered this terror with control issues and behavior problems. This would have been a much more difficult case if Joe had never experienced a loving relationship with anyone.

When a seriously disturbed child is as controlling as Joe, based on deeper insecurities, the therapeutic parents may need to be as controlling as Joe's mother was for months! Certainly, these children do not so easily apologize for misbehavior. Indeed, if Joe were a typical disturbed child, he would not be apologizing to the neighbors, he would be very convincingly complaining to them about how his mother was mistreating him. In fact, he would very likely be calling the nearest child abuse team from a neighbor's house!

The education of Joe's mother to enable her to deal with her son's problem by following out the instructions was a rather difficult task. She was a college graduate, a highly intelligent woman with a background of social and community interests and responsibilities. In the interview she was asked to describe, as fully as possible, the damage Joe had done in the school and community. With this description, the damage became painfully enlarged in her mind. (Plants do grow back, windowpanes and torn dresses can be replaced, but this comfort was not allowed to be a part of her review.)

Next she was asked to describe Joe "as he used to be": a reasonably happy, well-behaved, and actually a decidely brilliant child. She was repeatedly asked to draw these comparisons between his past and present behavior, more briefly each time, but with a greater highlighting of the essential points. Then she was asked to speculate upon the probable future of Joe both "as he used to be" and as was "quite possible" now in the light of his present behavior. I offered helpful suggestions to aid her in drawing sharply contrasting "probable pictures of the future."

After this discussion she was asked to consider in full the possibilities of what she could do over the weekend and the kind of role she ought to assume with Joe. Since she did not know, this placed her completely in a passive position so I could offer plans. Her repressed and guilty resentments and hostilities toward her son and his misbehavior were utilized. Every effort was made to redirect them into an anticipation of a satisfying, calculated, deliberate watchfulness in the frustrating of her son's attempts to confirm his sense of insecurity and to prove her ineffectual.

The mother's apparently justified statement that her weight of 150 pounds was much too great to permit putting it fully on the body of an eight-year-old child was a major factor in winning the mother's full cooperation. At first this argument was carefully evaded. The mother was helped to systematically marshal all of her objections to my proposed plans behind this apparently indisputable argument that her weight was too great to be endured by a child. As she became more entrenched in this defense, a carefully worded discussion allowed her to wish with increasing desire that she could do the various things I outlined as I detailed possibilities for the entire weekend.

When the mother seemed to have reached the right degree of emotional readiness, the question of her weight was raised for disposal. She was simply assured that she need not take medical opinion at all but would learn from her son on the morrow that her weight would be inconsequential to him. In fact, it would take all of her strength, dexterity, and alertness, in addition to her weight, to master the situation. She might even lose the contest because of the insufficiency of her weight. (The mother could not analyze the binding significance of this argument so simply presented to her. She was placed in the position of trying to prove that her weight was really too much. To prove this, she would need her son's cooperation, and I was certain that the boy's aggressive patterns would preclude any passive yielding to his mother's weight. In this way the mother would be taught by the son to disregard her defenses against my suggestions, and she would be reinforced in her acceptance of those suggestions by the very violence of his behavior.) As the mother later explained, "The way that bucking bronco threw me around, I knew I would have to settle down to serious business to keep my seat. It just became a question of who was smarter, and I knew I had a real job to do. Then I began to take pleasure in anticipating and meeting his moves. It was almost like a chess game. I certainly learned to admire and respect his determination, and I got an immense satisfaction out of frustrating him as thoroughly as he had frustrated me."

This is not a sick mother talking—this is a natural feeling, although we learn to believe that such a feeling is bad or unnatural. One mother, after being nonverbally reprimanded by an unthinking therapist, said, "How many times does your house have to be set on fire before it's okay to feel like wringing the kid's neck?"

"I had one awfully bad time, though. When he came back from the bathroom, and he started to lie down on the floor, he looked at me so pitifully that I wanted to take him in my arms.

But I remembered what you said about not accepting surrender because of pity but only when the issue was settled. That's when I knew I had won, so I was awfully careful then to be sure not to let any pity come in. That made the rest of it easy, and I could really understand what I was doing and why."

When working with disturbed kids, there is no compromise—it's either win completely or lose absolutely. Thus, the decision to disregard pitiful looks and pleading—no matter what other, well-intentioned people say—is of utmost importance.

For the next few months, until midsummer, all went well. Then for no apparent reason, except an ordinary quarrel with his sister settled unfairly to her advantage, Joe declared quietly but firmly that he did not have "to take that kind of stuff." He said he could "stomp" anybody, particularly me [Erickson], and he dared his mother to take him to see me that very evening. At a loss what to do, his mother brought him to the office immediately. As they entered, she declared, somewhat inaccurately, that Joe threatened to "stomp" my office. Joe was immediately told, disparagingly, that he probably could not stomp the floor hard enough to make it worthwhile. Irately, Joe raised his foot and brought his cowboy boot down hard upon the carpeted floor. He was told, condescendingly, that his effort was really remarkably good for a little eight-year-old boy and that he could probably repeat it a number of times, but not very many. Joe angrily shouted that he could stomp that hard fifty, a hundred, a thousand times if he wished. I replied that he was only eight years old, and no matter how angry he was he couldn't stomp a thousand times. In fact, he couldn't even stomp hard half that number of times, which would only be five hundred. If he tried, he would soon get tired, his stomp would get littler and weaker, and he would have to change off to the other leg and rest. Even worse, he was told he couldn't even stand still while he rested without wiggling around and wanting to sit down. If he didn't believe this, he could just go right ahead and stomp. When he got all tired out like a little boy, he could rest by standing still until he discovered that he could not even stand still without wiggling and wanting to sit down. With outraged and furious dignity, Joe declared his solemn intention of stomping a hole in the floor even if it took a hundred million stomps.

The mother was dismissed with instructions to return in the "square root of four," which she translated to mean "in two hours." In this way Joe was not informed of the time when she would return, although he recognized that one adult was telling another a specific time. As the office door closed upon his mother, Joe balanced on his right foot and crashed his left foot to the floor. I assumed a look of astonishment, commenting that the stomp was far better than I had expected of Joe, but I doubted if he could keep it up. I said that Joe would soon weaken, and then he would discover that he couldn't even stand still. Joe contemptuously stomped a few more times before it became possible to disparage his stomp as becoming weaker.

After intensifying his efforts, Joe reached a count of thirty before he realized that he had greatly overestimated his stomping ability. As this realization became evident in Joe's facial expression, he was offered the privilege of just patting the floor a thousand times with his foot, since he really couldn't stand still and rest without wiggling around and wanting to sit down. With desperate dignity, he rejected the floor-patting and declared his intention of standing still. Promptly, he assumed a still, upright position with his hands at his sides, facing me. I immediately showed him the desk clock, and I commented about the slowness of the minute hand and the even greater slowness of the hour hand despite the seeming rapidity of the ticking of the clock. I turned to my desk, began to make notes in Joe's case record, and from that I turned to other desk tasks.

Within fifteen minutes Joe was shifting his weight back and forth from one foot to the other, twisting his neck, wiggling his shoulders. When a half hour had passed, he was reaching out with his hand, resting some of his weight on the arm of the chair beside which he was standing. However, he quickly withdrew his hand whenever I seemed about to look up to glance reflectively around the room. After about an hour, I excused myself temporarily from the office. Joe took full advantage of this, and of several repetitions of my leaving, never quite getting back into his previous position beside the chair.

When his mother knocked at the office door, I told Joe, "When your mother comes in, do exactly as I tell you." She was admitted and seated, looking wonderingly at Joe as he stood rigidly facing the desk. Signaling silence to the mother, I turned to Joe and peremptorily commanded, "Joe, show your mother how hard you can still stomp the floor." Joe was startled, but he responded nobly. "Now, Joe, show her how stiff and straight you can stand still." A minute later, two more orders were issued. "Mother, this interview between Joe and me is a secret between Joe and me. Joe, don't tell your mother a single thing about what happened in this office. You and I both know, and that's enough, okay?"

Both Joe and his mother nodded their heads. She looked a bit mystified; Joe looked thoughtfully pleased. On the trip home Joe was quiet, sitting quite close beside his mother. About halfway home Joe broke the silence by commenting that I was a "nice doctor." As the mother later said, this statement had relieved her puzzled mind in some inexplicable way. She neither asked nor was given any explanation of the office events. She knew only that Joe liked, respected, and trusted me and was glad to see me occasionally in a social or semi-social fashion. Joe's behavior continued to be that of a normal, highly intelligent boy who now and then misbehaved in an expected and warrantable fashion.

Two years passed and Joe's mother became engaged. Joe liked the prospective stepfather but asked his mother one demanding question—Did I approve of the man? Assured that I did approve, there was then unquestioning acceptance.

In an undefined world where intellectual and emotional fluctuations create an enveloping state of uncertainty that varies from one mood and one moment to the next, there can be no certainty or security. Joe sought to learn what was really strong, secure, and safe, and he learned it in the effective way one learns not to kick a stone with a bare foot or to slap a cactus with the bare hands.

Therapeutic Parents

One of the most important concepts to take from this story of Joe, his mother, and Milton Erickson is that parents are an *essential* part of the treatment team. The parents involved—foster, birth, or adoptive—must become part of the process for any therapy to succeed with disturbed children.

An unconscious discounting of parents by professionals is a nearly universal problem. Privately, many professionals state that too many parents are noncompliant themselves; they won't do what they are told to do, and so undermine the therapy. I believe that the problem can be addressed if more professionals will take the time to properly train the parents. Not all professionals can deal with teaching parents; sometimes it appears easier to do it all by oneself rather than to train others. However, considering the waves of unattached children facing us and the lack of money for hospitalization, it makes sense to involve those frontline people who have the most invested in saving the children.

I use the term *therapeutic parents* when talking about parents with specialized training who can help reach difficult children. These can be birth or adoptive parents, but in most cases they are foster parents who are working with a child and a placing family in out-of-home placement. The placement may be for two weeks of intensive treatment or for longer periods, sometimes ranging up to a year or more. The therapist relies on these parents to make good therapeutic judgments with the children.

The first requirement for therapeutic parents is *training*. These parents must be extensively trained in normal and deviant child development. They must know normal and specialized parenting techniques, and how to handle the unusual problems of disturbed children: among these are the manifestations of sexual and physical abuse; severe control problems; and grief, loss, and abandonment issues.

Part of the training must be how to use therapeutic techniques and still remain within the guidelines set by various governmental departments. For instance, parents may be required not to touch a child against the child's will, or may be unable to restrain the child for any act other than one that physically endangers either the child or others. Simple reinforcers that may be effective with a disturbed child, such as withholding a meal until a job is done, may be against departmental guidelines, even though such a practice is carried out in many regular American households and is one of the underpinnings of the capitalist system. (If you don't work, you don't eat.)

Another thing parents must learn is that, whereas consistency and predictability are essential for most normal parent-child relationships, this is not always so when parenting unattached children. Certain things must remain constant—eye contact, touch, tone of voice, the child's safety, the parent being in charge. However, since it is necessary to "disturb the disturbed" to help unattached kids change, unpredictability becomes a crucial ingredient. When children act the most unlovable, parents need to act the most unpredictably. The parent must hug a child when he acts unlovable, not just when his behavior is good. The parent can pop a candy into the child's mouth when he does well, or when he doesn't; or ignore behavior when it happens, but impose a consequence at an unexpected time.

Therapeutic Parenting Techniques

The therapeutic techniques can be broken down into two areas: proactive and reactive. The proactive approach is used to avoid problems and encourage positive behavior. The reactive approach is used to respond to negative behavior. They are not exclusive; rather, they work hand in hand, and involve touch, eye contact, food, and smiles. Both approaches are action-oriented.

These techniques, used lovingly and with a high regard for children, a sense of humor and balance, a projection of strength even when it might be illusory, and a well-trained support system, will go far to making unattached children livable and lovable.

The following sections about proactive and reactive techniques were contributed by Deborah Hage, a therapist at the Attachment Center at Evergreen.

Proactive Techniques

Proactive techniques involve creating a home environment and relationship with difficult children so that being respectful, responsible, and fun to be around is a desirable goal for them. The parents must set a tone that is positive and makes valued behaviors worthwhile. There are several creative ways of doing this. One is planning family activities to maximize positives and minimize negatives, which helps the children be enthusiastic about the activities rather than apprehensive and defensive. Another way is for the parents to speak in loving ways, avoiding sarcasm and anger, so that the children will want to bond to them. The parents must spend a great deal of one-on-one time with each child to develop the parent-child bond: game-playing, cuddling, rocking, and occasionally feeding a bottle to an unattached child are all part of the life of a therapeutic parent. (Martha Welch, in her very good book *Holding Time*, goes into greater depth on proactive techniques.)

Tight control of television time is another proactive trait. Even so-called "good" programs are detrimental to kids, especially those with problem behavior, and it is not necessarily the content of the shows that is at fault. It is the passive watching that wrecks the kids. The TV does not relate, does not answer questions, and does not reward creative thinking. No matter if the show is *Sesame Street, Reading Rainbow, Where in the World Is Carmen Sandiego,* or some other highly acclaimed educational program, children simply sit and watch. They are not engaging in reciprocal smiles, eye contact, movement, or touch. None of the interactions essential to bonding are present. They might learn all about how high technology works, but they never get the chance to make a tin-can telephone with their parents or playmates! Therefore, proactive parents eliminate TV watching until unattached children have demonstrated good behavior over several months. (Yes, months—not a few days or a week.) Filling the TV time with fun time when earned gives children another incentive to work on their behavior.

Sincere encouragement is important as well. Proactive parents get excited when children are "caught" doing something right, rather than when they do something wrong. Bad behavior is dealt with matter-of-factly, while the pizzazz is saved for good behavior. Squealing with delight when children brush their teeth and ignoring them when they don't focuses on the positives in their personalities. The parents have to be aware of opportunities for such reinforcement, for they come unannounced: you might see a proactive parent suddenly grab a child in a hug and swing her around because she walked by another child and didn't hit him. "Wow! Did you see what you just did? You walked by Jim without punching him!"

Because unattached children are by definition self-centered, developing reciprocal relationships is part of the therapeutic parents' job, too. These children must learn to trust others to take care of them, and reciprocally, they must learn that they must take care of others. This is essential to the success of therapy. Participating in joint activities, doing chores, paying back those they hurt through their thoughtlessness are all learning tasks for unattached children. Therapeutic parents must provide many opportunities for disturbed children to interact in a reciprocal way.

All of these techniques sound child-centered, and I guess they are. However, concentrating on the child like this will burn out any therapeutic parent or couple. Therefore, the parents must be taken care of, too. Time off for the parents is important, and they must have some arrangement for someone else to watch the children periodically. The relief may come from family or from the program that the parents are involved with, but it must come. In addition, the parents must be sure to take care of themselves during family activities. When they choose to participate in something fun for the children, it must also be fun for them. On the other side of the coin, when a child's negative behavior requires a response, the parents must ensure that they feel good about themselves and the child, despite the child's reaction to the consequences of his behavior. In this way, the parents will be able to continue caring for the child, and the child will trust that the parents will be there for him.

Reactive Techniques

When children do not take advantage of the enjoyment life has to offer and make poor behavior choices, therapeutic parents must react to the choices. There are a number of ways for parents to demonstrate being "sad for" the child because of her behavior, rather than "mad at" her. These are the reactive techniques.

Reactive techniques can be seen as ranging along a scale from nonintrusive (ignoring behavior) to extremely intrusive (one-minute scolding). Underlying all reactive discipline techniques is *consequencing,* which is the concept of having children experience either a real-world or a simulated real-world consequence of their behavior. (*Parenting with Love and Logic,* by myself and Jim Fay, deals extensively with consequencing as a parenting technique.)

As the techniques become stronger in response to escalating negative behavior, the parent must remember that intrusive techniques can quickly become abusive techniques. During proper training in these techniques, parents will spend a lot of time discussing the slender line which divides discipline that makes the child confront and want to change her behavior from punishment that serves to satisfy the parent's anger. One common understanding is that when a parent becomes angry, discipline is no longer therapeutic and should not be attempted, at least until the parent is no longer overwrought. (This is a major reason why I keep telling parents that they must take care of themselves first, so that they can be therapeutic with their children.) Another important point that therapeutic parents agree on is that techniques which are not working should be changed, not applied with increased vigor.

As you read about these techniques, understand that most therapeutic foster parents are caring for children who are seen at least weekly by a therapist. Each session begins with parents and the therapist discussing the last week, what behaviors the therapist must attend to immediately, progress toward long-term goals, and what parenting techniques were used with which behaviors and with what results. Such consultation allows parents and therapists to decide which techniques need to be added, dropped, or modified. Intrusive techniques are used only as part of a specific behavior-modification plan, and only when parents and therapists agree that using them is in the best interests of the children. These techniques cannot be used in a vacuum—parents must use them with the consent and supervision of a trained attachment therapist.

Naturally, the least-intrusive reactive technique is simply to ignore all behavior that can be ignored, such as sloppy dressing and careless schoolwork. Of course, such behavior has its consequences: unkempt kids are not invited on family outings and poor schoolwork gets poor grades. The parents are not oblivious to what the child is doing, but they don't react to it when the behavior occurs. Later, misbehavior can be dealt with by the parents or the therapist, as they usually point to a larger problem.

The next step up the intrusiveness scale is a simple touch to remind children that the parent is present and is aware of their behavior. Very often, the parent need only rest her hand lightly on the child's shoulder to help the child become more thoughtful. If the child is out of reach, a smile accompanied by raised eyebrows can be effective.

"Mom time" or "dad time" is slightly more intrusive than touch, because the child is brought in close after misbehavior and is held or cuddled on the parent's lap. The goal of this is to make the child feel loved and valued while giving him a chance to regroup and choose better behavior. This may last for a few minutes, or it may go on for as long as it takes to read a couple of short storybooks. When that is finished, the child is given a consequence or sent off with a big hug to try again.

"Mom time" can be extended, if need be, into "line-of-vision supervision," in which the child is within the parent's sight at all times. Some therapeutic parents call this "the umbilical cord." The first effect is that the child is confronted with her behavior: she is told that until she is able to make good decisions—what to say, where to go to the bathroom, how to handle objects—she needs to be close to someone who can make good decisions for her. The second is that the child gets the chance to observe other people making good decisions. This modeling is an important part of the child's learning how to make such decisions. Line-of-vision supervision can be very tiring for the parent, for with unattached children it can go on for weeks or months.

Having "practice sessions" is another technique which is minimally intrusive. The goal of this technique is to get the child to enjoy cooperating, so the parent can be silly and use pizzazz. Practice sessions are held at the parent's convenience, and not necessarily when an infraction occurs. The parent starts with an unusual request, such as "Run to the door and put your nose to the doorknob." (This is sometimes done in a Simon Says game situation.) Once the child is cooperating on the silly things, the parent can make a command about what the child needs to practice: "Go flush the toilet." "Wipe your nose." "Get in the car and buckle your seatbelt." The child's response to the command is typically, "I didn't use the toilet," or some such objection, to which the parent says, "I know. This is just a practice session, so that when you need to do it you will know how."

If the child refuses to follow the command, the parent lets it pass, but the next time the child asks the parent to do something, the parent repeats the command. Very often, dinnertime is the next opportunity to get compliance. When the child asks, "Please pass the milk," the parent replies with a gentle smile, "Please go flush the toilet." The child might get mad, but not to worry. Sometimes anger is what the child needs to change his behavior, and he is the one who needs to get mad, not the parent.

Another technique that can be fun for parents is the "double bind." This paradoxical technique allows for, and sometimes encourages, oppositional behavior in a way that keeps the parent in charge. In essence, the parent tells the child to do what she is going to do anyway. If she does it, the parent is in control. If the child doesn't do it, she has made the right choice.

For example, the parent might say, "Go clean up your room; but first, whine and cry." The child might actually declare that she can pick up her toys without whining and crying, and then go clean her room. Or, the child will whine and cry, and then go clean her room. Either way, the parent has won. Other situations also lend themselves to this technique: "It's your turn to do the dishes, but dawdle around for a while before you start." "Feel free to not study for tomorrow's spelling test. Your dad and I are just as capable of loving a bad speller as a good one." "Keep practicing your cursing. If you're going to do something, you might as well do it until you're the best at it!"

Parents can use this technique in conjunction with others. For instance, parents might use pizzazz for good behavior with a double bind: "Wow! Did you see what you just did? You walked by Jim without punching him! I bet that was an accident—you meant to hit him and you forgot. Walk by and try it again. I want to know if I saw what I think I saw."

One of the beauties of the double bind is that parents can give children permission to make bad choices. Then, when the kids do make a bad choice, parents are ready for it and don't get sucked into an angry response. Since many children display negative behavior just to enrage their parents, parental permission to behave poorly often robs them of the reason to do so.

Sometimes the best response to continued bad behavior is for a parent to declare, "You are draining my energy. Which chore do you want to do to fill me back up?" Next, the parent lists some of the things that need to be done and has the child choose one. This creates a win-win situation: the parent is taken care of, and can continue loving the child without being blocked by anger. The child feels good for doing something right, and therefore entitled to his parent's approval. Of course, there must be a way to check that the chore was done properly; assigning a chore without proper follow-up is signing a death warrant for winning control and subsequent trust.

One technique used to deal with lying and stealing is to impose a consequence on the basis of who is probably responsible. This gets parents out of the "prove it" game, which they almost always lose. If the child protests, the parent asks, "What do you think I believe?" The child's petulant response is normally, "You think I did it!" to which the parent says, "That's right." The parent imposes the consequence while assuring the child that if she has been wrongly held responsible, then as soon as the parent becomes aware of the mistake, the wronged child will be repaid. This is a fairly safe technique with unattached children; despite their protestations, they usually are responsible. Rarely do therapeutic parents have to repay the wrong.

Very often children misbehave because they don't want to be involved in something in the first place. Forcing children to be where they don't want to be, do what they don't want to do, and see people they don't want to see guarantees that no one will have a good time. Setting a contract—verbal or written—with children beforehand often mitigates poor behavior, for it helps children choose to participate and lets them know what behavior is acceptable. Sometimes the contract might involve a reward for appropriate behavior—the children will get to do something they want to do, too. Other times, it might involve consequences for poor behavior—getting a babysitter, whom the children must pay for, so the parents can attend a function. If plans have to be canceled, the natural consequence is that the children will have to do something for the parents to make up for the lost activity. In therapeutic homes, that translates into chores, and lots of them.

Having a child who has made a poor behavior choice go to a "think-it-over" spot is often effective. Instead of the parent confronting the child over misbehavior, the child confronts herself. Whenever the child's behavior needs attention, the parent tells her to sit in a designated spot (in whatever position works) until she can say or write what happened, how she felt, how she behaved, and how she will handle the same situation in the future. If the child is so noncompliant that she cannot sit, or the parent doesn't want the hassle of making sure she is sitting, she can be sent to her room and allowed out as soon as the mission is accomplished. Or, the child may be required to simply sit with no directions as to what to think. At the end of the allotted time, the parent lets her get up, gives her a hug, tries to get a reciprocal smile, gives her a "good luck" message, and sends her off to try again.

Since touch is such a critical element of attachment work, it becomes an integral part of almost any therapeutic technique. Grabbing a child up in a big bear hug and lightly tickling him while encouraging him to get a task done gets the child laughing and into a compliant state. To accompany the tickling, the tickler might laughingly say, "Who's the best bedmaker in all the world?" or "Who can empty the dishwasher all by himself?" until the child giggles, "Me!" A pre-teen will usually fairly skip off to do what is required with just a light tousling of his hair and a last little rib tickle.

When a child has behaved badly, the parent might mock-wrestle the child while tickling. As both parent and child laugh, the parent says, "Do you think I'm the kind of mom who can love only good kids?" Although the goal is for the child to laughingly reply, "No," unattached children are so resistant that the first response will ordinarily be, "Yes." However, as long as both parent and child are having fun, the play can continue for up to sixty seconds or until the child answers, "No." If the minute passes and the child hasn't answered as desired, the parent stops the interaction and says, "Sorry you believe that," and then gives the child a quick hug and lightly explains the consequence for the behavior, if one is needed.

So far, the techniques discussed range from nonintrusive to mildly intrusive. With the proviso that therapeutic parents must regularly consult with a trained attachment therapist, we shall now discuss some of the more intrusive techniques.

A helpful way to create thoughtfulness in a child is to have her do something that requires her to expend a lot of energy. If the child is not completing a task well, the parent might say, "In my experience, a lot of kids find it easier to get their brain in gear when they get their blood moving. Do twenty-five jumping jacks, and see if that is true for you, too." This is a jazzy activity, not a chore, which makes for better compliance. (The activity might be running around the block, sit-ups, waddling like a duck, and so on.) If the child does this, the compliance will often carry over to the task. If it doesn't, the parent can get the blood flowing again: "I'm sorry. I didn't know that your brain was so hard to engage. This time do thirty-five jumping jacks and see if that helps you think more clearly." The parent can repeat the activity once or twice with some escalation, but if the child isn't prompted into thoughtfulness and compliance, the technique must be changed. Never continue with the same discipline technique if it is not producing the desired results, or the child will dig herself deeper and deeper into a morass of consequences and will see no way out. She will think she is in a lose-lose situation, get discouraged, and quit altogether.

Shocking children into compliance can occasionally be accomplished with a one-minute scolding. One of the most intrusive techniques, it requires the scolder to have a good sense of timing. The goal is for the scolder to recreate in the child the bonding cycle in about one minute. The child needs to be aroused and then comforted by the parent to reestablish the sense of trust. (See *Who's the Boss?* by Gerald Nelson and Richard Lewak for more information about this technique. Also, a cassette called *The Sixty-Second Scolding* is available from the Cline/Fay Institute; 800-338-4065.) The parent places his hands on the child's shoulders, looks him in the eyes, and scolds him severely and rapidly, concentrating on what the child did and why the parent is angry. When the child tears up or shows some sign of emotion, the difficult part begins. The parent must slacken his intensity and make a clear transition to nurturing. The parent draws the child in close, tells him how much he is loved, lets him know how much the parent wants a better life for him, and explains the effect of the poor behavior on the child. The scolder now ends with a hug, a reciprocal smile (if possible), and a short question-and-answer session on the matter. The whole technique has to be over before the child's brain disengages, which happens at about ninety seconds. It must be used sparingly, for the sudden shock is what gives it much of its power. When used daily or weekly, the one-minute scolding loses its effectiveness.

Often, a child who misbehaves or is noncompliant is so blocked up with rage that she cannot function. Unlocking that rage frees her to act correctly. This can sometimes be accomplished by getting the child to scream what the parent knows she is thinking or feeling. In doing this, the parent's goals are to have the child experience love and acceptance, even at the height of rage; and to get the child to release her rage in a way that can be controlled. If the rage stays inside, the subsequent explosion can be dangerous. And when the child does blow up, she will have to deal with the damage and hurt that she caused while enraged in addition to the underlying problem. This will leave her less able to concentrate on changing her behavior.

In this technique, the parent faces the child and lays her hands on the child's shoulders. The parent calmly suggests what she believes the child is thinking, and has the child repeat it. This might come out in a number of ways: "I won't do it your way." "You can't make me vacuum the floor." "I hate doing the dishes." "You're not my boss." "You're a bitch." "You fucking asshole bitch—I want to kill you!" Using a louder tone, the parent tells the child to repeat the statement louder, and moves her face closer to the child's. The cycle is reiterated until the parent and child are almost nose-to-nose, and the child is screaming into the parent's face. When the peak of screaming is reached, usually in less than two minutes, the parent drops her intensity and brings the child close in a hug. The parent shows her love for the child with gentle words. The sense of relief and trust that tends to flood the child when she stops screaming is locked in with the hug and reciprocal smiles—this release is critical for the child to be trusting and compliant in the future. After establishing a feeling of closeness, the parent has the child say, "I don't want to do it your way (or whatever is the matter), and I'll do it anyway." With one last hug, the parent directs the child back to the interrupted task.

While the child is screaming, the parent must focus on how hard she is working to release her rage rather than on the anger directed toward the parent. Otherwise the parent will get sucked into the rage, and will end up punishing the child instead of disciplining her.

The most intrusive technique is reserved for when a raging child is lashing out physically and there are no alternatives for regaining control. The point of this crisis intervention is to keep the child and other people and things safe. Touch used in this technique is so controlling as to be confining. If there is a chance that a child's behavior may escalate to the point where force is required, special training is essential. At the Evergreen Center, therapeutic parents are given a twelve-hour course entitled "Nonviolent Crisis Intervention" that teaches approved, safe holds, and which is sponsored by the National Crisis Prevention Institute. (The institute can be reached at 3315-K North 124 Street, Brookfield, WI 53005.)

First-Hand Account of Therapeutic Parenting: Bob and Kathy Lay

The next section of this chapter was written by Bob Lay. He and his wife, Kathy, are therapeutic foster parents who have worked with unattached children for a number of years. This material gives a good sense of how therapeutic parents can make a real difference with difficult children.

My wife, Kathy, and I have extensive experience living and working with disturbed youth. We have taught classes for state Departments of Social Services and are therapeutic parents.

Our therapeutic parenting journey began when we became specialized foster parents and took George, who had up to that time been unreachable. We planned to use timeouts and various clever consequences to turn George around. But by the time George had been in our home three months, we were ready to delay his birthday celebration indefinitely. We had taken many of his belongings out of his room and grounded him for the next two months. When we sent George to his room to think about what he had done and to get his act together, he would stomp off angrily and slam the door. Five or ten minutes later when I would go to check on him, he would be happily playing with his toys. One day I stripped his room of everything but a bed and dresser, and sent him in to think. Two minutes later I went into the room, and he happily called out, "See these specks of dirt? I'm playing GI Joe with them."

We realized that to-your-room timeouts, consequencing, and deprivations don't change certain hard-core troubled people, and in some cases these tactics make them worse—more subtle, clever, and sneaky. We also saw that George was devoid of a conscience and had very limited emotions. When nobody was directly confronting him and he was allowed to do his own thing, most of the time he was "happy" (a very shallow happy) in a somewhat obnoxious way. When we confronted him, he was either resistantly rebellious (a sort of covered-over, contained anger) or a masked and uncooperative scared. When we weren't watching him, he destroyed things and stashed things that didn't belong to him. During those three months, we never saw George sad.

Obviously, George was not responding to the techniques we were using. It was then that we began our search for literature on how humans develop internal moral, ethical, and empathic faculties. We felt that this would be the key to parenting George. As we read more on the subject, we recognized five areas in which therapeutic parents show love: touch, eye contact, facial expressions, sounds, and food. These are the basic first-year-of-life elements that promote bonding in the child.

The primary need of any personality is reciprocal intimacy with another. This is achieved by reciprocal positive strokes—if I make you feel good, you will make me feel good. The more positive strokes a person receives, the more he attaches. If the person gets only negative strokes, he begins to believe that he doesn't deserve positive strokes, and he remains unattached. He has a love deficit. In a sense, his battered ego goes into hiding behind fear, and is then covered over with anger, defiance, and cruelty.

It is the goal of therapeutic parents to cut through the disturbed child's anger and destructiveness to get right at his primary need. However, the unhealthy behavior of a severely troubled child is so obnoxious that it is extremely difficult to form the rapport necessary to modify behavior. When parents are able to involve the child in reciprocal love for long enough, the child begins to fill up his love deficit, and his behavior changes for the better.

The challenge lies in giving love to someone who does not want to reciprocate—if parents try to get closer to the child emotionally and physically, they quickly become emotionally drained. The natural response would be to distance oneself from the person. The answer to that response is therapeutic holding, "in-close time," and emotional-age-appropriate training.

There are three basic types of holding. *Simple restraint* is used to keep an out-of-control child from endangering himself and others. The message the holder gives the child is, "Too much stimuli sets you off. I'll limit it. You can calm down, and I'll protect you in the meantime."

In *compliance restraint,* the holder expects and works toward compliance from the child. The holder uses various safe means to make the noncompliant child uncomfortable. When the child capitulates and agrees to do whatever is asked, the holder rewards him by ending the holding. (If the child refuses to cooperate, the holder may end the holding and impose a consequence for the child's behavior.)

Restraint holding has the goal of reciprocity, and works on two levels—replacing obnoxious behavior with benign behavior, and getting at the child's primary need.

Because a troubled child forms his ego under duress (abuse, neglect, abandonment) and usually at a very young age, he doesn't develop emotional and interpersonal skills as he grows. If parents consequence him according to his chronological age—"Get away from me until you're fun to be around"—he will lock into negative behavior because he accepts these consequences as his lot in life. Therapeutic parents respond to the child according to his emotional age—which is perhaps two years old—with in-close contact such as holding and snuggling. The goal is to give positive reciprocal strokes no matter how hard the child pushes for negative strokes with bad behavior.

The following case studies from our own experience illustrate these principles of therapeutic parenting.

Jerry came to us from a psychiatric unit at the age of nine. He was considered suicidal and possibly homicidal. He was unable to carry out simple commands, and could not play with other children without getting mad and starting a fight. He hated closeness and touch and was terrified of the dark. He enjoyed being in trouble, was sexually abusive to others, and prided himself on his ability to lie without remorse. We saw no evidence of remorse for hurtful behavior and no interest in helping others. He liked to lie down in front of oncoming cars and get up just in time to avoid being hit. He also came in with new scrapes, cuts, and bruises every time he played outside.

We immediately implemented an in-close program, in which Jerry was always close to us, either in our laps or within eyesight, until his behavior improved. Only then would he be given out-of-sight play time. Jerry's first holding lasted about ninety minutes, and the basic issues were, "I'm afraid to be held. I have claustrophobia." "If you don't leave me alone, I'll kill you." At the end of the holding, Jerry snuggled in, rested, and then played on my lap for forty-five minutes.

During the first three months, we held Jerry whenever we had time and he had an aversion to closeness—about every third day for the first month, then about once a week the second and third months. After the first two weeks, Jerry was able to play with others unsupervised and without getting into fights as a regular occurrence. Jerry also liked to spend one to two hours, two or three times a week, snuggled on one of our laps watching television. He had been sexually active with adults at a younger age, but never made any inappropriate moves or statements on our laps.

Since we were relatively new at therapeutic parenting and Jerry was doing so well, we began giving him out-of-sight play time. At about the two-and-a-half-month mark, he regressed when we took a vacation. Upon our return, we learned of secretive and serious negative behavior, which led to a series of four holdings, each one or two hours long. After the fourth session, Jerry looked at me and said, "Dad, you know how you encourage us to tell on each other if we think a brother needs help? (We had two other troubled boys in our home.) Well, I'm afraid to tell on my brothers because I do more wrong than both of them put together."

"What do you want to do about that?" I asked. "I want to tell you all the things I've done wrong for the last two months," Jerry said, and he proceeded to do that for the next twenty minutes. At the end, he looked at me in amazement and said, "I can't believe what I just did! I've always liked not telling people when I'm wrong, even when I'm threatened. Yet, I've just told you every wrong thing I can think of and you didn't even ask." Then, with a genuine smile, he held one hand a couple of inches from his ear and said, "Dad, Jiminy Cricket has been born."

This was a real turning point for Jerry and for us. He and I went upstairs to his two brothers and announced that he had cleared his conscience and would be turning them in if he thought their actions were harmful to themselves and others. Their immediate response was, "Oh, yeah? Has he told you about this? And this?" They listed four or five things Jerry had done, and to each one I could answer, "Yes, he told me about that." And Jerry did start reporting on some important matters without coming across as a tattletale. We also tightened controls, becoming more aware of where our boys were and what they were doing.

Jerry became a hard worker in school, and a successful basketball and football player. He showed much more nurturing and cooperative behavior during the sixteen months he was with us. After leaving our home, he needed more time in a highly structured, loving environment to maintain the level of behavior he had achieved with us, but he did not revert to the person he had been.

Sam arrived at our home at age nine, when Jerry was still with us. He came across as very shallow—no reciprocity, no strong emotions other than oppositional anger, no empathy, no conscience, and totally self-centered. On the second day in our home, as I finished a thirty-minute holding with another boy, Sam jumped into my lap and said, "Okay, Dad, it's my turn." Seeing a holding obviously didn't scare him.

Because Sam took things as soon as he was out of sight, we quickly implemented our in-close and holding program. After three months, we had received no depth of feeling from him, and his home behavior stayed unchanged. However, we were making progress, as shown by his school reports. Before he came to us, Sam was in special education classes and was noted for disruptive behavior, including exposing himself. With us, he went directly into normal classes, and was never even sent out of the regular classroom.

Since his home behavior stayed so sneaky and shallow, for about three weeks we instituted a "blame Sam" policy. Any time something went wrong and we couldn't ascertain the guilty party, we blamed Sam. We told him, "Since you are responsible for more thefts and damage in the home than anyone else, and since you never own up to what you do even when you are caught, we are holding you accountable for all our unsolved crimes. So you need extra lap time and extra careful watching." (I recommend this technique only as a short-term measure and only with a consequence similar to ours.)

Sam made some progress—he started to own up to some of his behavior. The policy also had a strong impact on Jerry. After two weeks, Jerry took me aside and told me he was feeling bad "because I'm doing some things that Sam is getting blamed for." He learned a valuable lesson about taking responsibility for his own actions.

The real turning point for Sam came when we brought his birth mother into our home for three holdings. Kathy and I began each holding, and then turned Sam over to his mother while coaching her on what to say and do. For the first time, Sam showed powerful emotions as his mother talked about her feelings and the ways he had tried to hurt her and push her away from him. He also developed a yearning to reunite with his mother.

His mother began to connect emotionally with Sam, and felt she could reach out to him and help him. She started getting her own life together. Sam spent six months in our home, a few months in another therapeutic home, and then went home to his mother, who had met and now lives with a nurturing man. The last time we talked, they had all been together for more than a year and Sam was doing well. According to his mother, the in-close and holding times were the key to the success.

When Susan came into our home at age thirteen, she identified herself as having three separate parts named Sue, Susie, and Susan. There was no amnesia between the parts, although when Sue or Susie were active, it was extremely difficult to activate Susan. She stayed with us for about nineteen months. She was an extremely troubled young lady during most of her stay—running away, sexually acting out, lying, and stealing—and required close watching.

The part called Sue described herself as a worldly wise adult, and talked as though she were an alien visitor who wanted to use Susan's body for her pleasure and had no concern about any pain that Susan might experience. During one holding, Sue agreed to be totally honest with us, and the following conversation took place. (This may have been Susan's imagination, but the discussion was serious.)

"Sue, who is your worst enemy?"

"You are, because you want to keep me from using Susan's body the way I want to."

"How's that?"

"I want to have lots of sex, some of it painful. I want to get with a man who'll beat Susan up. If she has babies I don't care, but I don't want to care for the little bastards. I've been hanging around in this body since Susan was one year old, waiting for this chance, and now that she's old enough you're trying to stop me."

"So what do you want to do about that?"

"I want to take a butcher knife and carve you up in little pieces. You have no business in our personal affairs."

"Why haven't you cut us up?"

"Because Susan likes you and won't let me!"

"Why did you come into Susan's life?"

"Because Susie was real scared and wanted to hide from grown-ups when they were being mean. So I came in so Susie could hide and I could enjoy the pain."

"Do you have any plans for nice things for Susan's life?"

"None. I like pain and thrills."

Some therapists believe that a person can appear to swallow a concept of another person, without integrating the concept into her own self. Thus, the swallowed concept comes across as an alien presence, just as Sue did.

After further discussion with Sue and Susan, we and Susan could find no redeeming qualities in Sue, so we told her we didn't want her around anymore. This was about the tenth month that Susan was with us. Sue said she could find another body in which to have her fun and said goodbye, and Susan never felt Sue's presence after that. During the remaining months of her stay, Susan's behavior was less tough and arrogant.

Susie described herself as about four years old, although her emotional behavior seemed closer to a troubled two-year-old's.

Susie was very fearful of grown-ups and thought her body and sex were dirty but essential. She believed the only way she could feel loved was by having sex. She also had a strong yearning to run away whenever problems seemed overwhelming.

In the early stages of holding, Susie would cry, fight, and beg to be let go, but then calm down, snuggle in, and enjoy closeness much the way a two-year-old would. We would then talk to Susan about the importance of learning to love, care for, meet the needs of, and direct the troubled Susie. Susan did learn that if she ignored Susie for long and didn't give her time to express, Susie would cause embarrassing, inappropriate behavior.

About three months before she left our house, Susan made remarkable improvement. She had been gaining depth, responsiveness, and reciprocity all along. Although Susie still existed inside her, Susan considered herself the healthy and age-appropriate part of the personality. Susan would usually take charge during talk therapy, and came across as a pretty normal, balanced person. However, she had difficulty being in charge when no one was watching.

When Susan left, it was our opinion that she still needed time for her new life to solidify, for during the three months of improvement she would regularly allow herself to be a little girl. We felt we needed at least another month with her. While Susan liked us to nurture her, she had difficulty with self-nurturing. Perhaps Susie wasn't responding to the positive strokes we had been supplying, so she tried to get negative ones. Susie would do some fairly bizarre things to get her strokes. Unfortunately, the county responsible for her care put her in a residential setting where teenagers were expected to be self-nurturing. Susan went downhill fast.

The key to our therapeutic parenting is closeness and touch: a quick touch when walking by; holding hands, or hands on arms or shoulders when giving directives; time spent being close so that we can regularly be near the children, reach over and ruffle their hair or sit quietly on a couch with arms draped across their shoulders. When these contacts are rebuffed, we switch to across-the-lap, face-to-face holding.

After youngsters have been in our house for a while, they willingly take the lap position. If they don't come willingly, we put them in that position. Another holding position we use is laying a child on the floor, face up, with one parent across his legs in a wrestling hold and the other straddling his upper body while controlling his arms and head. The two holders make sure they are bearing most of their own weight, and not hurting the child. This may sound extreme or even ludicrous to parents who have not used therapeutic techniques, but it is sometimes the only way to bring an out-of-control teenager into compliance.

During the compulsory holding, our attitude is, "I'll do nothing physically to the child that a normal, emotionally healthy person wouldn't enjoy having done in the right setting. I'll acknowledge the howls, complaints, and ramblings caused by the disturbed state of the child, but I will keep pushing for the child to feel the interaction, the attachment, that is occurring." We key on the child's voice during the holding. In his anger state, his cries come from the high chest and throat, but when he is making progress, when we are reaching him, the voice comes from the diaphragm. Sometimes it has a guttural sound that makes our hair stand on end. During one holding, an eight-year-old boy was being fussy and distant when, suddenly, an evil look came across his face and with a deep growl he said, "I'm the devil." We were startled, but continued the holding, for now he was being *real*. Within ten minutes he was cuddly, playful, and reciprocal.

During holdings, it is best to control the activity and behavior you are able to control, and put your stamp of approval on what you can't control. Point out to the child what will happen when behavior is not reciprocal; encourage correct behavior—don't demand it. When you get the reciprocal behavior, reward the child with smiles and compliment him with pizzazz.

It is an excellent practice to model anger, sadness, and fear with these children. Sometimes the child joins in after I've spent thirty minutes modeling strong emotions; sometimes this occurs after only a few seconds. Younger children benefit from being wrapped tightly in a blanket and held tightly to your chest. Sometimes, after resistance has died down, giving the young child warm milk or juice in a baby bottle is effective in helping attachment.

Remember that the severely troubled youngster believes he deserves between zero and twenty percent positive strokes. He's not used to positive strokes, and will concentrate on negative ones. During holding, push for one hundred percent positive strokes. As the child becomes accustomed to receiving these strokes, he will become less inclined to hide behind negative behavior. Positive reciprocity negates the need for disturbance.

During holding, the child will complain that the holder is hurting him. The parent should check that he is not putting excessive pressure on the child and then regularly state something like this: "Pains you may feel are old memories. Being close brings up past pain. Let it out. Free yourself from it." During one holding, an eight-year-old girl told me, "No, *you're* causing the pain now!" This is the child's reality. I asked, "Who are you trying to convince?" and she responded, "Me." She stopped crying, looked at me in surprise, and started giggling. "I'm trying to convince myself the hurt is happening now. You really aren't hurting me."

When a child claims that a particular touch or position causes serious discomfort, make sure that the position is not dangerous. If it is not, maintain the touch or position until the discomfort is gone. This helps drive home the point that it is the memories that are causing the discomfort, not the touch.

It helps us to look at our parenting as a war for the child's sanity, emotional health, and future. Therefore, we don't get overly concerned about winning or losing individual battles as long as we can see that we're winning the war. When we get positive reciprocity going, we know everyone is winning.

Dangers of Unknowledgeable Outsiders

The Lays are so good at what they do that it may seem that they have continual success without any negatives from the outside world. This, of course, is not true. As shown in Chapter 5, even a couple as skilled as the Lays can be victimized by unknowledgeable neighbors, school authorities, and government officials. However, the Lays and other therapeutic parents know that reaching the children in their charge is so important that the flak which they get from outsiders becomes trivial in the wider perspective.

It appears to me that there is no group more misunderstood than the parents of unattached children. These children generally have severe control problems at home, although they appear charming and cute to strangers. The techniques that the parents must use to reach such children are frequently misunderstood by the professional community. There is little support for the parents from any quarter.

The following story is synopsized from a book about adoption titled *Suffer the Children,* by Carole McKelvey and JoEllen Stevens. The mother involved in this story, Sharon Osborn, is an outstanding parent of four adopted children. Her story is significant for several reasons:

> It is unfortunately common. Reliable sources have estimated that every day in America, three families are falsely accused of child abuse. Many of these families are adoptive or foster families raising extremely disturbed children.
>
> It is typical of the problems faced by many adoptive parents.
>
> It is a typical "horror story" that can occur when protective services have trouble differentiating strong consequences from abuse.

Osborn was taken to court for alleged child abuse after her adopted daughter, Sophia, attracted the sympathy of kindly passersby when she was being consequenced with techniques Sharon had learned in classes for parents with difficult children. Sharon had also been involved in Sophia's therapy. With an amazing lack of bitterness, considering what she went through for her child, she told of her life being turned upside down.

"Sophia and my sons had been swimming, they're on the swim

team at their school, and I told them they had to be ready to leave when I got there to pick them up," Osborn related. "I had an important phone call coming in that I had to be home for."

The boys were ready, but Sophia was a picture of noncompliance. "When I walked in she was sitting playing cards with some friends. When she saw me she said, 'I'm not ready yet, mom.' I helped her gather up her things and we went out to the car." But when Osborn told Sophia to get into the front seat, Sophia replied, "No, I don't want to ride in the front seat with you." She was put in the back seat, but angrily stated, "I don't want to ride home with you. Let me out!" She started to kick the back of the seat.

Osborn continued, "Her voice can be very shrill when she's angry and she started to get louder and louder, screaming and jumping up and down, even though she had her seatbelt on. It got worse and worse and she started hitting her brothers. It was a fifteen-minute drive and she was escalating the closer we got to home."

With less than a mile to go, Sharon decided it was best for her daughter to walk the rest of the way. She had considered pulling over until Sophia's fit passed, but that would have given the child too much control. After all, there were others in the car who wanted to get home and eat, and it was 8:20 PM. It was a "rather nice, crisp fall day," and Sophia was well acquainted with the three-block route she would have to take to get home. It should have taken her about fifteen minutes, allowing for play along the way.

When Sophia did not return in thirty minutes, Sharon went looking for her. It was now dark. Sharon and her son drove around, covering all the normal routes Sophia could have taken. When this failed, they took flashlights and went out on foot, calling Sophia's name.

When they got back home without Sophia, Sharon noticed a police car with its spotlight on at the end of their cul de sac. "When he pulled up in front of our house I went out to ask him if he had my little girl. He ignored my questions and then asked, 'Are you Sharon Osborne?'" The officer kept asking questions, finally answering Sharon's demands with, "Your daughter's tucked away safe and sound for the night," and refused to give further information. He then asked to come into her home and began asking all sorts of questions: "Who is in the family? Who lived where? If my husband and I were separated (which we were)," and so on.

Sophia was a manipulative child and had been undergoing therapy for an attachment disorder caused by deprivation prior to adoption. True to form, Sophia had lied to the police and the couple that picked her up. She was manipulating a situation in which she was in control. At the time, the police officer asked many questions and made Sharon feel like she was a bad mother. He never read her rights to her or said anything about an investigation.

"And he never tried to contact my husband, even though he knew where he was. No one [from social services] ever came to my house to check it out. They just made the decision and placed her [in a foster care situation] that night."

Although she was told the hold would be overnight, Sharon was not to see her daughter for many days. And she was ordered to appear for a hearing at 1 PM the next day. "I thought I had lost her . . . and I literally spent the most hellish night of my life."

A friend from Arapaho County Social Services in Colorado accompanied Sharon to the hearing, telling her he was "amazed that they had taken Sophia and not returned her the same night." He suggested that it was all a mistake, and that Sophia would be back at home soon. However, the hearing was continued from Wednesday to Friday, and Sharon still did not get to see her daughter. Eventually she was charged with child abuse because of the incident and had to fight to retain custody of Sophia. This was the second time that Sharon had to battle for Sophia, for she and her husband had first adopted her and her half-brother only after much difficulty. "From the beginning, it was clear to us that Sophia, in particular, had numerous problems around being separated from her birth mother, foster parents, and her half-brother, Alex. We had made it clear we wanted to adopt both children when we got Alex, to carry out the birth mother's wishes that they be kept together." Finally, after much maneuvering, the Osborns got the two children.

In midsummer 1990, Sharon was charged with abusing Sophia because she forced her to take a short walk home on a fall evening, and she stood trial. Once twelve reasonable people on the jury heard the facts, she was acquitted. However, the process leading up to the trial and the trial itself cost Sharon thousands of dollars and much mental anguish.

Why adopt difficult children? For the Osborns, the medical reality was that they would never have birth children, and for a number of reasons, they decided that they wanted to adopt older children instead of babies. Other parents have different reasons to adopt children who might have attachment problems. What this chapter shows is that parents can survive these children, and that they can turn these children around so that they can lead normal, loving lives.

9

GOVERNMENT CAN HELP

Despite the general ineffectiveness of government attempts to attack the social problems that produce severely disturbed children, and the restrictive attitude its agencies have toward people who have to deal with the results, there are things that the government can do to help handle the tide of unattached citizens that is threatening to overwhelm our therapeutic community, our justice system, and our society.

Changing Attitudes About Entitlement

Primary among these is a new attitude toward entitlement in this country. Ever since social welfare programs were begun on a large scale during the Great Depression, critics have been bewailing their effects on society as a whole: Welfare is against God. It is a communist plot. It costs too much. People will never get off the dole. The middle class will be taxed out of existence. The basic issue is that social welfare programs are based on the idea that every American is *entitled* to a certain standard of living, no matter what poor choices they make in their lives.

This concept cuts against the capitalist idea of a dog-eat-dog world of competition, an idea that supposedly undergirds American society. When the stock market crashed in 1929, this competitive notion drove the country. However, the massive suffering of the 1930s was generally acknowledged to be beyond the control of individuals; therefore, the government did what it could to help out. There was still plenty of resistance to the idea of government entitlement programs, but the social welfare nonetheless became the government's responsibility.

The Great Society experiments of the 1960s solidified this attitude in the government, and it was generalized to other areas such as education, health, employment opportunities, and housing. With the widely publicized "bailout" of the Chrysler Corporation in the late 1970s, the government proved that it was willing to help out even corporate entities which, through their own mismanagement, were in competitive trouble.

There have been tangible benefits of these social welfare programs—the standard of living, until recently, was rising; millions of people were clothed, sheltered, fed, and employed; expectations of a "better" society were raised. However, the idea of entitlement—that everyone *deserves* certain things—was ingrained in our collective consciousness. This is a dangerous attitude, because it makes people look to the government (or private philanthropic agencies) for help when they should properly be looking to themselves.

Here is how this affects the unattached population in America. The unbonded people walking our streets generally cannot hold jobs that pay living wages since they cannot relate to bosses and co-workers. They float through relationships, using up sympathetic people and moving on to someone else. They commit crimes of varying degrees, including abusing any children they have, because they don't care about anyone and don't care about consequences. And they go through life blaming everyone but themselves for the troubles that follow in their wake.

These selfsame people are guaranteed by the government a place to sleep, food to eat, and clothing to wear. They are given acute health care when they require it, are educated if they can sit still for it, and are even offered job placement services. If they are laid off a job, they can apply for unemployment insurance; if they can somehow claim injury due to a job, they can apply for disability. If they have children and can qualify, they can receive AFDC funds.

Now, all of these sources of aid certainly do not guarantee these people a royal or even a middle-class life-style—subsistence is more like it. However, they validate the poor choices that these people make in life. Unless they are caught abusing their children or committing other crimes, they will continue to be paid their monthly stipend by the government. They are not required to take any responsibility in working on their problems so that they can become functioning members of society.

As the success of Alcoholics Anonymous and other twelve-step programs has shown us, there is no hope that a person will reform himself unless he feels a compelling need to do so. The only way a person can feel this need is if he is faced with the loss of everything—job, family, home, food, even life. It's called hitting rock-bottom, and the only way to go is up.

Most unattached people are never allowed to hit rock-bottom. The government "safety net" catches them, and keeps them suspended just enough so that they don't have to face up to the fact that their condition results from their own actions. And although the life-style that the welfare system provides seems squalid and scary to most Americans, it is good enough for the unattached. They're not expecting luxury—they simply want to take whatever they can get.

For years, social engineers have been striving to find a way to "break the cycle of poverty" for the millions of poor, undereducated, unemployed Americans. More often than not, the answer has been to increase welfare payments of various sorts, to improve educational opportunities, to provide new housing, and so on. The emphasis has always been on having the *government* do something to help.

Preventing New Generations of Unattached Citizens

What government must do is to flip this emphasis. We as a people must once again accept the consequences for what we do. I can fairly look into the minds of the campers who defiled the Glen Canyon cave with their excrement and shocked guide Larry Jensen (see Chapter 5). What did it matter if they used the cave as a latrine? Someone else would clean it up.

We have to create in the minds of our people the impression that perhaps no one else will clean up after us. What this means for the welfare system is that recipients of funds must learn that our patience is not endless. Unless they change their ways and start making better life decisions, they could face serious consequences. In other words, people who accept stipends have to agree to certain restrictions on their behavior—they have to get therapeutic help, stop using drugs, start using birth control, and so on. Only when the people themselves make the decisions to do these things can we begin to think about breaking the cycle of poverty.

Once the individual has taken definite steps to being responsible, the government can reach out to help. Prenatal medical services must be available for pregnant teenagers. Young mothers with babies need child care services in order to hold jobs or take classes. They need parenting classes to learn how to care for their children without abusing them. They need support to keep them from using drugs or alcohol again. Young fathers need the same support. Contraception must be a requirement to keep young parents from having too many children (for many of them, one child is too many), and it must be available at a reasonable price. It can't be free—that's entitlement again.

Government at all levels can work with school authorities to promote the only form of birth control that seems effective for teenagers—delaying the age at which they begin having sexual relations. The average age is now about sixteen for white teens and fifteen for black teens, and it has been dropping for some years. What this means is that as the average age for starting to have sex drops, more children become active. This negates the effect that family planning services has on the older children. The younger the girl, the less likely she is to use contraception. Statistically, the earlier a girl bears a child, the more children she is likely to have. And when a teenaged girl has a child, it is better than even money that she will not finish high school.

Some who are involved with children's issues see the crux of the matter as an economic one. Marian Wright Edelman of the Children's Defense Fund, an organization that is in the forefront of improving the lives of America's children, says, "The best contraceptive is a real future." She is probably right. For a long time, many teenagers of minority families in our country have believed that they have had no prospects for their future—few jobs, poor pay, slow advancement, no way out of the ghetto. This attitude is influencing white teenagers, too, as the idea that the bulk of jobs in the twenty-first century will be low-paying service jobs gains wide acceptance. So why should teens delay having sex when they perceive no significant future ahead? It is important that this fatalistic attitude be changed.

To change this attitude will take a concerted effort on the part of parents, teachers, administrators, school boards, businesses, and government, for a way must be found to provide our children with the education they need to compete for better-paying jobs in the worldwide economy. Work-study programs could be expanded, or even become mandatory, as they have in some school districts. Government could become more involved in education, which means providing more funds for programs that have proved effective, not only with high-risk children, but with the average students, too. School officials must come up with true competency standards, and a way to make sure that students meet them. Requirements for advancement in school must be spelled out precisely, not in vague language about "understanding concepts." And parents must become more involved in their children's education.

A way must be found through the morass of legal entanglements and interest group lobbying to promote laws, policies, and regulations that will help families—biological parents and children—stay together. Study after study has proven that the best situation for children—economically, psychologically, socially, and educationally—is to live in a household with the two birth parents. Day care, after-school programs, and television can provide only so much to children; ultimately, the sort of people they grow up to be depends on their parents.

And we need to take positive steps to promote the institution of the family quickly. As one obstetrical nurse in a large private hospital in Denver recently told me, "Hey, America has no idea what we're in for down the road. I just completed twenty-eight days of shifts on the obstetrical wards. Not one child was born to a mother in wedlock."

The ultimate wish would be that all children would have at least one birth parent caring for them in their home. There are too many variables involved with this to make this a feasible government goal, but there are things that the government could rightly do that would help push the country toward the goal. For instance, the Secretaries of Labor and Commerce could begin a campaign to influence business to offer more flexible-time solutions for parents with young children at home. Perhaps a special tax break could be given to companies that provide their employees with personal computers so they can work at home instead of commute to the office. Or the government might influence the growth of day care centers in offices, so that more companies take advantage of this "innovative" idea.

Speaking of day care, there is a generally acknowledged lack of licensed, regulated, affordable child care services in the country, especially in low-income areas. (Care for children is almost always better for those who can pay well for it than for those whose children are in danger of being left alone because the parents have to work.) The government could make a special effort to promote the opening of such centers, perhaps with tax abatements or specialized professional assistance. In addition, it could influence high schools and colleges to give courses in the field, so that there will be trained people to staff the new centers.

Saving the Current Generation of Unattached Citizens

The matters I have discussed so far in this chapter deal with preventing a new generation of unattached children from arising. This is our best hope of saving ourselves in the long run; if we stop producing conscienceless children, we will see a significant decrease in the mayhem on our streets and in our homes. However, it would require a transformation in how government operates its social services agencies for these policies to be realized.

While waiting for this change, we need to deal with the products of our present flawed child-rearing—those unattached infants, children, adolescents, and teenagers. We might include unattached adults in our discussion, but most of these are beyond the reach of therapy of any sort. Thus, we are talking about changes in a small area of government—child-protective services.

The greatest change that protective services could make is in their attitude toward intrusive therapy and therapeutic parenting. What these agencies must recognize is that not all strong parenting tactics are abuse. The standards for judging whether techniques are abusive should not be how they appear or what a disturbed, manipulative individual says about them. The standards should be what effect such techniques have on the physical and mental health of the individual. Is the child's overall condition improved? Is the child seriously injured, or simply discomfited? Has the child stopped antisocial behavior? This is not a question of the end justifying the means, as some critics of intrusive therapy have complained. Rather, it is a matter of seeking a wider perspective. Protective agencies should not cry "abuse" when a child experiences physical discomfort and is pushed to rage if the child stops self-destructive behavior and thereby stays out of jail.

Once they have taken this changed stance in regard to intrusive therapy, protective agencies must educate their employees to what unattached children are like. They must train them to recognize the manipulative nature of these children and to view the testimony of these children with great skepticism. Instead of treating children who complain of familial "abuse" with gentleness and regard, they should immediately call people who know about the case—the parents, the therapist, perhaps grandparents. Protective services should determine whether the child has really been abused, or if the child is simply unhappy about his treatment.

Protective services should also work to increase treatment options for unattached children. Agencies should reduce the number of onerous restrictions that have been placed on therapeutic parents and institutions over the years, and allow more touch and holding. This will have three salutary effects. First, children in therapeutic situations will be less likely to become violent, for a touch or a hug can often help these children become more thoughtful about their actions and what they are doing to others. Taking just such actions is now forbidden to foster parents in a number of states. Second, the children are much more likely to bond, as touch is one of the primary elements of the first-year-of-life attachment cycle that these children need to have recreated. Third, more couples will be willing to become foster parents, increasing the chances that unattached children will have the opportunity to live in therapeutic homes. As it stands now, couples are leaving foster parenting because of increasing restrictions.

And instead of acting as Big Brother who oversees foster homes and institutional care, and who slaps punitive sanctions on parents and therapists who step out of line, protective agencies should become stronger partners in helping prevent the next generation of unattached children from getting started. These agencies should place more emphasis on preventing or mitigating abuse and neglect by birth parents, rather than searching out alleged abuse by therapeutic foster parents. "Child" protection could be extended to prenatal care so that there are more professionals involved in giving children a better start in life. The present publicity campaigns, with their shock ads which seem better suited to getting more people to report abuse by their neighbors than to stopping parents from abusing their own infants, should be scrapped, and the money should be used to provide family planning and psychiatric services in schools for the teenage parents who really need them, and who may be abused children themselves.

There is much to be done to reclaim our society from the unattached people who walk the streets. Essentially, attitudes must be changed—attitudes of government officials, attitudes of professionals, attitudes of citizens. As the therapeutic parents who are involved with the Evergreen Center know, it is better to change techniques than to intensify techniques that aren't working. What we need to do as a society is to take that idea and broaden it so that government agencies begin to promote therapies that work with these children, not spend their time disputing those whose style is not in the mainstream.

10

EPILOGUE

You recall the story of the clinical psychologist from California who grew up as an unattached child that ended Chapter 1. She knew that she functioned well as an adult, but she also realized that she narrowly escaped living a fruitless, unproductive, possibly violent life. When we left her story, she had reached the seventh grade, and was an out-of-control teenager. Now she continues:

> The summer before high school I met the man who saved my life. Before the workshop [the intrusive therapy workshop that I was giving where I met this woman] I had never been quite sure as to just how or why I decided to trust him. At first I thought he was a jerk, like all other adults. The first time I remember meeting him (although he says he had known me for years, probably through my parents) was after a friend and I had ridden across a parking lot and were sitting on the hood of someone's car. He put his hands heavily upon my shoulders to let me know he was in charge, locked his fingers behind my neck, and started talking to me about how I was too smart and had too much going for me to throw my life away by falling off a car and getting run over. I refused to look at him, as I didn't want him to have any control over me, so he lifted my chin with his thumbs until I had to look at him. Then I closed my eyes to show him that he couldn't make me do something that I didn't want to do. He put his thumbs on trigger points behind my jaw and pushed on them. Not hard enough to hurt me badly, but hard enough to let me know he meant business and he *could* hurt me if he wanted to. I remember clearly the surprise I felt that someone would actually *care* enough about me to make me mind him. Of course, I was furious when he let go. I decided to try to outsmart him at every chance I could get, and this decision led me to join a youth club that he was sponsoring. At first I made noises and

214

picked pockets every chance I could get. Eventually, he helped me get my life together and stop being so oppositional, although I continued my oppositional behavior with other adults I did not like or who thought they could control me just because they were adults.

For most of my life since that time, I have wondered many times what it was that made me respond to him when I hadn't responded to anyone else. When I participated in your workshop and saw your technique of letting kids know that you are in charge because you hurt them just a little bit, or make them mind you and let them know you could hurt them if you wanted to, the pieces of the puzzle began to fall into place. What had forced me to connect with him was his pressure on my jaw trigger points. I had to open my eyes and look into his, where I could see his concern and caring for me as a person. In the workshop I saw the children you work with making the same connection with your eyes and it was if a lightbulb went off in my head.

I think your belief that you have to let some disturbed kids know you are in charge and could hurt them a little bit with pressure over a rib is exactly correct. I know, now, from my own experiences that this is what made me sit up and take notice. Some people may not understand this and I'm not sure I really do either, but I know, deep inside me, that you are *absolutely* correct about this.

More and more people—therapists, parents, government officials, school authorities—are coming around to the idea that we have to "disturb the disturbed" to gain ground against the generation of conscienceless individuals that confronts us. As I travel around the country giving seminars on how to parent lovingly and therapeutically, I meet many people, professionals and laypersons, who have realized that traditional therapy does not work with what they perceive as hard-core problem children. Some of these people have been searching for years for therapy that will help them escape the hell they have been living with their children.

Learning how to be therapeutic parents is the answer for many of these couples. They know that becoming a therapeutic family is not easy: all sorts of painful issues must be confronted in holding sessions. Very often, the parents are damaged individuals, and need holding themselves before they can start holding their children. It is a difficult, demanding way to parent, but it is a most rewarding way. Those who choose that path almost always see results with their children that they thought were impossible.

And such positive results *are* impossible without intrusive techniques, because the children are not in touch with anyone else. By recreating the first-year-of-life bonding cycle through holding and a push to rage, parents and therapists can bond with the children. The children learn that giving up control to another person can be a positive, not a painful, experience. And the crust of anger, fear, and hatred that surrounds the children's hearts is burst apart, allowing the children to work through their emotions and become healthy again.

As I've stated previously, intrusive techniques do not work with all clients who seem likely candidates—the long-term follow-up that was done with Evergreen Center clients demonstrates that. However, severely disturbed children have a much better chance of getting their lives on track after undergoing intrusive therapy sessions. Certainly it is better to trade short-term discomfort (very often only one session is needed to open children up to others) for a long course of nonproductive "talk" therapy. For those children who are at risk of being lost to the streets, and for the society that is at risk of losing its right to walk the streets safely, time is of the essence.

TRANSCRIPTS FROM THERAPEUTIC SESSIONS

The transcripts included in this appendix were chosen because they illustrate different aspects of intrusive and confrontive techniques, not because all the children were suffering from reactive attachment disorder. Intrusive techniques are often used as "door-openers" so that the usual methods of therapy can be effective with otherwise unresponsive children. Family therapy, sand-play, general play therapy, activity therapies, and all the usual, less-confrontive individual techniques are therapies of choice if the child can be effectively and efficiently reached. All of the good intrusive therapists I have known would rather use less-confrontive methods if at all possible. But one method of therapy never has all of the answers for all of the problems all of the time. A good therapist needs to have many different tricks in his bag.

As you read these transcripts, keep in mind the limits of the printed page. Although I have included parenthetical remarks about facial expressions, movements, and so on, there is really no way to express length of silences, voice inflections, sighs, newly discovered insights, depths of sorrow, and intensity of rages. Nor can I show the caring touch during heavy verbal confrontation, the smiles, the concern in the therapist's eyes, the joy at the development of insight, the reciprocal smile, and other body language. While tenderness often comes through in a look, a touch, or a smile, therapeutic confrontation is almost all verbal. Thus, these transcripts emphasize the confrontation without highlighting the equally important support.

Prior to the recording of these transcripts, each of the children had, for varying lengths of time, been unresponsive to the usual techniques. Candy and Cindy were extremely self-destructive and overtly suicidal. Long hospitalizations had proved ineffective with Candy, Matt, and Tina. All of the children had been unwilling to make therapeutic contract, and Eddie simply refused to talk. Four of the children—Matt, Cindy, Tina, and Christy—were reactive attachment disordered, having suffered abuse and neglect during infancy. Candy and Paul were raised in loving homes, but were stuck in therapy. Candy's father had committed suicide, Eddie's father had a life-threatening illness, and both children were adept at avoiding their feelings through denial.

Candy: Use of Intrusive Therapy to Motivate an Adolescent for Psychotherapy

At the time of this session, Candy was a sixteen-year-old alcoholic who had been in and out of a hospital for the previous eighteen months. Her childhood had been traumatic, although she managed to do well in grade school. Her alcoholic and abusive father shot himself in the head when she was thirteen. (Reportedly, the bullet ricocheted off the ceiling and landed on a pillow in Candy's bedroom!) After her father's suicide, Candy went downhill in all areas. She started running away from home and began abusing alcohol and drugs. When she was hospitalized, she never got down to business, never gave therapeutic contract, and never had any real progress. Noting the superficiality of her emotions, her therapist said, "I can't get anything *real* out of this kid. I've only seen her upset once, and that was when we wouldn't give her a pass!"

Candy was manipulative with other adolescents on her unit, and her major purpose when in the hospital was getting out. Throughout her time in the hospital, she was filled with denial, blamed anyone but herself for her problems, and refused to look meaningfully at her substance abuse and family issues.

The intent of this session was to form contract for Candy to work on her issues in the hospital. Because of her denial, we helped her feel her emotions, and then followed with intrusive verbal confrontation. During the session, Candy broke down for the first time. She screamed, vented her frustration and hate, and most importantly, looked at her own issues without denial and saw the bleak future she faced if she didn't get her act together.

Six months after this session, her therapist wrote to me to tell what a success it had been: "After you saw Candy, it was like doing therapy with a different individual." He related that Candy herself told him that she divided her life into "B.C." (Before Cline) and "A.C." (After Cline).

Candy's case illustrates three important points: (1) Without contract, therapy is usually not successful. (2) Intellectual understanding of a problem without catharsis does not help a patient. Patients need to resolve (feel and deal with) their emotions, not just talk about them. (3) Confrontation must be used with an equal dose of support. The session was recorded in front of a small audience of the institution's staff.

Cline: So, Candy . . . what's been going on?

Candy: It just . . . it seems like my parents were divorced and my dad shot hisself [sic] and I just thought life isn't very fair, so why should I be fair to it? And I just got kind of headstrong and it took me. One of my things is it took me fourteen years to get this way, and I thought, by God, I won't change.

Cline: So you were getting back at life, sort of, by screwing yourself up? What was in your gut was, "I'll show you, life."

Candy: *(Laughing, taken aback)* Yeah . . .

Cline: You were a fairly angry little kid, would you say? And you had temper tantrums and were oppositional and all those kinds of things?

Candy: I was a spoiled little brat. I'm not proud . . . I mean, you know, if I got grounded, I knew how to get out of it. If I wanted something, I knew how to get it. And

I'm not proud of it, but it's true.

Cline: Um-hmm.

At first, I didn't think that Candy was proud of it, but this denial showed the truth. She was proud of it.

Candy: It's just . . . I kinda knew how to throw the words. And when I got older, I just kept it up and just pushed the point to where my mom didn't know what to do but put me into here. I mean, I asked for everything I got. If I had listened a long time ago, I wouldn't be here now. When I was little, I was jealous of my mom's job a lot, and one of the things was she never made me breakfast and all of the other kids' mothers made them breakfast. And she would say, "Are you jealous of my job?" And I'd go, "No, I'm not jealous of anything of yours. I don't need anything you've got." Really, I was . . . I can see that now. I was just putting up a wall and it was like I just have to show life a thing or two and I took everything out of life and everything I was gettin' was because of my actions.

Cline: So what you're saying is that while you were giving it to life, you were really giving it to yourself?

Candy: Indirectly, I didn't realize it at the time. I was spitting at life, but it was really spittin' on me. *(Laughs)* Massively.

Cline: Now that you're here in the hospital, what are the major feelings that you go through life with, right now? Are you mainly at peace? Are you mainly frustrated? Are you mainly angry, or what? What do you go through life with a lot right now, Candy?

Candy: Kinda mixed, because, like, I'm on an "in-room" program and I hate stayin' in that room because I have nothing to do but think and when you're in the room, all you can do is think. And I get mad because of the things I did to put me here and I get depressed because of the rules and I want to be at home and I kinda mess up on the things I do . . . the things that I thought were fun really weren't that fun. It's like (Changing to a very maternal tone) "How in the world could you do that!" But, I'm just . . . I think it's punishment in a way, but *(doubtfully)* I'm getting something out of it.

Cline: Well, evidently you've been doing some heavy thinking right now. But it's one thing to talk the talk, which you are very good at . . . I mean, I believe you believe what you're saying and probably you are going to make some changes in your life, but it was only six weeks ago that you ran away and got drunk, right? What makes you think you can walk the walk? If the doors were open today and they said, "Candy, go for it," what makes you think you can walk the walk right now?

Candy: Part of the reason I got busted when I ran away is because I didn't want to go out and get drunk that night. I mean, I went, and I was sittin' in the basement, and everyone was passing around joints and there was food going around, and yeah, I took a drink, and the whole time, I was thinking about, "Are you really enjoying yourself?" And I thought, "God, you've had too much psychiatry!" And then I watched Chad fall down, bounce down a flight of steps and hit the bottom. And then he picked up the fifth and it took me and about five others to pry it out of his hand and I thought, "Now, I *really* enjoy this." And, I mean, I got sick that night, too, and I just thought . . . I finally just put the bottle down and said, "I don't want to do this."

For the next few minutes, Candy chattered on about the party. Basically, this is a young woman in denial, filling the vacuum of denial with adolescent talk and hopes for a better future. This kind of talk is not therapy, however; if it continues too long, it simply reinforces the adolescent's unrealistic hopes (overfocus on the future) and hinders real work. I attempted to convert Candy's externalized problems into internal ones. To help do this, I turned to Candy's mother, who had been sitting quietly by.

Cline: *(To Candy)* Ask your mom what kind of men turn her on. The ones that are best for her, or the ones that screw up her life.

Mother: It looks like the ones that screw up my life. *(Mother and Candy laugh insightfully)* 'Cause, I've had a long time to sit and think about my life, too. And, I've had to look and see where I was and how I got there and now, what am I going to do about it?

Cline: *(to Mother)* And what was your relationship like with your parents?

Mother: My father was on the road, so I really didn't have a father.

Cline: So you didn't have a father image . . . So we have a mom without a father image and she marries two alcoholics, and we have a kid who's drinking and six weeks ago goes to a place and drinks and has some boy falling down, and *(To Candy)* I'm saying, what kind of men do you think are the men that are going to turn you on? Candy?

Candy: Yeah, but I hope . . .

Cline: *(Interrupting)* But let us not hope! Let us look at statistics. You're old enough now to be thoughtful. What kind of men are going to turn you on?

Candy: Probably the kind that turned mom on.

Cline: Yeah. Son of a bitch!

Candy: *(Laughing reluctantly)* Yeah.

Cline: That's the type of men who are going to turn you on, Candy, sons of bitches. Unless you work that out, right here, in a really strong way. Any time someone comes to you sounding like a son of a bitch, you'll be turned on. And way down deep inside your heart, you'll think, "That's the boy for me!" *(Turning to Mother and speaking louder)* Is that what happened to you?

Mother: Yeah, that's exactly what I came up with after the last two months by myself. Exactly, that's it! Because I can look back and see guys that would have been an absolutely wonderful father image [to Candy] and I thought, "Ugh!"

Cline: Boring!

Mother: Very boring.

Candy: *(Laughing, with insight)* You said that they were too good.

Mother: *(Laughing)* They were! And . . .

Cline: They treated you like a princess!

Mother: Absolutely!

Cline: And you weren't used to that, were you?

Mother: Absolutely! Absolutely!

Candy's mother's experience is, unfortunately, typical. Women who were, as children, psychologically or physically abused by men often tend to view "nice guys" as "boring"—and they use this exact word over and over! Thus, we often find a woman who was mistreated by her father married to an angry or abusive man. An extension of this syndrome is that women who were abused by their fathers tend to raise (and be abused by) out-of-control little boys. Their response to their sons' behavior? "You know what men are like!"

Cline: This type of thing goes on for generation after generation with women. I give you about a fifteen percent chance of changing it, Candy, if you decided to work very hard at it. But you're going to have to keep looking at your dad and what he taught you about life and what went on with him, and if all men were like your dad what they would be like. You have a lot of feelings that you have buried and you need to get them out and you can get them out here better than anyplace outside of here. I'll show you something. *(Standing over Candy, indicating a very major point in the treatment session)* Close your eyes for a second, Candy. Sit back in the chair . . . take a few breaths. I just want to show you something so that you understand some of the feelings that are way down deep inside. So you take a few deep breaths—slow breaths. Good. You let your mind start going back to when you were thinking you wanted to hurt the world, and the world was not a very good spot for you, and you let your mind go back to the house you lived in when you were in fifth or sixth grade. See the way the house looked. *(Silence—timing the speech with Candy's breathing)* And you remember going home to the house from school, and your trip home, and you let your mind go back to before your dad committed suicide, to when you were a little kid. *(Silence)* With easy deep breaths I will make sure this works out well for you, Candy. I will take good care of you. You remember the rooms that you saw your dad in . . . With each breath you soak in your feelings for your dad—the feeling a little kid would have mixed up in her mind with love and abusiveness . . . *(Speaking softer)* hatred and kindness . . . each breath . . . you're soaking in memories of your dad . . . *(Silence)* and you remember so well the way he acted. That would be painful to a little kid, a pretty little girl growing up, not knowing what's coming off, that the ways he is acting are going to influence her life and the type of boys that appeal to her; and the things that are going on, the mom who allowed them to occur to her, who picked abusive men to marry and then had a little girl . . . *(Silence)* And you let your mind go back, Candy, to the times when you saw him acting in ways that would be very frightening to a little girl . . . *(Whispering)* with each breath . . . you're soaking in your feelings . . . so you feel them building like a bomb inside you . . . *(Silence)* and you look at your dad's face and you think about the way he ended his life . . . and you think about his raising a little girl who thought the same things about her life at times. *(Silence)* You think about his drunkenness and raising a little girl who gets drunk, and you think about the times that you loved him and how you felt as you see him . . .

At this point, I saw that tears were welling up in Candy's eyes. This brings up an important point about technique. It is often best not to ask patients to respond out loud until emotions have been tapped; otherwise, many individuals will slide into rationalization. If emotions are expressed, they can be heightened by asking the patient to repeat the words louder. It is safer to encourage individuals to repeat their own words. The therapist can feed the patient statements or ideas, but generally this is best only if the patient is unable to come up with much on her own, or if the therapist definitely has a track that can be followed therapeutically. Encouraging the patient to talk after the emotion has been tapped helps the therapy progress easily.

Cline: And if your dad was sitting across from you, Candy, right now, in that chair, you tell your father what it was like being a little girl growing up in a home here. Tell him what life was like with him, just as if you were talking to your dad right here. What do you want to say? Tell him.

Candy: Tell him?

Cline: Yeah, just as if he was sitting right there . . . what you remember.

Candy: *(Her voice shaking)* At the time I came home? I didn't know if he'd be drunk or yelling or talking real slow and I'd know he was all screwed up.

Cline: *(Louder and pushing)* You tell him that. Say, "I never knew whether you'd be screwed up or not." Say it again, Candy.

Candy: I never knew if you were going to come home so
       fucked up that you could not talk straight. I never
       knew if you were going to break things in front of peo-
       ple. Whenever I took my friends over to my own room
       you used to hit my mom in front of some of them, like
       in front of Shannon. You used to break things, every-
       thing, that meant anything to my mom. *(Voice quiv-
       ering)* You . . . you broke everything you could get
       your hands on when you were mad. You even hit me
       twice when you were mad.

Cline: Tell him how you were feeling when that was going
       on. Tell him how you were feeling when those kinds of
       things were going on and he was hitting you, Candy—
       what kinds of thoughts and feelings did you have?

Candy: *(Beginning to cry profusely)* I wanted to run out of the
       house, and I wanted to go to another one's house, but
       I couldn't because a lot of the parents wouldn't let me
       go to their house because of what was going on at my
       house.

Now I could use the issue of running away and metaphorically
push it to the hilt, because running away was Candy's problem. It
was part of her life-script. This could be generalized into the present situation in the hospital. Candy had been running away psychologically, and would like to have run away physically, as well.

Cline: So you tell him really strong. You tell him. You say
       that really strong to him. Say, "I felt like running
       away" to him.

Candy: I felt like running away because of the shit you were
       putting me through.

Cline: *(Loudly and pushing)* Say that louder, because that's
       the story of your life, Candy. Say that louder to him.

Candy: *(Louder)* You really fucked me over. I mean because
       now my entire life, you fucked up. You hit my mom.
       Then you fucking go out and shoot yourself and you

expect me to put up with it. *(Wailing)* You made me make promises that you knew I couldn't keep. And you said that if I didn't keep them, I didn't care. And I did everything I could to keep them. And then when the adults went over my word because they were over me, I felt like shit because of it. It was not my fault, the things that happened! *(Continuing to sob)* I get so sick and tired of comin' home, and I hear somethin' break or hear somethin' slam and I think, "Here he goes again!"

Cline: *(Returning to life-script issue)* You tell him, "I felt like running away!" Say that to him strong. Come on, Candy.

Candy: I felt like runnin' away.

Cline: *(Standing behind Candy and pushing a little on a pressure point at her wrist)* Louder than that. You look right in his face and you say it really loud. You say, "I wanted to run away" really loud. Trust me, Candy.

Candy: I wanted to leave because I didn't want to be around you. When you died I felt good for a while because the tension was over. I wouldn't have to listen to the fights anymore. I didn't understand it wasn't permanent, but I just knew you were gone and all the screamin' was gone and dishes breakin' and the food getting thrown on the floor and then watching you hit my mom and break things. *(Almost pleading)* I just got so sick of watching. I mean, if I brought a friend over, what was I supposed to do if you hit someone when you were drunk. You kicked out glass. You broke everything. You busted the phone.

Cline: *(Strongly)* And you tell your dad who's growing up just like him. Who's doing the same thing after he stopped busting things? You tell him. Then who has a temper tantrum and who busted things? Tell him! Just tell him how messed up your head is, Candy.

Candy: And I grew up thinking that drugs are okay and that getting drunk was okay.

Cline: And you tell him . . . are you growing up just like him?

Candy: *(In agony)* Yes!

Cline: Tell him that. Say, "I've grown up just like you."

Candy: I would throw things, and I would scream, and I would cuss, and I would bitch, and I would blame my mom for shit, just like you did! You said you were a drunk because of her, and I said I got in trouble in school because I got in so much trouble at home, and I'm in this place because of all the patterns I saw. It's not fair! Because you fucked me over!

Cline: Yeah. You tell him, "I hate your being in my head!" You tell him . . .

Candy: *(In agony)* Oh . . .

Cline: You like being like him?

Candy: No, I want him to stay dead and stay the hell away from me. He fucked me over enough!

Cline: You tell him, "I wish you were out of my head." You say that loud.

Candy: *(Still wailing)* I wish he was gone. I wish I could forget everything. I wish I could forget his voice, forget his face, forget every part of him because I don't want anything to do with him. I don't care anymore. I'm tired of defending a man who fucked me over my entire life. I'm sick of sticking up for him. He was never a father to me. All he would do is drink, and he would run around with beer, and he'd run around with his friends, and he'd go get fucked up, and he would take me in the car so the cops wouldn't pull him over. If he had wrecked the car, I'd have been killed, too. But at least they wouldn't have got busted. That was his attitude. *(Sobbing)* I wish he'd stay the fuck away from me. *(Wailing)* Don't you see I want to go home? I want to be with my mom. I don't want to be around you or your family! Or anything to do with you! Because of the shit you did I have to sit here so I won't do the same thing. You stay away from me!

Cline: *(Sits down beside Candy, places arm lightly on her shoulder, and motions to Mother)* Put your arms around her and tell her, "I love you."

Mother: *(Sobbing)* I love you, Candy.

Candy: Oh . . .

Mother: It's all right.

Parents sometimes are reassuring, when it is support for real work that must be given. The two are not synonymous.

Cline: *(Interrupting)* It's not necessarily all right.

Candy: Oh—I want to go home.

Mother: It's all right, we'll do it together, okay? But you have to make decisions.

Cline: Yeah, and when you want to go home . . . who never faced things? Candy—who never faced things?

Candy: Me.

Cline: You bet! *(Candy continues to hold her mother and sob.)* Now what male staff member do you know in this place, Candy?

Candy: Steve Tracy.

Cline: Is he here?

Mother: No.

Cline: *(Addressing the hospital audience)* Who here knows Candy? *(A hand is raised.)* Larry, come up here and sit across from Candy. *(To Candy)* Larry tried working with you for an unhappy year, right?

Candy: *(Laughing a little in spite of herself)* Yeah.

Cline: *(To Larry)* Tell her how she impressed you when you knew her. *(To Candy)* Ask him. Say, "How did I impress you?"

Candy: How did I impress you? What was I like?

Larry: As someone who didn't want to work. As somebody who wanted to stay the same, continue rebelling, continue being angry. Somebody who didn't want to get through things.

Candy: It's true. I just timed off my hour and left.

Cline: Ask her if she would handle it any differently now.

Larry: Do you think you would handle it any differently now,
        if you were doing it?

Candy: *(Voice quavering)* Yeah. I wouldn't lie. I wouldn't
        come to sessions stoned. And I wouldn't sit there and
        try to convince you that I didn't have any problems . .
        . that I was a normal kid and leave me alone. That's
        exactly what I did the entire time.

Cline: Ask her if she thinks she's a normal kid right now.

Larry: Do you think you are normal now?

Candy: I don't think I'll ever be normal.

Cline: *(Putting arm on her shoulder)* You will if you work
        hard.

Candy: I know, but I've been through a lot and I feel like I'm
        being punished, and then I'm here, and I put myself
        here, and that's what hurts! *(Sobbing again)*

Cline: *(Speaking strongly)* As long as you feel punished,
        you're going to make squat progress. Do you under-
        stand this isn't a punishment? This is an opportunity.
        How many kids get to spend time in a psych hospital?
        (Candy and the audience laugh.) I mean really, when
        you get right down to it, how many have the chance?

Candy: Half my friends have. *(Audience laughs.)*

Cline: Yeah, with the friends you have, probably. *(Candy and
        the audience continue to laugh.)* But if the general kids
        out there really use their time here . . .

Candy: Some of them do, some of them don't.

Cline: *(Strongly)* That's right! And if you go through here,
        and every moment that you're here you think of this as
        a punishment instead of an opportunity, you're just
        playing your dad all over again.

Candy: I know . . .

Cline: How would your dad feel about . . . if your dad were
        in an alcohol rehab center, would he consider that an
        opportunity, or would he consider that a punishment?

Candy: Punishment. He'd probably con the psychiatrists into a prescription.

Cline: I bet he would!

Candy: That's what he did when he had 'em.

Cline: Yeah. And now, who would like to con their way out of here?

Candy: I'd love to go home . . .

Cline: *(Interrupting loudly)* Who would like to con their way out of here?

Candy: I would. I'd love to but I don't want to.

Cline: *(Going with her thought and hoping for a healthy side)* You bet you don't want to! But there is a part of you that would love to con your way out of here. You would, Candy.

Candy: *(Capitulating)* Everybody would.

Cline: Well, that's because people who are here are not too bright yet. Otherwise they wouldn't be here! You'd love to con your way out.

Candy: *(Agreeing with excitement)* Yeah, I would! I know I would if I wanted to, but I don't want to. I want things to work out. I want to look at this thing.

Cline: Well, I hope so! And would your dad consider the alcohol rehab place punishment or an opportunity? What do you say?

Candy: A punishment.

Cline: Yeah. Well, why don't you just be like him and consider it a punishment while you are here?

Candy: Well, I don't know . . .

Cline: Are you going to consider it an opportunity or punishment? Which?

Candy: An opportunity.

Cline: You better believe it! Because you're not going to get it again. Because the insurance companies are getting a lot tighter, I'll tell you that. Consider it an opportunity or punishment? Which?

Candy: An opportunity.

Cline: You better believe it!

Candy: It's not very easy. *(Self-conscious laugh)*

Cline: It's not that easy. But your strength is your honesty.

Candy: Yeah. It costs a lot.

Cline: *(Kindly)* Do you think you're worth a lot?

Candy: Yeah, with all the psychiatrists I've seen.

Cline: Well, it's an expensive row to hoe, right? And you'll never have the chance again. So you can either get out of here a little prematurely and go blow it with your first and second husbands, or you can get it together here and make it help to last. That's where it's at. And . . . and you need to really use this time 'cause you don't have very much of it. At the most, how long could you be here? I mean how long would you be here at the limit of what you could be here?

Candy: They don't tell me.

Cline: Well, how long do you think? What's your suspicion?

Candy: My insurance runs out in September.

Cline: Well, that's a pretty good idea. That's the most possible, 'cause a place like this can't afford kids when the insurance runs out. So, if your insurance runs out in September, that's the longest you can be here.

Candy: But I don't think I need to stay here.

Cline: Well, maybe you don't, maybe you don't. That may be true Candy. You don't, but right now, until you start considering this place an opportunity and start talking to staff members about your feelings . . . until you can talk to them as well as you talk to your mom, then you're not going to make it with your first husband. I'm just telling you that, flat out, because I'm a wise old shrink who has been through the mill with many people. 'Cause someday you're going to want to talk to your husband intimately and thoughtfully and carefully. So you might as well practice here on people and go to the summit. Some people get close to the summit. If they would just give it that extra bit, they would go on a roll and they would make it. What they do is they go up and they say, "God, I've come so far and I've done so much, I can't make it anymore," and then they roll back down to the starting point. And you could roll right back down to the starting point, and you could go out and you could get drunk so fast it would make your head spin. You know alcoholism is genetic, too. You know that, don't you? Do you know it?

Candy: It goes through the generations.

Cline: Not only psychologically, but genetically.

Candy: You mean like the Smiths? *(Referring to her father's side of the family)*

Cline: Yeah, like the Smiths. And when you get it, you get drunk. It runs in families and you are an at-risk kid. Your father's side of the family is not genetically super.

Candy: *(Voice quavering)* No, I know they're not.

Cline: And then there's that, and you have half of his genes in you. And for you, alcoholism is a great risk. And I'm not talking about all the psychological ways you have fucked up your head. I'm talking about your genetics. You take a drink and you're at risk for alcoholism. You better use your time here and get your head together. You better thank your lucky stars you have insurance that lets you be here. How do you think you'd really handle it if you were let out of here in three months, Candy? How many binges would there be?

Candy: What do you mean, binges?

Cline: I mean, how many times would you drink too much?

Candy: I know my friends drink too much. I wouldn't want to be around them, 'cause I don't want to come back once I leave *(Starting to sob)* and the only way not to come back is not to do the same things over.

Cline: *(Somewhat accusingly)* And did you say that same thing four months ago?

Candy: What do you mean four months ago?

Cline: Four months ago were you saying the same thing, "Boy, if I ever get out of here I won't drink, if I ever get out of here." Were you saying that four months ago?

Candy: No, four months ago I made my mind up not to do that. But I did my time, and I was so glad when I got out and I wanted to be back with my mom, but I didn't really make up my mind to quit. But after I saw Chad bouncing down the stairway, I decided I didn't want to be a part of that.

Cline: Well, you're going to see people bouncing down the stairway all your life if you live the way most kids of alcoholics grow up.

Candy: *(Quivering)* Yeah, but I was thinking . . .

Cline: Well, tell me about it. Look at the average smoker. Is he real happy about smoking? No. What do you want to do?

Candy: Quit.

Cline: When you see them three months later, what do you see hanging out of their mouths?

Candy: A cigarette.

Cline: Yeah. Candy, that is the way your life is going to be if you don't use this time. This is your last best chance.

Candy: *(Starting to sob)* But it's really scary.

Cline: *(With concern)* To look at yourself?

Candy: I want to stay home.

Cline: Well, that's part of your dependency. That's part of your sickness. How old are you?

Candy: Sixteen.

Cline: And how old do you think you're sounding when you say, "I need to stay home with mommy"? *(To Mother)* And you encourage it by saying, "Mommy loves you"! *(To Candy)* How old do you think you sound—"I need to stay home with my mommy." Really, how old is that?

Candy: Ten.

Cline: Probably.

Candy: But I never wanted . . . I mean when I came in here, I was too independent. I didn't even want any . . .

Cline: *(Interrupting)* Oh, you weren't independent. You were just rebellious. Don't ever get the two confused. You just knew what people wanted so you went the opposite way. But who is in charge? If I say, "Go left," and you go right, who calls the shots?

Candy: Me.

Cline: Huh-uh.

Candy: You?

Cline: Sure, 'cause every time I want you to go left, what do I say?

Candy: Go right?

Cline: Go right, Candy. *(Candy and the audience laugh.)* All rebellious people think they're independent, but they're just allowing someone else to call the shots. If I wanted you to kill yourself I would say, "Don't drink, be nice, don't hurt yourself," and what would you do? You'd go out and do it. You've never been independent! You've never had a chance with your dad and mom to be independent, and you're not independent now. You're a dependent, lonely, needing-mommy little girl. And until you get over that, and *if* you get over it, and I don't know whether you can or not, but I think you can because you're a gutsy kid . . . but until you get over being with your mommy, you're not going to be independent, you're not even going to be close. *(With love)* Candy, I'm telling you that because you're a gutsy kid.

Candy: *(With a wail)* But what's wrong with wanting to be home?

Cline: *(Accusingly)* The way you want to be home? What's wrong with the way you want to be home, Candy? You tell me. What's wrong with the way you want to be home? *(Candy gives a slight and honest shrug.)* You want to be home because you *need* her. Is that right or wrong?

Candy: I don't know.

Cline: Do you want to be home because you want to be home or do you really feel like you need to be home?

Candy: I want to be home with my mom because . . .

Cline: I don't think so.

Candy: I want to be with my mom, but I want to be home.

Cline: I think you're a dependent little girl, still. And I think you can change it. I think way down deep in your heart you can. Now you're ten. But a little bit ago you were two. You're making great progress, but you're not even close to being sixteen. *(Giving Candy a big hug)* I love you, Candy. You're doing okay. Do you understand what I'm saying? *(Candy nods her head.)* But you don't like it?

Candy: *(Crying)* No.

Cline: You know why I'm telling you things you don't like?

Candy: It's reality.

Cline: Yeah. And you can handle it. Some kids, I don't tell them reality 'cause they can't handle it. I think you'll hurt, but I think you'll make it. God bless you, Candy. *(Giving her a hug)* I know it's going to hurt . . .

I then told Candy's mother that I thought she had raised a super daughter, but that she needed to tell Candy that she hoped Candy would make a better choice of men than she herself did. I helped her tell Candy that she hoped Candy got her act together. On this note, with love between the mother and daughter, the session ended.

Five years later, I spoke with Candy on the phone to obtain her permission to use the tape of her session for training others. She bubbled and responded thoughtfully, occasionally talking to her three-year-old in the background. She laughed and said, "I turned around and did exactly what you said I would do, and stayed for five years with a man who abused me. If I can save someone else from being a repeat of me, I want to do it! I am sure the only thing I ever understood was fighting, because that's all I saw from my mom and dad. I'd love to see others not make the same mistake. Here I am, five years and one child later, but it's not going to continue!

"I'm going out with a new guy now who talks to me! He acts like I'm his friend. It's so strange! He's nice to me, and it feels weird. I have to sit down and think about it. People have to learn to trust people, and it's like reprogramming myself. I sit there and think about it, and it's strange, but then I think, 'That's the way it ought to be!' That's the way people ought to act when they like each other. I think, 'Why did I do that five years!' It's not going to happen again. People are not toys. People are not someone to play games with. I'm a person! If you want to use the videotape and that helps other girls not make the same mistake, use it!"

Matt: Confrontive Sit-Down Therapy with an Eight-Year-Old

This transcript demonstrates how intrusive techniques are used in a sit-down, eyeball-to-eyeball confrontation. It also shows the therapeutic persistence needed to help some extremely passive-resistant children to express their true emotions and come to grips with their rage and loss so they can work through these difficult emotions.

Matt, an eight-year-old boy with reactive attachment disorder, had suffered abuse and neglect during his infancy and toddlerhood. His father was physically abusive and his mother was neglectful. After he was removed from his birth parents' home, he had failed in a number of foster homes. When I saw him, he was institutionalized. His psychiatric consultation sheet noted, "In more than ten months of therapy, there has been no notable progress. In therapy, Matt is superficially obnoxious and generally noncompliant. In the cottage, he is superficial and always noncompliant." The psychological report stated, "This kid does not 'wear well' to say the least. He answered everything with 'yeppy' or 'nopper.' Even in the beginning this fell a little short of amusing. . . . While completing the WISC [Wechsler Intelligence Scale for

Children] I asked Matt, 'How do you make water boil?' and he said, 'You bubble it.' I asked him, 'How do you do that?' And he answered, 'Too hard.'" A staff member at the institution commented, "Matt has never given the right answer in the right way at the right time to anyone!"

Matt had no good friends his own age. Even more critical was that the staff at the institution found him very difficult to like. Knowing the staff as I do—they are a group of professional "likers"—and discovering that there was not one among them who really liked Matt was a bad prognostic sign.

I decided to start the session with fairly heavy confrontation, even without good contract, for three reasons: (1) Matt was young. (2) He had had years of unsuccessful therapy. (3) His history indicated that he would attempt to make contract a joke to gain control of the session and to hide his real feelings of hopelessness and rage.

The session was recorded from behind a one-way window in a child treatment center. Matt's counselor, Mike, introduced me to Matt, and the transcript begins as we completed the introductions and sat down together.

> Cline: *(To Mike)* Try it again and see if he won't give a straight answer. If he does answer, okay? *(To Matt)* Don't snap off a good answer, okay? Don't act your age. How old are you?
>
> Matt: Eight.
>
> Cline: Don't give an eight-year-old answer. Give kind of a dumb answer, or no answer, or a "noppy" or a "yeppy," but something kind of stupid. You know, so it's just kind of two-year-old-like, okay?
>
> Matt: You want me to do it?

This was a pretty good shot at acting stupid in the face of fairly stiff early confrontation. If I had answered Matt directly, he would have been in control of the session. So I ignored him and directed my next comment to Mike.

I was also using a paradoxical technique that is effective in reaching very resistant children by asking Matt to do or say what he insisted on doing anyway. As you will read, I then congratulated him for his behavior, taking control of the session by redefining his passive rebellion as compliance. This unsettles children, because they are uncertain whether they are acting the way they want to or as the adult is demanding. This technique often raises the child's anger, anxiety, and helplessness to a conscious and even expressed level, where they can be worked through and resolved.

Cline: *(To Mike)* Ask him the question.

Mike: Okay. What does Dr. Cline do? *(Matt is silent.)*

Cline: *(Slapping leg)* Good! Very good! Shake! Well done—very well done! Quite good! Ask another. Can he do that on all questions coming up? Ask him another question, Mike. This is good, Matt.

Mike: How are you feeling today? *(Matt remains silent.)*

Cline: Good! *(Laughing)* This is really good. Yeah, you're very good. So lots of the time when you talk to Matt, he's more or less kind of two-year-oldish, right?

Mike: Yeah, but lots of times it's more like this: I ask him if he is nervous and he says "no," and I know that everyone gets nervous. Then I ask him again, "Are you nervous?" and he says, "yes."

Cline: *(Surprised)* Really! *(To Matt)* Oh, you mean you told him the truth?

Matt: *(Laughing nervously)* Yeah.

Cline: Oh, Matt, how could you do that? *(To Mike)* Ask him that again. *(To Matt)* Don't tell the truth! I hear you don't tell the truth very much!

Mike: Are you nervous? *(Once again Matt is silent.)*

Cline: Good—that's very good, Matt. Ask him another question.

Mike: How old are you, Matt? *(Matt is silent, and wrinkles up his nose.)*

Cline: *(Laughing and slapping leg)* Very good—very good.

You kind of get a nose right there. All right. I'll talk to him for a while.

It is best to carry out heavy confrontation when alone with children or with well-tutored parents or therapists who can help with the confrontation and any necessary holding. Children needing intrusive techniques tend to be manipulative, and look to adults for sympathy. Unfortunately, those in the helping professions are often all too ready to give it when it is least needed.

Mike: Okay.

Cline: And really, he makes a very good two-year-old. Probably one of the better two-year-olds. But you know, when you're eight and it's hard for you to trust people or to be very loving, then what you do is kind of flunk out and act two. And it's understandable, because it's very hard for people who have had hard times to act eight when they're really eight.

This statement balanced the confrontation with support, helping Matt feel safe to express real feelings. However, I didn't give too much support too soon, or Matt would never have felt hopeless or helpless enough to get to the deeper emotions.

Cline: *(To Matt, as Mike leaves the room)* A sad look. Are you looking sad?

Matt: No.

Cline: Well, are you looking happy? *(Matt doesn't reply.)* You don't know how to look. Give me any kind of look. Very good! You're very good at any type of look. Let's see. You kind of like doing things wrong, right? I mean, don't you kind of like it, and then after you do something, don't you say, "Hey, look, I did this wrong, I did that wrong." I mean, you're really into doing things wrong, right? Why do you think you do that so much? Why do you think you like doing things wrong so much?

Matt: I don't know.

In a few minutes, after only a little confrontation, Matt would be entirely honest, giving an entirely different answer to basically the same question!

Cline: Good answer! Good dumb answer! Shake. Very good. Okay, now why don't you tell me that again. Why do you like doing things wrong so much, Matt?
Matt: *(Softly)* I don't know.
Cline: Really, do you want to know what I think?
Matt: What? *(Slight ring of honesty—for the first time)*
Cline: Do you really, or do you not want to know what I think?
Matt: I do.
Cline: You do want to know what I think?
Matt: Yeah.
Cline: I think you don't like to do it anybody else's way except yours. So if somebody else's way is the right way, then you'll do it your way even though it's the wrong way because you don't like doing anything the way anybody else tells you to do it. 'Cause you don't have much trust in your heart. You don't trust people enough to do it their way. So you'd rather screw up and do it your way. Okay? Let me see how you can do it here. *(Taking paper and drawing)* I'll draw something and then you draw it your way, okay? I think you did this for Dr. Lyke. And then say things like "noppy" and "yeppy," you know, dumb stuff. It's easy to say kind of dumb stuff, Matt, when you don't trust other people. . . . Okay, draw this. Do it your way, though, okay? You can either do it the right way or your way. Either way you want to do it is okay. The right way or your way. *(Matt draws.)* Okay, all right. Now, which way did you do that? Did you do that the right way or the wrong way?

Matt: The right way.

Cline: Hmm?

Matt: The right way.

Cline: *(With an intimidating tone—no niceness)* Why? Why did you do that right when you do things wrong so much?

Matt: Just wanted to do it.

Cline: *(Sternly)* Why? I think you did it the right way because I said you could do it the wrong way, so you decided to do it the right way. Why do you think you did it the right way? Why do you think you have tears in your eyes right now, Matt? *(Harshly)* Why do you think you're feeling a little unsettled? *(Louder)* Why do you think you have tears in your eyes right now? Why do you think you're looking that way? Why do you think you're not saying anything and why do you think you did that the right way instead of the wrong way? What do you think the answers to all these questions are, Matt?

Matt: *(Pouty)* I don't know.

Cline: Why do you think you screw off so much? Do you think that you're easy to like or do you think you're hard to like?

Matt: Hard to like.

Cline: Well, say it louder to me. I want you to say that louder! When you talk to me, I want you to talk up! Got it?

Matt: Yes.

Cline: I don't want you to say "yes" when I say "got it." Got it?

Matt: Got it.

Cline: Louder than that. Got it?

Matt: Got it!

Cline: I want you to say "got it" louder to me. Got it?

Matt: *(Louder)* Got it!

Cline: That's what I want you to say. Got it!

Matt: Got it.

Cline: Why do you think you screw up so much?

Matt: *(With emphasis)* I want to!

What a great answer, and so different from the previous "I don't know." With just a little push and some support, children meet higher expectations. Regardless of how awful this exchange may sound to certain people, Matt's answer indicated that he felt safe with me.

Cline: All right! That's an honest answer. Why do you think you want to, Matt? Why do you think you want people not liking you?
Matt: *(Mumbling)* 'Cause they don't want to be my friends.
Cline: They don't want to be your friends or you don't want to be friends with them?
Matt: I don't want to be friends with them.
Cline: Say it louder.
Matt: *(Clearly)* I don't want to be friends to them!
Cline: I want you to shout that. Say it louder to me.
Matt: I don't . . .
Cline: Say it loud: "I don't want to be people's friends!" Say it!
Matt: I don't want to be people's friends!
Cline: Say it again! I want you to say it loud to me, Matt! Go!
Matt: I don't want to be people's friends.

In spite of the push, Matt was plateauing. Thinking he might do better when encouraged to express his anger directly at me, I changed my approach.

Cline: Say, "I don't want to be your friend," to me. Say it!
Matt: I don't want to be your friend.
Cline: Say it louder!
Matt: I don't want to be your friend!
Cline: I want you to scream that at me, Matt. Go!
Matt: I don't want to be your friend!
Cline: Say, "I don't want to be anybody's friend!" Say it loud!

Matt: I don't want to be anybody's friend!
Cline: Louder!
Matt: I don't want to be anybody's friend!

Matt was loud and compliant, but not really into deeper emotions. His experience of compliance and honesty for the first time in months was not to be taken lightly, but if the session had ended at this point, there would have been no real change for him, and no connection with the therapist. As the subject of friends was not proceeding, I switched to another issue.

Cline: I want you to say it with all the anger you have in you. You have a lot of anger in you, do you know that? You have to have a lot of anger to goof off as much as you do and goof around. Do you goof around a lot?
Matt: Yes.
Cline: Do you goof off in school?
Matt: Yes.
Cline: Name three ways you goof off in school, and say it fast. Go!
Matt: Don't do my papers right.
Cline: Okay. What else?
Matt: Stand in the corner.

This was Matt's attempt to regain control with a stupid answer. He wanted me to follow his lead and say, "No, Matt, standing in the corner is what you do right, but I want to know why you stand in the corner." The rhythm of the session would have been broken, and I would have been operating on Matt's own passive-aggressive terms. My reaction surprised Matt.

Cline: Louder!
Matt: Stand in the corner.
Cline: Say, "I stand in the corner," loud. Go!
Matt: I stand in the corner!

Cline: Okay, and what else? What else do you do?

Matt: And I play games with the teacher.

As he was trying to do with me!

Cline: Say it loud.

Matt: I play games with the teachers!

Cline: Why do you think you have tears in your eyes right now?

Controlling children always tear up when controlled. The first tears are never sorrow; rather, they are anger over losing control. Feelings of hopelessness and helplessness are buried much deeper.

Matt: I don't know!

Cline: *(Doubtfully)* You don't? I think it makes you mad doing it someone else's way. Say, "I hate you for this." Say that to me right.

Matt: *(First real feeling)* I *hate* you for this!

Cline: Say that louder.

Matt: I hate you for this.

Cline: You look at me when you say that to me, Matt. Go! Loud!

Matt: I hate you for this.

Cline: I want you to say it like you mean it. Do you understand what I'm talking about? I don't like this crappy halfway stuff that you've been giving me. Got it?

Matt: Yes.

Cline: Got it?

Matt: Got it.

Cline: *(Louder)* Got it!

Matt: *(Louder)* Got it!

Cline: All right. Say, "I hate you for this." Say it louder than that. Come on, Matt, let's go. I want it just like you're feeling it right now.

Matt: I hate you for this!

Cline: Louder than that!

Matt: *(Angry and frustrated—the first hint of losing control)* I am!

Cline: I don't want any of that cry stuff. Do you think you have a lot of anger in your heart?

Matt: Yes.

Cline: Do you go around with it very much? Does it hurt you very much? Do you go around with a lot of hate in your heart or do you go around with a lot of love? Which do you go around with?

Matt: Hate.

Cline: Louder!

Matt: Hate!

Cline: Say it in a sentence.

Matt: I go around with hate.

Cline: Louder than that, Matt. Come on, I want to hear it loud.

Matt: I go around with hate!

Cline: Good. That's the way I want you to say it. Say it again! I want you to say it twice as loud. Got it?

Matt: Got it.

Cline: Do I want a dumb little "got it" like that, or do I want a loud "got it"? Got it!

Matt: Loud. Got it!

Cline: *(Louder)* Got it!

Matt: *(Louder)* Got it!

Cline: Good! Say that sentence again.

Matt: I go around with hate . . . hate in my heart.

Cline: Louder than *that*. One more time.

Matt: *I go around with hate in my heart!*

Cline: How do people end up feeling about you?

Matt: Not very nice.

Cline: Do they love you a lot?

Matt: No.

Cline: How do they feel about you, Matt?

Matt: Not too good.

Another plateau. I decided to go abruptly from "here and now" to "there and then," picking up on issues about Matt's dad. I knew from Matt's chart that he must have had feelings about those issues.

Cline: How did your dad feel about you, Matt?
Matt: He loved me.
Cline: Louder.
Matt: He loved me.

I was careful not to get sucked into an argument or a go-nowhere exploration here.

Cline: Really, how did he treat you, Matt? Come on, you've told people how he's treated you. You gave him a real nice present. What was the present you gave him at Christmas? What was the present? What did the bank say on it? That you gave him? Come on, let's go! Do you want to play your dumb act? Let's go, loud. What did you give him for Christmas?
Matt: I gave him a boxing glove.
Cline: Louder.
Matt: I gave him a boxing glove!
Cline: Louder than that!
Matt: I am!
Cline: I want you to say that loud, "I gave him a boxing glove." Say it loud!
Matt: I gave him a boxing glove!
Cline: Um-hmm. And what did it say on it, Matt?
Matt: I don't know.
Cline: Oh, come on, Matt.
Matt: I'm telling you the truth!
Cline: Oh, what a bunch of . . . you don't know what it said! I doubt that very much. It said, "Sock it to me." Say that loud.

Although I was fairly certain that Matt remembered what was written on the gift, if I had tried to push his remembering too much I might have lost control of the rhythm of the session. To head this off, I simply gave the answer. The other option was to push through with hints and help him remember. Each method has pluses and minuses.

Matt: Sock it to me.

Cline: Louder! Say it louder!

Matt: Sock it to me.

Cline: Is that what he did to you, Matt? Then you sit in there and think about your dad and say, "He beat me all the time" when you were with Mike, or "I'm here because my dad beat me." Is that what you said?

Matt: Yes.

Cline: Louder!

Matt: Yes!

Cline: Are you just going to sit there and play the dumb act all the time?

Matt: No.

Cline: Do you like playing the dumb act?

Matt: No.

Cline: Say, "I like playing the dumb act."

Matt: I . . . like playing the dumb act. *(Crying—first real sob)*

Cline: Say it again. Say it again to me. "I like playing the dumb act."

Matt: I like to play the dumb act.

Cline: Is that true or not, Matt?

Matt: Not true!

Cline: I say it's true. Aren't you honest enough to look at that? Are you a dumb person or a smart person?

Matt: Smart.

Cline: I think you are, too, Matt. How do you act?

Matt: Dumb.

Cline: Look at me! Do you or do you not act dumb?

Matt: Not act dumb.

Cline: Do you act dumb or do you not act dumb?

Matt: I act dumb.

Cline: *(Holding Matt close)* Really cool. Then, how do you think people like to treat you? How do people end up treating you, Matt? Just like who treated you?

Matt: My dad.

Cline: Do you want to go through life having people kick you around? And treat you like your dad treated you? Is that what you want out of life, Matt?

Matt: No.

Cline: Say, "I want everybody to treat me nasty." Say it!

Matt: I don't want . . .

Cline: Say, "I like people to treat me nasty." Say it!

Matt: I don't want people to . . .

Cline: No, I said you do like people to treat you nasty. Say, "I like people to mistreat me." Say it.

Matt: I like people to mistreat me.

Cline: Say it again.

Matt: I like people to mistreat me.

Cline: Is that true or not true?

Matt: Not true.

Cline: Well, how do you act around people, Matt?

Matt: Not very good.

Cline: Then how do they treat you, Matt?

Matt: Just what I said to you.

Cline: They don't treat you very nice, do they?

Matt: No.

Cline: Just like who treated you?

Matt: *(Loud, frustrated, and aware!)* My dad!

Cline: Do you want everybody to treat you that way, Matt?

Matt: No.

Cline: That's what you act like, Matt. You act like you want everybody to treat you the way your dad treated you. A lot of kids do that. Do you think you are a very lovable kid, or do you think you're very hard to love?

Matt: Very hard to love.

His response was quick! Kids can easily handle the fact that they are hard to love. Obviously, it is less helpful to have them say, "Nobody loves me," no matter how true that may be.

Cline: What do you think the staff thinks? If I ask them, "Is Matt a lovable kid?" what do you think they would say?

Matt: No.

Cline: That's right. Dumb! Are you a dumb person, though?

Matt: No.

Cline: How do you act, Matt?

Matt: Smart.

Cline: *(Doubtfully)* Do you really!

Matt: Yes.

Cline: I say you act dumb most of the time. Is it smart to have people not love you?

Matt: No.

Cline: You're really blowing it. All that stupid stuff like "Righto" and "Yeppie" and that kind of crap! Who does it hurt?

Matt: Me.

Cline: You better believe it! Do you want to go through life like that?

Matt: No.

Cline: Tell me how you want to go through life, Matt.

Matt: Liking the kids and stuff.

Cline: Do you really? They don't like you very well, do they? I don't blame them. I think you go through life really a bummer. Do you understand what I'm saying?

Matt: Yes.

Cline: Does it make you feel bad for yourself or not?

Matt: Yes.

Cline: *(Softly, lovingly)* Or are you happy with the way it goes, hmm?

Matt: Sad.

Cline: When are you going to change?

Matt: Today.

At this point, I was trying to wind down to a conclusion, leaving Matt in a good spot. I was a little concerned because he became very angry and honest, but not rageful. The session seemed incomplete, although perhaps it was the best that could be done on a first consult. But Matt was about to surprise me.

Cline: *(Hugging Matt)* Really?
Matt: Yes.
Cline: Well, don't say it if you don't mean it. When are you going to change?
Matt: *(Nasty)* I meant it!

Wow, nastiness! Following the hug, it really meant, "I still have some anger, and I feel safe enough to work on it with you." I thought, "Well, super, kid. Let's go for it one more time!"

Cline: Did I ask you to talk to me that way?
Matt: No.
Cline: Say, "I hate doing it your way."
Matt: I hate it doing your way!

Note the change in wording. Passive-resistant children often change the wording, although this may be unconscious.

Cline: Say it again. Say it louder. That's the way you live your life! Say, "I hate doing things your way." Say it again, Matt.
Matt: I hate things doin' your way! *(Right words, wrong order)*
Cline: Say it again, Matt. Good for you. That was saying it good. Say it again like that.
Matt: I hate things doin' your way!
Cline: "I hate doing it your way." Say it like that.
Matt: I hate . . . it doin' your way. *(Right words, wrong order, wrong rhythm)*

Cline: I said, "I hate doing it your way." Say it that way. I hate doing it your way. Say it that way.

Matt: I hate doing it your way.

Cline: Say it louder.

Matt: I hate doing it your way.

Cline: Say it really loud to me now, Matt. Say it again. Say it again. Come on, let's go!

Matt: I hate doing it your way!

Cline: Is that the truth?

Matt: Yes.

Cline: Is that the way you live your life? Hating doing it other people's way?

Matt: Yes.

Cline: Who gets hurt, Matt?

Matt: Me.

Cline: Bummer, isn't it?

Matt: *(Snuggling in, sniffling)* Yes.

Cline: And when I make you do it my way, how do you feel about me?

Matt: *(Honest anger)* Not too good!

Cline: Oh, "not to good." You hate my guts when I make you do it my way! Say, "I hate your guts when . . ."

Matt: I hate your guts when I do it your way!

Cline: Say it again, Matt. Come on, say it again. Let's go, Matt.

Matt: *(First real rage)* I hate your guts when you do it . . . your way.

Cline: Just say, "I hate your guts!"

Matt: I hate your guts!

Cline: Wrinkle your nose more when you say it. Wrinkle your nose more when you say it and say it like you mean it. Make me believe it. Say it again, Matt!

Matt: I hate your guts!

Cline: Say it again, Matt.

Matt: I am saying it!

Cline: Well, good. Say it again, anyway. We're doing it my way, got it?

Matt: Yes.
Cline: Got it.
Matt: Got it.
Cline: Who is boss here?
Matt: You.
Cline: You better believe it. Say, "I hate your guts."
Matt: *I hate your guts!*
Cline: Good, I want it three times like that. I want you to say
        it like that three times.
Matt: I hate your guts!
Cline: Good, say it again.
Matt: I hate your guts!!
Cline: *(Softly)* Good, say it again.
Matt: *(Screaming at the top of his lungs) I hate your guts!!!*

At last—real rage! When children actively express their feelings
without pushing by the therapist, this shows they are able to cope
with their emotions and feel safe doing so with the therapist. The
key is the expression of feelings directly to the therapist at the therapist's request. All rage-filled children express themselves just fine
out on the playground, at parents, or at another (often younger)
child. However, that sort of expression is not under another's control, and certainly does not help these children work through their
emotions.

Cline   And why do you hate my guts?
Matt: *(Through clenched teeth)* 'Cause I have to do everything
        your way.
Cline: I know. And whose way do you like doing it?
Matt: Mine.
Cline: Who gets hurt when it all goes your way, Matt?
Matt: *(Sobbing)* Me.

Matt's rage was solid, and his capitulation was complete. With
a good and loving ending, bonding would lock in. Bonding with
the therapist is easily transferable to more important others, for

loving people are able to love more than one person. Now Matt could move in therapy. But for a proper ending, I had to get Matt to give me a reciprocal smile.

Cline: Look at me. I don't like a pouty mouth. Open your mouth. Not that wide open. I want you to look like . . . close it. Now, I want there to be a slight smile on it. Get ready . . . No, just a nice . . . No, I don't want a fakey smile. Got it!

Matt: Yes.

Cline: Got it! "Yes!" What do you mean?

Matt: Got it!

Cline: Say, "I really hate you right now."

Matt: I really hate you right now.

Cline: Good, say it again. That was good, Matt. You did a really good job on that one. Say it again.

Matt: I . . .

Cline: Sorry, I said you did a good job. It almost blew your mind, right? You hate doing a good job, don't you?

Matt: Yes!!

Cline: Why, Matt?

Matt: It's because I'm doing it my own way!

Cline: I know. Look, when you were a little kid, if you did it your dad and mom's way, do you think you would have been very happy? Or do you think you had to learn to do things your way?

Matt: Had to learn to do things my way.

Cline: Are you living with your mom and dad right now?

Matt: No.

Cline: Look at me when you talk to me. Are you living with your dad and mom right now?

Matt: No.

Cline: So whose way do you have to make it every time?

Matt: My way.

Cline: Um-hmm. Does that make sense?

Matt: No.

Cline: It did when you were a little baby. I'm sorry you got beat up. *(Lovingly)* And I'm sorry you were around people you couldn't trust. That's too bad. It really is. Any time a kid gets treated that way, it's too bad. But if you're going to live like you're living with your folks your whole life, you're really going to get hurt. You got the picture? Am I your dad?

Matt: No.

Cline: How do you treat people? Do you treat them really nice or do you treat them like you treat your dad?

Matt: I treat them like . . . my dad.

Cline: Well? Do they end up liking you or do they end up feeling like they'd like to take boxing gloves to you? Is that the way people end up feeling about you?

Matt: Yes.

Cline: And who did you give the boxing gloves to?

Matt: My dad.

Cline: Do you want to treat everybody like your dad?

Matt: No.

Cline: Well, then, who has to change, Matt?

Matt: Me.

Cline: You better believe it. And when I said you were doing things really good today, the first thing that flashed through your mind was, "Good, well then I'll screw up." Right?

Matt: Yes.

Cline: Do you think that way?

Matt: No.

Cline: We're going to try something two ways. I'm going to say, "Good, you did a really good job today, Matt." And you say, "Oh, well then I'll screw up." Say that to me. Hey, you did a really good job today, Matt.

Matt: Then I'll screw up.

Cline: Say it a little louder. Hey, Matt, you did a really good job today.

Matt: Then I'll screw up.

Cline: *(With pizzazz)* Hey, Matt, you did a really good job today!

Matt: Then I'll screw up.

Cline: That's the way you go through life. Does it feel good to you?

Matt: No.

Cline: Now I want you to say, "Thank you."

Matt: Thank you.

Cline: No, after I say it. Hey, Matt, you did a really good job today.

Matt: Thank you.

Children who have routinely done things wrong need to be taught exactly how to do things right. It does no good for the therapist to say something like, "Act appropriately." Unfortunately, there are many adults who don't know exactly what that means! It helps lock in the new behavior when the child is asked to do something wrong, and then is asked to do it right, as just transpired above. It is best to follow this up with exploration or congratulations about the correct response.

Cline: A sweet thank you, not a cruddy thank you. Got it?

Matt: Yes, got it.

Cline: *(Slapping leg)* Got it!?

Matt: Got it.

Cline: Thank you. Hey, Matt, you did a really good job today.

Matt: Thank you.

Cline: Is that a sweet thank you?

Matt: No.

Cline: Did I ask for a sweet thank you?

Matt: Yes.

Cline: A really nice thank you.

Matt: Yes.

Cline: You'd better give it to me. Got it?

Matt: Got it.

Cline: Good. I like it when you do things my way. It just

makes me feel good all over. Hey, Matt, you did a really good job today.

Matt: Thank you. *(Better)*

Cline: Hard, isn't it? Let's try it again. You're doing very good. Well, Matt, I declare, you've done quite a good job today.

Matt: *(Sweetly)* Thank you. *(Super response)*

Cline: Very good! That was a very good thank you! In fact, that was a fantastic thank you! . . . What are you supposed to say?

Matt: What you said.

Cline: No, no, no. When I say something nice about you, whenever anyone says anything nice about you, what are you supposed to say?

Matt: Thank you.

Cline: Very well done. Very well done. Do you want to go through life like that little baby who had to have things go his own way all the time, or whose folks were mad at him, or do you want to grow up?

Matt: Grow up.

Cline: *(Lovingly)* And part of growing up, Matt, is doing it other people's way. You got the picture? It's hard to do it other people's way, right? What are you going to do, Matt?

Matt: Do it their way.

Cline: Are you really? It will be kind of strange at first, won't it? You're not used to it, right? *(Hugging Matt)* Do you think you can do it?

Matt: Yes.

Cline: All right, there's some staff in the other room. I want you to go in there and I want you to tell them that from now on you're going to try to do it their way. That their way is the best way for you. Do you believe that or not?

Matt: I believe it.

Cline: How have you been acting?

Matt: Not doin' it their way.

Cline: Okay. You ready?

Matt: *(Softly and nicely)* Ready.

Cline: That was good. That was a really good "ready." That was fantastic!

Matt: Thank you!

Cline: Okay! Good! All right! Come on, let's go.

Matt's last "thank you" had taken me by surprise. As we walked out of the room, he surprised me again by reaching up and putting his hand in mine.

In the time between this session and his next consultation, Matt's cottage behavior was entirely different. He was helpful and relatively compliant, and he was much better able to control himself around others.

Following is a portion of the transcript from the short follow-up session in which Matt laughed and played with me. One of the major risks of intrusive techniques is that children will relapse and begin to feel invaded, intimidated, or angry at the therapist. This is usually entirely mitigated if several fun follow-up sessions occur. Only after a session like this one are unattached children ready to work on their feelings and behavior and benefit from the usual techniques.

At the beginning of this session, Matt was a little whiny. This was easily overcome with a little playful intrusiveness, leaving Matt feeling good about himself, the therapist, and the relationship.

Matt returned to his foster home after six more months in residential treatment.

Cline: Like you mean it! Curl your nose up and say it with some meaning!

Matt: I am.

Cline: Well, if I say you're not saying it with enough meaning, what are you doing?

Matt: Not saying it.

Cline: Right. Okay, say, "I hate being bossed around."

Matt: I hate being bossed around.

Cline: Again, come on, Matt, I want to hear it loud from you. If I don't hear it loud, I'm just going to tickle you. Just really say it loud. Okay, go . . . come on.

Matt: I forgot what you said.

Cline: I hate being bossed around.

Matt: I hate being bossed around.

Cline: Really loud. That was good. Say it again like that.

Matt: I hate being bossed around.

Cline: Come on, get into it.

Matt: I am.

Cline: More than that. I want you to get into it a little bit more than that. I want you to say it like you really mean it. I want you to get mad. Say it again to me. Say, "I hate being bossed around," really loud.

Matt: I hate being bossed around!

Cline: Oh, you tell me when you're ready. *(Tickling)*

Matt: *(Laughing)* I'm ready.

Cline: Oh, now I don't believe you.

Matt: *(Continuing to laugh)* I'm ready.

Cline: Are you? All right then, I better hear it a lot louder.

Matt: I hate being bossed around!

Cline: Well, good. It's really a shame that the little old spider had to come along and start giving you some tickles to get you to say it good and loud. Isn't that a shame?

Matt: *(Giggling)* Yes.

Cline: Wasn't that a bummer. *(Matt is still giggling.)* You should have said things loud in the beginning, right?

Matt: Yes.

Cline: Yes!? What are you supposed to say?

Matt: Right!

Cline: Right!

Matt: Right!

Cline: That's what I want from you. I like the laugh, and I like the smile, and I like you doin' it my way, right? Then you and all people will get along fine. 'Cause you're just a little squirt, and you're going to have to learn to do it everyone else's way. So you can learn to be a really good big squirt, right?

Matt: *(In typical resistance tone and cadence)* Um-hmm.

Cline: Sure! That's the way it is, pal. How'd you feel about coming up here today? Scared?

Matt: No.

Cline: Mad about it?

Matt: Mad about it.

Cline: Were you so mad about it you didn't enjoy the trees?

Matt: Yeah.

Cline: Were you so mad about it you didn't enjoy the sunshine?

Matt: *(Laughing)* I enjoyed the sunshine.

Cline: Were you so mad you didn't enjoy the clouds?

Matt: *(Laughing)* I enjoyed everything!

Cline: Are you sure?

Matt: Yeah, I'm sure.

Cline: Well, that's good. You always want to enjoy everything, right?

Matt: Yeah.

Cline: Right?

Matt: Right.

Cline: Got it?

Matt: Got it.

Cline: For sure . . . I want to hear the "for sure," too.

Matt: For sure!

Cline: Right?

Matt: Right.

Cline: Got it?

Matt: Got it.

Cline: For sure.

Matt: For sure.

Cline: That's my pal.

Eddie: A Thirteen-Year-Old Who Wouldn't Talk

This transcript is included as an example of light and fun confrontation that can be so effective with pre-teens and sometimes with teenagers. These kids can sometimes relate easily with a little cajoling and light, playful touch. Such playfulness often changes pouting, withdrawn children into laughing children who then can begin to look at their issues more realistically and begin to work on them.

This session with Eddie echoes my previous assertions that therapists must use the *least intrusive methods possible*. Eddie was not an unattached child, but he was a major behavior problem at home and school. In seventh grade, he acted out angrily at school and cursed at teachers. He was brought unwillingly to therapy by his parents, and distrusted adults and did not want to relate to them. At the beginning of the session, Eddie simply sat there in silence, with his coat on and his arms folded.

I recognized that Eddie was refusing to converse with me, and so decided to use the tape recorder for a "man in the street" interview routine. The goal was to help Eddie go from silence to monosyllables to reciprocal and responsive relating. The transcript starts where Eddie is beginning to talk.

Cline: Oh, I know! *(Picking up recorder)* Let's have a man in the street . . . *(Mock reporter voice)* This is a man in the street interview with . . .

Eddie: Me.

Cline: And me. You're going to school right now. Are you one of those people who hate school or loves it?

Eddie: Hate.

Cline: Hate. Do you hate with a deep felt passion or with slight hate?

Eddie: Deep.

Cline: Deep hate. Tell me, when people hate with passion in school, what is it they hate about school? Is it because it's a bore? Or is it because of the kids? Or is it because of teachers or . . . why is such a deep hate present in so many of today's American students?

Eddie: None of your business, you bum.

Cline: There, now that's a typical example of a junior high attitude that probably has something to do with the reason you hate school. Would that be correct, average junior high student?

Eddie: Scat.

Cline: "Scat," like "s-c-a-t," like that type of scat?

Eddie: Um-hmm. Scram.

Cline: Like "scram"? I think your attitude is just . . . absolutely irrepressibly horrible! *(Eddie starts to giggle.)* How does the average teacher put up with a kid like you? I mean, what does the average teacher do with a kid like you?

Eddie: *(Continuing to giggle)* They don't put up with us.

Cline: *(Enthusiastically)* They don't put up with you? Well, what do they do?

Eddie: They go sit in the corner and cry.

Cline: Really! You mean you make life that miserable for your junior high teachers. That unhappy! You mean, when they see you coming into the room they have a big smile on their faces and do they say, "Oh, good, that ol' Eddie is walking in," or do they not say it?

Eddie: They don't.

Cline: They don't say it!

Eddie: They just say, "Eddie, sit down."

Cline: *(Teasing)* Do you have a feeling that your teachers love you, care about you from the pits of their hearts or they don't, or what do you think the average teacher thinks about the average student with a lousy attitude?

Eddie: They hate 'em.

Cline: *(Shocked)* Hate 'em? But, do these teachers who hate kids like teaching or do they dislike teaching?

Eddie: *(Taken aback)* I don't know.

Cline: Well, they probably like teaching. But would you say

that the fact that this teacher hates you has to do with the way he is as a teacher, or does it have to do with the way you are as the average American junior high student in this day and age in present, modern-day America?

Eddie: *(Confused)* What?

Cline: Is it because of you or is it because of them that there is trouble in school?

Eddie: Both.

Cline: *(Interested and curious)* Both? How is it their problem? Tell me so that maybe we could use this tape in the future to help teachers know how to relate to miserable students, students who give them a hard time, students who don't do their work. What should the teacher do? I mean, in your opinion, what do teachers do that makes life more miserable for you and them?

Eddie: They teach.

Cline: What do they do that makes life better for you and for them?

Eddie: They get sick and they don't teach.

Cline: Well now, those sound like two very unhappy possibilities—either they're making you sick and teaching or they're getting sick and not teaching. Are there any other alternatives that you see at this particular point in time?

Eddie: *(Belches)* Excuse me.

Up to this point, Eddie had been giving brief, fairly negative responses, and generally appeared passive-resistant. After this, I used his belch therapeutically, and the tenor of the conversation changed, allowing Eddie to be more open and responsive. We began a generally enjoyable interaction. I took what I could get and ran with it!

Cline: Did you . . . did you just put the grossity of belching on tape?

Eddie: *(Laughing)* Yup!

Cline: You can apologize greatly for that. You can say, "My god, I apologize greatly!" I'm waiting for an apology for belching on the tape!

Eddie: *Laughing)* I apologize that I didn't belch on your lousy . . .

Cline: *(Interrupting loudly with mock indignity)* Oh, you better apologize for belching on this tape. You apologize for belching on this tape! Say, "I apologize deeply, deeply." I'm waiting for a deep apology from you, a deep apology. Do you apologize that you belched on this tape? Yes! *(Touching Eddie for the first time, shaking him lightly)*

Eddie: *(Continuing to laugh)* Uh-uh. *(Belches again)*

Cline: *(Mock rage)* You don't apologize for belching? *(Poking at Eddie)* You don't? You know what I do with kids who don't apologize? I take them apart piece by piece. I tear them apart in their ribs. *(Tickling)* I tear them apart in their arms. *(Poking lightly in Eddie's armpit)* And I tear them apart in their knees. *(Poking lightly around his knees, and then pulling Eddie down to the floor)* I pull them apart all over their bodies until they say, "I greatly apologize for belching on the tape." *(Eddie continues to laugh loudly.)* It's rude. It's crude. It sounds just terrible. Terrible. Terrible!

Eddie: Hold it—we'll compromise. Bring the mike over here.

Cline: *(Giving the recorder to Eddie)* Okay, we'll compromise.

Eddie: I apologize shallow . . . Oh, what's that word? *(Looking questioningly at Cline)*

Cline: Yeah, "shallowly."

Eddie: Shallowly for belching on your tape. *(Whispering)* I lied.

Cline: *(Grabbing the recorder)* You gave a shallow apology? *(Laughing)* A shallow apology just won't make it. Do you know what "shallowly" means? It means like algae covering the pond . . . not going to the bottom. It means like the fungus floating on top.

Eddie: *(Practically hugging Cline)* That's the way I feel about you sometimes!

Cline: *(Mock menacingly)* You feel . . .

Eddie: *(Enticingly, loving the touch)* I better take off my coat here.

Cline: You feel fungus about me? Is that what you said? Is that what I heard from you?

Eddie: *(Laughing)* Yes.

Cline: Do you know what I do? Do you know what I do with little toadstools like you?

Eddie: *(Interrupting, laughing)* Oh, geez . . .

At this point in our nonsense we accidentally knocked into the recorder and turned it off. The fun interaction was used as a nucleus around which deeper issues were explored. Following this beginning, Eddie was able to talk about his feelings about teachers, parents, and school in a reasonable, accurate, and two-thirds-thoughtful manner.

Christy: Intrusive Therapy to Motivate a Fourteen-Year-Old

Christy had a history of abuse and neglect. Early in life, she had been in and out of a number of homes, including her birth mother's, relatives', and friends'. Her birth mother was reportedly an alcoholic and a prostitute (Christy was probably sexually abused by her mother's boyfriends), and parental rights were terminated when Christy was seven. At that time, she was adopted by a loving couple, who found her to be an extremely difficult child.

In her adoptive home, Christy was generally defiant and sexually provocative with the other children. She was brought to Evergreen for treatment, but shortly after being placed in a therapeutic foster home, she ran away.

The following transcript is from a videotape of my first session with Christy. The goals of the session were to help Christy admit to some conflict around her running away and sexually provocative behavior, and to get treatment contract. Christy had never before made contract for productive work. She denied, repressed, and rationalized her feelings, maintaining that "I am the way I am; that's the way I am, and I don't care." The intense push that I gave her in this session, followed by support and affection, helped her bond and make contract.

Christy's birth mother, Cynthia, traveled from military base to military base and reportedly had a number of children fathered by different men. When I went to get Christy for this session, she was in an angry, sullen pout since she had just been brought back by police after a runaway attempt. Christy's chart noted an earlier remark to her therapist that "if I grow up like my mother, I don't care." This statement was unprovoked, and so I knew she must have had strong feelings about that issue. I decided to attempt to reach her by calling her by her mother's name. This shocked her into a response. The transcript begins as I walk into the treatment room with Christy.

Cline:	I'm Dr. Cline, and you're Cynthia, right?
Christy:	Cynthia?
Cline:	Cynthia, right? Isn't that right?
Christy:	Christy. *(Softly)* I act like Cynthia.
Cline:	Do you have ringworm?
Christy:	No.
Cline:	Are you going to be pregnant at seventeen?
Christy:	No, I'm not going to be pregnant at seventeen.
Cline:	Why don't you think you're going to be pregnant at seventeen? Do you like kids to throw balls at your rear when you're bending over?
Christy:	No, I didn't like it.
Cline:	You have your hands over boys from eleven to fifteen . . . Cynthia, where are you going with your life? Do you know what I think? About twenty years from now, you'll have a kid in some therapy place, somewhere, crying. That's what I think, Cynthia. I think

you'll go from Air Force base to Air Force base and will be pregnant by somebody you don't even know and you'll have a screwed up little kid who will want to act just like you. Cynthia, that's what I think. You'll have a little kid who has so little happiness in her life that she has to feed ants by putting sugar around the outside of the fence. And you'll be so unloving, Cynthia, that you're not going anywhere in life, Cynthia, and you won't be anything! And you'll raise a little kid who will grow up to be the same way. And do you know what, Cynthia? Your little kid will have one of the best therapists around, and your little kid will say, "I don't want to work, I just want to feed the ants. And I want to fondle boys. And I want to grow up just like you, so I can have a kid like me." *(Pause)* Look at me. You are Cynthia. *(Caringly but sad)* You are Cynthia. You don't have to work at it, Christy, you are already there. *(Christy is crying.)* What are you crying about? I thought you wanted to be Cynthia.

Christy: *(Continuing to sob)* I don't want to be Cynthia.

Cline: *(Moving closer and looking directly into Christy's eyes)* I say you do want to be Cynthia.

Christy: *(In a pleading whine)* I say I don't.

Cline: Look at me and say it like you mean it. Say, I don't want to be Cyn . . .

Christy: *(Interrupting, shouting)* I don't want to be Cynthia!

Cline: *(Shouting)* You better scream it at me!

Christy: *(Shouting at the top of her voice)* I don't want to be Cynthia!

Cline: You better scream it to me.

Christy: I don't want to be Cynthia. *(Breaking down and sobbing deeply)*

Cline: Is that true?

Christy: *(Continuing to sob)* Yes.

Cline: *(Kindly touching Christy)* Are you Cynthia?

Christy: Yes, but I don't want to be her . . . when I ran away on Friday I knew I was going to be just like her because it was what she did. *(Sobbing)* That's why I wanted to turn back, but Karen didn't want to. *(Continuing to sob)* I hate Cynthia!

I had to be sure not to let Christy lead me into talking about issues around running away with Karen or Karen's lack of responsibility. I had to help Christy look at her feelings about her mother, her sense of loss, and her own irresponsible behavior. The important issue is Christy's feelings, not her projective blame of others—at which most disturbed children are experts!

Cline: Let me know louder.
Christy: *(Screaming) I hate Cynthia!*
Cline: Scream it—you love being Cynthia.
Christy: I hate Cynthia!
Cline: Because she lives inside your heart.
Christy: *(Continuing to scream during this interaction)* I hate Cynthia!
Cline: Because she lives inside your heart.
Christy: I hate Cynthia!
Cline: Because she lives everywhere around you.
Christy: I hate Cynthia! *(Deep sobbing)*
Cline: *(With kindness)* It's tough to change, isn't it.
Christy: Yes.
Cline: *(With great caring)* You are mostly Cynthia, aren't you?
Christy: Yes.
Cline: *Christy* almost sounds like *Cynthia.* How much of you is Christy and how much of you is Cynthia?
Christy: *(Sobbing)* About ninety percent Cynthia and ten percent Christy. There is only ten percent me.
Cline: Well, there are a couple of things that you might have going for you. How well did Cynthia do in school?
Christy: Not very good.

Cline: And what was her music like? How did she light up people with her music? How did she light up their lives with music?

Christy: By not handling it very good.

Cline: Was she musical?

Christy: Yeah.

Cline: *(Surprised and doubtful)* Was she as good as you?

Christy: No!

Cline: Are you better?

Christy: No.

Cline: Are you better than Cynthia?

Christy: Probably the same.

Cline: But you do better in school?

Christy: *(Crying)* My grades, probably. But I don't know about everything else.

Cline: Do you think you're smarter?

Christy: Yeah. In math and stuff like that. But not in everything else.

Cline: Well, you have three things going for you, then. *(Raising voice, pushing for eye contact with Christy, who has been sniffling in her handkerchief)* Are you listening to me!?

Christy: Yes.

Cline: What are the three things you have going for you? *(Christy just sits and sobs.)* I want to know the three things that you have going for you that make you different . . . what's the ten percent you . . . that's not Cynthia, Christy?

Christy: *(Sobbing)* I have a good therapist.

Cline: *(Laughing)* Right. That's one good thing. Right, sweetheart, you have a good therapist. What else.

Christy: I have good parents. *(Referring to her adoptive parents)*

Cline: You have good parents, right.

Christy: And I have a good home. *(Referring to her therapeutic home)*

Cline: You know what else you have? This is the most important thing of all. Do you know what else you have?

Christy: What?

Cline: *(Softly)* You care. That is your hope—that you care. *(Christy continues to sob.)* And when do you think you're going to be ready to work?

Christy: I don't know.

Cline: *(Mockingly)* Oh, why don't you take your time. Why don't you wait till you're seventeen and you have your first baby. To grow up sick and acting like you act. Maybe you want to wait until you're seventeen and have your first pregnancy. Maybe you'll have your first pregnancy before you're seventeen. When do you want to start working? I'm serious.

Christy: As soon as I can.

Cline: Louder than that.

Christy: *(Screaming)* As soon as I can!

Cline: *(Shouting)* Is that true or is that bullshit?

Christy: *(Shouting)* It's true!

Cline: Well, whom do you need to tell that to?

Christy: Mike. *(Her therapist)*

Cline: Well, I'll see if I can round him up! You better decide whether you're Cynthia or Christy because you don't have much time. Do you have the picture?

Christy: *(Continuing to sob)* Yes.

Cline: *(Hugging Christy and speaking softly)* Is that really true? Am I telling it to you true?

Christy: *(Softly)* Yes, that's true.

Cline: *(Going to get Mike)* I'll see if I can round him up. *(The door opens and closes. Christy sits and sobs.)*

As Christy's consulting psychiatrist, I saw her about once a month. She made excellent progress, with ups and downs, and about six months after our first session, I decided to check Christy's memory and feelings about that session.

Cline: How did you say things are going for you right now?

Christy: Really good.

Cline: And why are they going really good?

Christy: 'Cause I've been doing my chores right and I've been giving good answers—"yes, Mom; yes, Dad" and stuff like that.

Cline: Um-hmm. And how do you feel about yourself these days?

Christy: Really good.

Cline: Are you feeling really good? Great. You know I remember one time I saw you after you had just run away. Do you remember that?

Christy: Yah.

Cline: You're laughing. What are you laughing about?

Christy: It was stupid.

Cline: What was stupid?

Christy: Running away.

Cline: I thought you thought seeing me was stupid.

Christy: No.

Cline: What *did* you think? Didn't I give you a really hard time that day? Didn't I say that you were ending up like your mom, or something like that?

Christy: Yah.

Cline: How much do you remember of that session?

Christy: Well, I remember that you said that I was ending up like my mom and then I got really mad 'cause you were saying that, and then you started calling me Cynthia.

Cline: How were you feeling when I was calling you Cynthia?

Christy: I was pissed off, man.

Cline: Have you been pissed off very much in this program? I mean, is this program good at pissing you off at times?

Christy: Yah.

Cline: How has that pissing you off affected you?

Christy: To get stronger.
Cline: Really. Like in what ways?
Christy: Well, it makes me learn to deal with those problems that piss me off.
Cline: So, are you saying you cope with anger and so forth better and better?
Christy: Yes.

Tina: Confrontive Techniques with an Eleven-Year-Old

I saw Tina several times in consultation at a Denver institution. The consultations were requested by her therapists in the hopes that I could "mobilize her anger." The cottage staff and I reviewed the problem. Tina had suffered a great deal of early abuse and neglect. She had zipped unsuccessfully through a number of foster homes and two adoptive placements. After more than six months in residential care, she was making very little progress. None of the children really liked Tina, for problems seemed to follow her like the dust cloud that follows the character Pigpen in the comic strip *Peanuts*. Wherever there was an uproar, there would be Tina, standing in the middle of it but apparently not overtly participating in it. One of the staff related, however, "You just know that somehow she precipitates things. You just don't know how she does it."

To adults, Tina was a dream—to their faces. With blond pigtails and freshly scrubbed appearance, she acted as if nothing troubled her at all. However, she never had anything nice to say about anyone behind their backs. She was extremely manipulative, setting kids against staff, staff against kids, and even staff against staff.

In six months of weekly therapy, Tina had always been superficially pleasant. Her therapist noted, "At times I catch glimmers of something nasty in her eyes. But it's so transient. When I ask about it, she pulls away. She has no problems she wants to talk about. She skirts issues that took place in her adoptive home." These issues included instigating sex play with other children and the death of a puppy under mysterious circumstances.

A few nights before I met Tina, the cottage had two workers

scheduled on, instead of the usual one: Bill—a large African American, and a real teddy bear of a man who was loved by most of the children—the regular worker, and Jim. As the children were all in bed, Bill walked past each door to wish them good night, opening with, "Okay kids, time to quiet down."

Bill said this to Tina and her young roommate, and then continued down the hall. Unbenownst to the two children, Jim was following seconds behind Bill. As Jim passed Tina's room, he heard her hiss in a guttural voice, "No fuckin' nigger can tell me what to do!" Jim was shocked. "I never heard anything said with that much hate." He reported the incident in team meeting, and the team agreed to call me on a consultation.

Tina came to the consultation friendly and vaguely nonresponsive, as she usually was. She was all blue eyes, blond hair, and freckles, and had a slight air of "victim."

At the beginning of the transcript, Tina was operating in her usual "interview mode." She appeared thoughtful, slightly blaming, slightly apprehensive, and superficially responsive. This attitude causes many such children to be diagnosed as depressed, and often their therapists go to work to "help them feel better about themselves." This involves the type of therapy Tina had received for so long: gentle, talk-it-out therapy, with the professional trying to build a trusting relationship. At best, though, only a shallow relationship is built because the professionals allow the children to give shallow responses. Frightened of their own emotions, these children unconsciously think, "They wouldn't like me if they *really* knew me!" Thus, the professionals never get to the root cause of the problem.

As the transcript opens, Tina had just finished repeating with her counselor some of the reasons that she was having this consultation with me, the most important being to get her anger out.

> Cline: All right . . . How did you feel about coming down here today?
> Tina: I didn't want to come.

Cline: Why?

Tina: I was pretty scared and nervous.

Cline: Why?

Tina: Well, I get scared when we have like systematics or consultations.

Cline: Do you get scared when somebody you don't know is going to talk to you?

Tina: Uh-huh.

Cline: Why do you think that is, Tina? I mean, is there something going on inside your head that you have to worry about, that people will know or find out or talk about? Why do you get scared? Why don't you say, "Oh good, I get to meet a new person?"

Tina: 'Cause I have more problems.

Cline: What? I mean what do you see as your problems? What do you *really* see as your problems?

Tina: Whaddaya mean?

Cline: Well, what scares you? What do you really see as your problems?

Tina: Well, I haven't told people my feelings before and then I got all those stirred up.

Cline: I know you don't. I don't think you tell people your feelings very much. I'm suspicious of you. I like you. It doesn't have anything to do with not liking you. But I'm suspicious. You want to know what my suspicions about you are? I mean if you were suspicious about me, I'd certainly want to know about it, right?

Tina: Yeah.

Cline: The suspicions I have about you are that you act like a very nice little girl on the outside and you have a lot of anger on the inside. And every so often, when you think it's really safe, you let it out. What do you do when the other little kids are around you?

Tina: I blow up. I argue with them and stuff like that.

Cline: Yeah. Well, then what do you do with the adults? Do you blow up and argue with the adults?

Tina: No.

Cline: But I wonder what kind of thoughts you have about the adults when you're not blowing up with them. What kinds of things you think in your head but you don't say. That's what I wonder about with you, Tina. Do you want to tell me about that?

Tina: To tell what thoughts that I think about adults?

Cline: Yeah.

Tina: When I'm not blowing up?

Cline: Yeah. What do you really think about adults? You know, what's really going on inside you?

Tina: In some ways I think they're nice and some ways I don't.

Cline: What ways don't you?

Tina: When they tell me to do something and I don't want to do it.

Cline: When they tell you to do something and you don't want to do it makes you mad? Do you think you trust adults, or you don't trust them, in general?

Tina: I think that I don't trust them.

Cline: You think that you don't trust them. Good. I would agree with that. Why do you think that is? Why do you think you don't trust adults? *(Pushing her for the first time)* Now, that should not be a very hard answer for you to come up with. Why do you think someone with your history wouldn't trust adults?

Tina: I can't answer that question.

What follows is an amazing example of denial. No wonder this child was making no progress—in her head, she was still living at home. If this type of denial were allowed to continue, real splitting and even multiple personalities could result.

Cline: You can't? Who gave you away?

Tina: My mother.

Cline: Then who gave you away?

Tina: Nobody.

Cline: Really? Didn't you live with the Smiths for a while?

Tina: Yes.

Cline: What happened there?

Tina: The judge had them send me back to my mother.

Cline: And then what happened?

Tina: The judge took me back and gave me to the Smiths.

Cline: And then what happened?

Tina: Then the Smiths kept me.

Cline: And then what happened?

Tina: *(Starting to lose composure, becoming hard to understand)* And I been living with them.

Cline: And then what happened? Are you living with the Smiths at this minute?

Tina: No.

Cline: Then what happened?

Tina: I came to the children's home.

Cline: Why?

Tina: To work on my problems?

This answer is really no answer, but therapists let children get away with it.

Cline: Why? What's happening at the Smiths', Tina?

Tina: I had problems.

Cline: I know. But what, Tina? What was happening at the Smiths'? What were the problems?

Tina: *(Quavering voice)* I didn't tell them my feelings.

Cline: What were you doing?

Tina: I was doing bad things. *(Starting to sob)*

Cline: Like what?

Tina: Stealing things, lying . . .

Cline: These are people you love and care about, right?

Tina: Right.

Cline: Do you really love them or do you not really love them?

Tina: In some ways they don't when they treat me nice.

Cline: So some ways you do . . . you don't when they treat you nice?

Tina: When they're nice to me I like them.

Cline: What does "being nice" mean to you?

Tina: When they do nice things for me.

Cline: What does being . . . well, when they are not nice, what does that mean?

Tina: When they tell me to do things that I don't want to do.

Cline: Right, and they treat you like a kid. When they treat you right they want you to do something and that makes you mad, right? Do you have to be in control? I mean, do you think you always have to be in control?

Tina: Not all the time.

Cline: Do you know what's making you mad? How do you feel about me right now?

Tina: I didn't want to talk to you! *(Strongest and straightest statement so far, but still not a feeling)*

Cline: How do you think about me this minute?

Tina: Mad! *(First feeling, obliquely directed—she did not say "Mad at you!")*

Cline: Do you really?

Tina: Yes.

Cline: Tell me how mad you feel. I want to see what you do when you get mad. If you're mad, tell me how mad you are.

Tina: I'm mad because I had to talk to you. *(Crying)*

Cline: Well, how do you feel about it?

Tina: I don't like you! *(First real emotion directed to me. It is still oblique—this is how she doesn't feel—but it was said with good congruent emphasis.)*

Cline: Good! Just say it like you really mean it, Tina.

Tina: I don't like you!

A little pushy encouragement can go a long way. Tina was now matching my cadence and relinquishing all control of the conversation.

Cline: Good! That's what I mean. Do you have a lot of hate in your heart right now toward me?

Tina: Yes.

Cline: Well then, tell me about it, Tina.

Tina: I don't like you . . . the way you talk to me.

Cline: Say, "I don't like the way you talk" really loud. Snarl when you say it. Pucker up your nose.

Tina: I don't like the way you talk to me.

Cline: Scream it!

Tina: *(Screaming)* I don't like the way you talk to me!

Cline: Why don't you keep saying it until you get it out of your soul. Keep going.

Tina: *(Screaming)* I don't like the way you talk to me!

Cline: Good! Say it again.

Tina: *(Good rage)* I don't like the way you talk to me!

Cline: Good, again.

Tina: *(Screaming)* I don't like the way you talk to me!

Cline: Good, again.

Tina: I don't like the way you talk to me!

Cline: And any time an adult makes you do things their way, how do you feel about it?

Tina: Mad!

Cline: Do you? Tell me about it. Say, "I hate doing other people's ways."

Tina: I hate doing other people's ways!

Cline: Come on, say it loud!

Tina: *(Screaming)* I hate doing other people's ways!

Cline: Good! Say it again.

Tina: I hate doing other people's ways!

Cline: Good. Again, Tina.

Tina: *(Screaming)* I hate doing other people's ways!

Cline: Do you? But what you do is you do it anyway and you just think nasty thoughts in your mind, right?

Tina: Right!

Cline: Is that what you do?

Tina: Yes!

Cline: Tell me what you do when you do that.

Tina: I do it anyway, but I think, I won't do it again!

Cline: Now, what do you think in your mind? Do you think, "You bitch, you bastard," or something like that?

Tina: Yes!

Cline: Tell me what you think in your head.

Tina: They can go to hell!

This answer took me by surprise. It was probably valid—it certainly wasn't something that was in my head.

Cline: Good. Say it again.

Tina: *(Screaming)* They can go to hell! *(The most rageful statement yet)*

Cline: Say it again.

Tina: *(Screaming)* They can go to hell!

Cline: That's what's going on inside your heart when you're doin' it somebody else's way.

Tina: Yes!

Cline: And when they tell you in the cottage to do things, what are you thinkin' in your heart, Tina?

Tina: They can go to hell.

Cline: *(First softness and acceptance, showing love that Tina is honest)* That's what's in your heart—a lot of that anger, right?

Tina: Right!

Cline: Look at me and just scream.

Tina: *Right!*

Cline: Good. Again.

Tina: *Right!*

Cline: Good. There's a lot of mad in there, isn't there?

Tina: Yes!

Cline: I know, and all the time you're going around acting like a really good little girl, and inside you're thinking what?

Tina: I'm mad.

Cline: They can go to what?

Tina: Hell!
Cline: Do you think it would help very much?
Tina: No. *(Said like a question—indicating her ambivalence about the answer)*
Cline: Really?
Tina: Really.
Cline: I'm not sure I believe you. I mean, you might be telling me the truth. But are you an expert liar?
Tina: Sometimes.
Cline: So do you think I believe you right now?
Tina: No.
Cline: But you might be telling me the truth, right?
Tina: Right.
Cline: So, if you are telling me the truth and I don't believe you, whose problem is that?
Tina: Mine.
Cline: No! If you're telling me the truth and I don't believe you, then whose problem is it?
Tina: Yours.
Cline: Right. But if you're not telling me the truth and I don't believe you, who's problem is it?
Tina: Mine.

The preceding exchange is standard procedure for handling probable or possible lying when the facts are not clear.

Cline: Right. *(Pause)* I know kids like you often think about hell and stuff like that, and the devil and stuff like that. Maybe you don't. *(Pause)* But what do you think I think?
Tina: About how they act outside and inside.
Cline: Um-hmm. *(Pause)* How do you think you are inside?
Tina: Mad.
Cline: A lot?
Tina: Anger.
Cline: Are you? A lot of the time?
Tina: Yes.

Cline: All the time, aren't you? You know it would really be a help to you to get all that anger out. Now do you feel mad at me that I see all the anger inside? Does that make you mad or do you think, "Yeah, it's there."

Tina: I *know* it's there!

Cline: What are you going to do about it?

Tina: Work on it with Ms. Davis.

Cline: You're working on it today?

Tina: Yes.

Cline: *(With an accepting smile)* Really hard, right?

Tina: Right.

Cline: See, because that anger causes you to be a very sneaky person. Ve-e-e-ry sneaky. Caused Mike to be very sneaky, too. Caused you and Mike to be sneaky. Do you think you and Mike were sneaky?

Tina: Yes.

Cline: Did you do sneaky things?

Tina: *(Louder)* Yes.

Cline: And things that you felt bad about later on? Or did you not feel bad about them?

Tina: I did feel bad about 'em.

Cline: Did you? Is Mike a sneaky person?

Tina: Yes.

Cline: And are you a sneaky person?

Tina: Yes.

Cline: Ve-e-e-ry sneaky. And when you're sitting around with a bunch of other kids, who's kind of encouraging them to act out?

Tina: Me.

Cline: Yeah. How do you do it?

Tina: Play games.

Cline: How?

Tina: With my fingers.

Cline: Show me.

Tina: Like, I get really mad and I stop them. And they get really mad.

Cline: Yeah. Show me the games you play with your fingers to stir 'em up.

Tina: Well, like I will say, "Look at the flowers" and I point at 'em. *(Points with middle finger—darned if she isn't giving the other kids the finger when she is pointing at things. No wonder the cottage staff had trouble catching her!)*

Cline: So you tell the other kids how to act out?

Tina: *(Pause)* What do you mean?

Cline: Do you encourage the other kids to get into trouble?

Tina: Yes.

Cline: Say, "I made them act out," and say it loud.

Tina: *(Loudly)* I made them act out!

Cline: Say it again!

Tina: *(Shouting)* I made them act out!

Cline: And it's because of the anger in me! Say that again.

Tina: Because of the anger in me!

Cline: Say it again!

Tina: Because of the anger in me!

Cline: Say it again!

Tina: *(Screaming)* Because of the anger in me!

Cline: There's a lot in there, isn't there, Tina?

Tina: *Yes!*

Cline: *(Moving close and giving Tina a hug—she is stiff.)* Well, I know there is. It's a bummer, isn't it? And you know what? You don't take comfort very well from someone else, do you?

Tina: No!

Cline: Makes you mad, doesn't it?

Tina: Yes.

Cline: You hate getting loved, don't you?

Tina: Sometimes.

Cline: Right now, do you hate it?

Tina: Yes!

Cline: I know. You don't like it from me, do you?

Tina: Right.

Cline: Why do you think that is?

Tina: *(Accusingly)* The way you talk to me.

Cline: Yeah. How do I talk to you?

Tina: Mad.

Cline: Do I talk mad?

Tina: It sounds like it!

Cline: Who has the mad inside?

Tina: Me!

Cline: Do you know why I got mad at you?

Tina: Because you're trying to get all the anger out of me.

Cline: Yeah, right. Because if I said . . . Let me tell you what would happen if I were a nice guy. I'd say, "Well, hi, Tina. How are you today?" Answer like you would.

Tina: *(Immediate return to a sweet, conversational voice)* Fine.

Cline: How do you like it here?

Tina: I don't like it.

Cline: Mmmmm. What things don't you like?

Tina: *(Immediate return to victim role)* The way they treat us here and the way they tell us to do things.

Cline: Oh, did they tell you to do things that you think aren't fair?

Tina: Yes.

Cline: *(Pushing)* Now, would that ever get at your anger?

Tina: Probably not.

Cline: Would it? Would it? Yes or no!

Tina: No!

Cline: Say, "No, it wouldn't get at my anger." Say it louder.

Tina: *(Louder)* No, it wouldn't get at my anger!

Cline: Say it again.

Tina: *(Screaming)* No, that wouldn't get at my anger!

Cline: Say it again.

Tina: *(Screaming)* No, that wouldn't get at my anger!

Cline: No, you'd just sit there and be really sweet, right? And inside you'd have all that anger, right?

Tina: Right.

Cline: So who's way are we going to do it?

Tina: Your's.

Cline: Right. Say, "Thank God, we're going to do things your way."

Tina: Thank God, we're going to do things your way.

Cline: You betcha. *(Pause)* It makes you mad, though, doesn't it?

Tina: Yes!

Cline: Good! I'd rather you be mad and show it than sit there and think things like "dirty nigger" and all the other stuff you think, and then have it come out months later. And that man never knew how much anger you had inside of you, probably. Did he or did he not?

Tina: No, probably not.

Cline: And when he was around there, did you think "dirty nigger" a number of times about him?

Tina: Yes.

Cline: Did you ever say it?

Tina: No.

Cline: You just kept it inside, right?

Tina: Right.

Cline: Eating away at you, right?

Tina: Right.

Cline: This thing is very bad for you, that kind of anger. It's not going to hurt him any, not a bit. And if you're mad at the adults around here and me and all the other things, who's it hurting?

Tina: Me.

Cline: You better believe it. 'Cause I'm going to walk out of this door and I'm not going to be hurt by your anger, right?

Tina: Right.

Cline: Who's going to be hurt by it?

Tina: Me.

Cline: You betcha. And sometimes people grow up with that much anger inside and they never get rid of it. Do you want to be that way or do you want to be different?

Tina: I want to be different.

Cline: Do you? Really?

Tina: Yes.

Cline: You've got some changes to make, then. 'Cause who was your foster family?

Tina: The Smiths.

Cline: Yeah, and they knew what was inside you, right? That's why they had you here, right?

Tina: Right.

Cline: How did they know that the anger was inside of you? What did you do around there?

Tina: Sneaky little things.

Cline: Louder.

Tina: Sneaky little things!

Cline: Again.

Tina: *(Easily going into rage)* Sneaky little things!

Cline: Right, like what? Name three things fast.

Tina: Sneakiness, lying, and taking things.

Cline: You stole, right?

Tina: Right.

Cline: I'm telling you this anger and stuff inside you is not your fault. It's nothing you have to feel guilty about, but you better work on it, because you've got lots in there. You did a really good job today. See how you try to hold it in?

Tina: *(Quietly)* Yes.

Cline: You see that?

Tina: Yes!

Cline: See how hard it is for you to take a little bit of loving?

Tina: Yes. *(Sobbing)*

Cline: It's a bummer for you. Cry. Just let it out. *(Tina continues to sob.)* It would do you good to be held and sob for a while, you know that? This is the only way of getting at it, you understand?

Tina: *(Sobbing)* Yes.

Cline: See, you have a lot of crying inside you, and you don't let it out, but you know what? When you were a little girl, your first mom didn't hold you like this. And you cried and cried, but you know how babies cry and sob? You didn't do a lot of that—you couldn't. It's not her fault, either. But you understand what I'm saying?

Tina: Yes.

Cline: Do you also see how hard it is for you? Do you feel how hard it is for you just to relax?

Tina: Yes.

Cline: You're not a very relaxed person. Do you know that you turn when you look at someone? *(Demonstrating—rigidly)* You say "hi." You turn your head. *(Looking at her sideways, with poor eye contact)* That's how rigid you are! That can all be changed if you want it to change. But if you sit there and say you want to change and you don't inside, and you think, "I'm fooling them!" who are you hurting?

Tina: Me.

Cline: You better believe it! 'Cause I know you. It would be very easy for you to sit and say, "I've got to do this and I've got to do that," and inside you're thinking "Bullshit!" Now am I right or am I wrong?

Tina: Right.

Cline: I know I'm right. You did a good job today.

Tina: Thank you.

Cline: You're welcome. Sometimes people like to see who was behind the mirror and sometimes people don't. What would you like?

Tina: To see who was there.

Cline: Okay. Why should I let you see who was behind there? Why would that be good for you?

Tina: To see who people are knowing my problems.

Cline: Why would it be bad for you to see who was behind the mirror?

Tina: 'Cause I'd say I didn't want them to know my problems!

Cline: Right. Then you'd know who to be honest around, and who to be dishonest with. And then you could manipulate people, if you know who was behind there. You'd know who knows what.

Tina: Right.

Cline: I don't think it is a good idea for you to know who knows what right now. I think it is a very good idea for you to be *one* kid, and when people ask you to do something, to start liking it instead of acting like you do on the outside and thinking "bastard" on the inside. Say, "I hate you for not showing me what's behind the mirror."

Tina: I hate you for showing me who's not behind the mirror!

Cline: Say it again.

Tina: I hate you not, you won't show me who's behind the mirror!

Cline: Good for you! Say it again.

Tina: *(The encouragement leads to correct and nonresistant grammar.)* I hate you because you won't show me who's behind the mirror!

Cline: Good! That's what you're feeling inside, isn't it?

Tina: Yes.

Cline: You're just beautiful when you show it. Do you understand why we are doing this?

Tina: Yes.

Cline: I think you do, and you're doing a really good job! I think you can grow up to be a really straight **person.** Okay, I'll have someone come back in and take you upstairs, or wherever your cottage is. How do you feel about me now?

Tina: Still mad! *(Asking for more, but we are out of time.)*

Cline: Good. So nice of you to say so! Say it again.

Tina: Still mad.

Cline: Good. Do you want to leave that way, or do you want to leave saying maybe I'll get over it?

Tina: Yes.

Cline: Well then, do it my way and say, "Maybe I'll get over it."

Tina: Maybe I'll get over it.

Cline: Say it with a smile.

Tina: *(Perfunctory smile)* Maybe I'll get over it.

Cline: With a sweeter smile.

Tina: *(Better smile)* Maybe I'll get over it.

Cline: Say, "Maybe I won't hate you forever."

Tina: Maybe I won't hate you forever.

Cline: "Maybe I won't even hate you for a couple of weeks."

Tina: Maybe I won't even hate you for a couple of weeks.

Cline: Who does it hurt when you have all that anger inside?

Tina: Me.

Cline: Say, "Maybe you're not so bad."

Tina: Maybe you're not so bad.

Cline: Okay, you'll have to decide what you want to believe, right sweetie?

Tina: Right.

Cline: Okay, good. Excellent! Okay, she's ready to go up.

Five months after this recording, Tina returned to her adoptive home, where she did well.

About six or seven years later, just before Tina was graduated with honors from high school, she and her mother had lunch with me. I was preparing to give a speech at a fund-raising banquet for the residential treatment center she had been in. I remembered the tape we had made of her session, and mentioned to Tina that the average American has no idea of the hate underlying the severe problems she had overcome, and can't comprehend why some kids need residential treatment. I asked her if I could play the tape at the banquet, and then if she would be willing to speak to the audience. A few days later, she called me and agreed wholeheartedly.

At the banquet, I spoke briefly and introduced the tape. Then Tina took the podium and told of her trials and her efforts to become whole. The audience gave her a standing ovation. One member of the audience was so impressed that he invited her to speak at a meeting of his Kiwanis club, and she was later named "Kiwanis Girl of the Year" for that chapter.

In 1990, fifteen years after we recorded the session, I spoke with Tina again. She was twenty-six and a thoughtful young person. She had continued in therapy, and had had some additional successful therapy when she was twenty-one. She is married and has children, and called her situation "as happy a life as I think most people live." Of her session with me and her time in the residential center she said, "I had a hard time, but I really found out why my anger was there. Sometimes I'm not sure kids can really understand why they are so angry."

Cindy: A Sixteen-Year-Old Unattached Child

Cindy was a typical sixteen-year-old with an attachment disorder. She was adopted at six months but never formed a loving, responsive, or reciprocal relationship with her parents. (An older sister, whom the couple adopted at birth, did well, and the parents demonstrated excellent parenting techniques, but they found Cindy to be uncontrollable.) At thirteen, Cindy was hospitalized for a year at a metropolitan psychiatric hospital, where her frequent rages caused her to be placed in restraints. After she was discharged from the hospital, Cindy had difficulty in school, toyed with substance abuse, was sexually active, and continued to reject any parental limits. After years of traditional therapy, her parents didn't know where to turn.

When I first saw Cindy, she had dropped out of high school, had had two abortions, and continued to show reactive and uncontrollable rage toward her parents. These rages were occasionally followed by periods of fleeting remorse and suicidal ideation.

After taking a history from her parents, I talked with Cindy. She admitted to having a great deal of rage and emptiness, but said, "I don't have any today." I explained to Cindy that I would treat her according to how she was acting, regardless of her chronological age, and she agreed that when she was in a rage, she acted as if she were two years old. I said that if she showed two-year-old rage, I would hold her in my lap. Her response was, "Well, that will be interesting." I considered her response to be good contract for the work we would need to do.

The second session was uneventful. Cindy was merely passing the time, and I dismissed her after only a few minutes, telling her that she was "bullshitting" herself and needed to get in touch with some deeper feelings. She left a little nonplussed, feeling angry and rejected.

On the morning of her third session, my secretary gave me a message from Cindy's mother: "This has been one hell of a week!!!" This was from a quiet, almost timid woman, and my secretary added, "She said to be sure to add the three exclamation points." When I called Cindy's mother, she related the events of the week, and told me that as a final straw, Cindy had stayed out all night. When the mother saw her in the kitchen making breakfast, she carefully asked, "Where were you?" Cindy responded by viciously hurling a canteloupe at her head. "I do believe that if I hadn't ducked, I could have been killed," her mother said.

Cindy's father brought her to the third session. I saw them sitting outside my office, Cindy in a definite angry pout with her arms folded. I said to her, "Well, you look happy today," and catching her father's eye, I asked how the trip to Evergreen was. He looked at me somewhat aghast, and simply gave me the thumbs-down sign. Cindy trounced into the office, refused to sit down, and yelled, "Well, if you wanted to see me fucking angry, I'm fucking angry now!"

I quickly grabbed Cindy and put her on my lap and held her. She exploded into a half-hour projective blaming rage, followed by sobbing, snuggling-in, and an admission that she had fouled up everyone's life, and most of all her own. I said, "It's great that you can launch into this insight with me, but who do you really need to work things out with?" She replied, "I know, my dad, but I don't know if he could handle this [her strong expression of rage]."

I brought Cindy's father in and had Cindy wait outside while I told him about the session, her need to go through the issues with him, and her belief that he wouldn't be able to handle her emotions. He gave a snort and responded, "Dr. Cline, what else do you think we've been dealing with for sixteen years?"

I called Cindy back into the room, and, following my instructions, her father went through fifteen minutes of solid rage with her, with magnificent eye contact. The following transcript is from this father-daughter session, and it begins with Cindy and I working together. She was sitting in my lap, and her father was watching the process.

Cline: How've you been acting this weekend? Like a what? How? You shouldn't even have to think about that, Cindy. You shouldn't even have to give it a thought. How've you been acting since Saturday when you stayed out all night? Like a what?

Cindy: Crazy.

Cline: Yeah. Say it louder. Say it louder, Cindy.

Cindy: Crazy.

Cline: Say, "I've been acting crazy." Put it in a sentence. Yeah, you're right, you have. Put it in a sentence. Go.

Cindy: *(Loudly)* I've been acting crazy.

Cline: Three times like that.

Cindy: I've been acting crazy.

Cline: Again, Cindy.

Cindy: I've been acting crazy. I've been acting crazy!

Cline: Yeah, and acting like you hate who?

Cindy: Everybody.

Cline: Say, "I hate everybody."

Cindy: I hate everybody.

Cline: Say it louder.

Cindy: I hate everybody!

Cline: And when you're telling me or you're telling anybody what you feel or how you're going to act . . . How do you feel toward me right now?

Cindy: *(Loudly)* I hate you!

Cline: You do. Say it louder to me.

Cindy: *(Louder)* I hate you!

Cline: Good. You just scream right now. Go. *(Cindy begins screaming her rage, and continues through the next comments.)* You keep going. *(Sobs mixed in with the screams)* Good, Cindy, you just scream. You open your eyes when you scream at me. *(Screaming continues.)* Good, Cindy, you look at me. Again. *(More screams)* You keep going. *(One last scream, and then Cindy breaks into sobs.)* And then how do you feel about yourself afterward?

Cindy: I hate myself!

Cline: I bet you do, because how do you want to feel toward the people you're around? *(Cindy's sobs slacken.)* Yeah . . . How do you really want to feel?

Cindy: I want to love 'em . . . be nice to 'em.

Cline: Yeah. Something keeps getting in the way, doesn't it? And you wish it didn't, huh? That's hard on you, isn't it?

Cindy: *(Crying softly)* Yes.

Cline: And you want it all to be different, right?

Cindy: *(Still crying softly)* Yes!

Cline: And most of the time you don't feel very good about yourself, is that right?

Cindy: No.

Cline: And how do you feel when you get some of this anger out?

Cindy: *(Sniffling)* I feel better.

Cline: I bet it's there all the time, it seems like, isn't it?

Cindy: Yeah. *(Sniffling)* Most of the time.

Cline: Okay. You sit over here. Dad, you sit here. *(To Cindy)* Is that where you are supposed to be sitting? What in the world are you doing?

Cindy: I'm supposed to sit down here.

Cline: I was talking to your dad, not you. You're getting tissues. Where are you supposed to be sitting?

Cindy: On his lap.

Cline: Right. *(Giving instructions arranging Cindy on her*

father's lap. He is sitting in an easy chair, and she is
draped across his lap, legs hanging over the side of the
chair. He is positioned so that he can hold her tightly,
with one arm free to control her head movements.)
Okay. And you've got her arm right behind you? Okay.
Tell her, "Try to get up." *(To Cindy)* Try to get up.

Dad: Try to get up.

The "try to get up" routine is used at the beginning of many
holding sessions with adolescent or latency-age children. When
they find they cannot get up—a surprise to narcissistic children
who think they can accomplish anything—they feel consternation
at being controlled, but they also know it is safe for them to really
lose control and let go of buried emotions.

Cline: Come on, Cindy. Try to get up. Don't act like a wimp!
Try to get up! Come on, Cindy!

Cindy was truly struggling to get up here, but my statement
implied that she wasn't really trying. This technique heightens the
child's feeling of helplessness and hopelessness.

Dad: Try to get up. Come on!
Cline: Geez, I've seen six-year-olds try harder, haven't you?
Dad: Yep.
Cline: *(To Dad)* Okay, now put your hand over her mouth
and ask her how she acts most of the time.
Dad: How do you act most of the time?
Cline: Don't smile when you say it to her. Say it to her really
strong.

If the therapist or parent is too nice, the child feels too guilty to
really hate. It is easier to hate a strong, demanding, and somewhat
demeaning person.

Dad: *(Stronger)* How do you act most of the time?

Cline: Good! Say it again like that.
Dad: How do you act most of the time?
Cindy: *(Muffled)* Sick.
Cline: Say it louder.
Cindy: Sick in the head.
Dad: Say it louder.
Cindy: Sick in the head.
Cline: Scream it to me.
Cindy: Sick in the head!
Dad: You scream that again!
Cindy: *(Screaming) Sick in the head!*
Cline: Three times.
Cindy: *Sick in the head! Sick in the head! Sick in the head!*
Cline: And ask her how it was like coming up here with her.
Dad: How did you act in the car coming up here?
Cindy: A real bitch.

Cindy's father was absolutely dumbfounded at her response, as Cindy was very good at blaming others and seldom took responsibility for her own actions. With an astonished, though satisfied, smile, he had to ask her to repeat herself.

Dad: What?
Cindy: A real bitch and real defensive.
Cline: And when she acts like this . . . Ask her how does she feel toward you right now? Ask her that.
Dad: How do you feel toward me when you're acting this way?
Cindy: *(Loudly)* That I hate you.
Cline: Have her say that loud four times.
Dad: Say that loud four times.
Cindy: That I hate you!
Cline: You look in your dad's eyes and say it loud when you say it.
Cindy: That I hate you!
Cline: You look at him and say it. Go!

Cindy: That I hate you!

Cline: Again.

Cindy: That I hate you!

Cline: Again, Cindy.

Cindy: *(Sobbing)* That I hate you!

Cline: Good, good. Ask her how she's felt about you a lot ever since she was a little girl.

Dad: How have you felt about me a lot since you were a little girl? *(Cindy sobs, and Dad becomes louder and more insistent.)* How have you felt about me a lot since you were a little girl?

Cindy: That I hate you.

Cline: Good. Try it again.

Cindy: *(Screaming)* That I hate you!

Cline: Good. Louder.

Cindy: *I hate you!*

Cline: And do you feel like calling him names?

Cindy: Yes.

Cline: Go ahead.

Dad: Call me names. Tell me what you really think. Call me names.

Cindy: *(Screaming)* That you're a bastard!

Dad: Call me again. Tell me three times.

Cindy: That you're a bastard!

Dad: Again.

Cindy: That you're a bastard!

Dad: Again. Louder.

Cindy: That you're a bastard!

Cline: And say, "How do you feel?" Ask her how she feels right now about herself.

Dad: How do you feel about yourself?

Cindy: *(Screams)* I feel better!

Dad: Feel a lot better?

Cline: *(Putting the conversation back on the right track)* Uh-huh, but after you act like a nasty little girl, then after you act like that to your dad, then how do you feel?

Cindy: *(Her yell becoming almost a wail)* I hate myself when I do that!

Dad: You hate yourself after you do that. Does that make you feel better?

Cindy: *(Sobbing)* No it doesn't, no! It makes me feel worse about myself.

Cline: And can you tell your dad how you'd like to feel toward him all the time? How would you like to feel toward him all the time?

Dad: How would you like to feel toward me all the time?

Cindy: I want to be nice.

Cline: How do you want to feel?

Cindy: I want to feel good and be nice to you and make you feel happy.

Dad: Do you want to love me?

Cindy: Yes!

Cline: *(To Dad)* Then how do you want to be toward her all the time?

Dad: I want to love you.

Cline: Whisper into her ear, "But you've made it pretty hard all your life." Whisper that in her ear now.

Here, Cindy and her dad had a soft conversation that the tape didn't pick up. Cindy's sobs subsided.

Cline: Now just hold her. That's good . . . just hold her. Whisper in her ear, "I'd like to love you all the time, but you made it hard." Whisper that in her ear.

Dad: I want to love you too, but you've made it hard all your life.

Cindy and her dad then held each other for about twenty minutes, and we ended the session.

About a month later, Cindy and I had a follow-up session, from which the next transcript is taken.

Cline: Okay, I'm here with Cindy. We're talking in my office and it must be, what, a month ago since we had a heavy session?

Cindy: About a month ago.

Cline: We had a heavy session with your dad. Now that you can look back at that a month later what do you think about that session—that it helped you or it didn't help you? What are your feelings about it?

Cindy: I think it helped me a lot.

Cline: In what way? I mean, how can you tell that it helped you any?

Cindy: It's hard to explain. Uh, it got a lot of anger out that I had toward him and for myself. And when I look at him I don't see that anger, or I don't feel that anger anymore, and I feel that our relationship is content now . . . I do!

Cline: *(Enthusiastically)* That's a nice word, content.

Cindy: Uh-huh.

Cline: After the session, when you went back down to Denver, what was that like? Do you remember?

Cindy: *(Laughs)* That was great!

Here Cindy related how she and her father had stopped at a restaurant and had talked in the parking lot for half an hour, and then all through a two-hour dinner. Cindy said, "We talked more in one day than I had ever talked with him in sixteen years."

Cline: Now you did that with your dad. Did it help any with your mom, or did it help none with your mom, or your behavior with your mom, or your feelings about your mom? Has it been the same or worse with your mom?

Cindy: It helped a lot with my mom, too.

Cline: Uh-huh.

Cindy: 'Cause I wasn't as angry at her.

Cline: Even though she wasn't involved you had a better time with her.

Cindy: Yeah.

Cline: Do you think that the results of that session have lasted
or not lasted? Is it lasting, or how do you feel about
that?

Cindy: Yeah, it's lasting. I haven't felt that anger since that session.

Cline: And right now you're doing a record for yourself. I
mean you're making a record for yourself in school,
right?

Cindy: Right.

Cline: Tell me how you're doing in school . . . how it's better, why it's better.

Cindy: Well, it's better because I'm *in* school . . . I don't know.

Cline: You're not cutting, right?

Cindy: Right. I go to class.

Cline: Now, when a person has that much anger in them, like
you were feeling, and I was helping you get it out, and
you were expressing it . . . Did you have any leftover
anger toward me, or do you feel good about me, or
how do you feel about a therapist who puts a person
through that, or helps a person through that? How do
you feel about that?

Cindy: I feel you were really helpful in doing that because I
probably . . . I couldn't have done it, you know, without somebody there telling me to do it and helping me
get that anger out.

Cline: Now, you've had some experience in a hospital, right?

Cindy: Uh-huh.

Cline: Did they do that kind of thing in the hospital, or not,
or what was it like in the hospital?

Cindy: Well, no. If you'd get angry they'd just put you either
in restraints or sit you down and talk to you. But they
didn't have any session where you'd get real angry.

Cline: There weren't any sessions then where you'd be
encouraged to get it out, so to speak?

Cindy: No. They just thought talking about it is the best way to get your anger out.

Cline: Uh-huh. You know, one of the feelings that you used to have quite a bit that concerned me was that you'd feel really guilty and bad, and then crazy, and sometimes like you just didn't feel life was worth living. Have you felt that way as much, or less, or a little bit, or a lot, or what?

Cindy: No, I've felt it less.

Cline: Okay. Well, can you think of anything that's pertinent that I haven't said? Do you think that the anger inside you will build up to the point where you might need something like that again, or it probably won't, or what's your thoughts on that?

Cindy: Huh. Good question. Uh, I don't know. It could build up. Yeah, I think it could. But I think if I just try to deal with it, you know, in a perspective way, I don't think I'd have to do that again.

Cline: Right. So in other words, there are easier, better ways of handling it than something like that.

Cindy: Right.

GUIDELINES
AND LIMITS FOR
INTRUSIVE TECHNIQUES

This appendix contains guidelines for holding and the intrusive techniques as they are currently being used in many different states. These guidelines may serve as examples to be modified and used in other institutions. What works for one institution may not be practical or workable for another institution.

The guidelines in this appendix were submitted to the Texas Department of Human Services by Catholic Charities, St. Teresa's Home. The Texas DHS is currently referring and paying for services at St. Teresa's Family Attachment Program and has approved and supported holding and intrusive techniques as described herein. Therapists Sheryl Jordan and Kathy Baczynski, the authors of these guidelines, originated the St. Teresa's program and studied extensively at Evergreen Consultants. These guidelines include treatment techniques as well as information found in *Understanding and Treating the Severely Disturbed Child* by Foster Cline and *High Risk: Children Without a Conscience* by Ken Magid and Carole McKelvey.

Program Overview

An expert multidisciplinary treatment team will supervise the treatment of children in care. The two therapists on staff have been trained in Evergreen and have been working with attachment disorders over the past several years. One of the consulting psychologists has also been trained in Evergreen and treats children with attachment disorders. The other psychologist has years of experience working with children in residential treatment, and the staff psychiatrist specializes in infant/child bonding.

Children are assigned a primary therapist who coordinates the professional team and directs their treatment. In addition to regularly scheduled therapy sessions, the therapist is available twenty-four hours a day as needed. The majority of treatment, however, occurs within specialized treatment homes by highly trained professional parents. The attachment process is facilitated through a close, structured family environment, coupled with the intensive therapy. The professional parents are key members of the treatment team.

Admission Process

Families or agencies who wish to place children in the program complete an in-depth admission process. Each child and family are carefully screened to assure that attachment therapy is appropriate. Other, less-restrictive forms of treatment must have been unsuccessful before these children will be considered. A psychiatric evaluation is completed by the staff psychiatrist. The primary diagnosis will be that of Reactive Attachment Disorder, but other secondary diagnoses may be Conduct Disorder, Depression, Attention Deficit Disorder with Hyperactivity, or Post-Traumatic Stress Disorder. The psychiatrist must recommend placement. The child must also possess an average IQ. Information regarding a child's parents is gathered through clinical interviews and psychological testing. Living with unattached children is very difficult and often the placing parents appear physically and psychologically exhausted. Careful screening helps to assure that the family is able to handle the intense nature of the treatment and that successful reintegration of these children into the family is a definite probability.

Theoretical Framework

Philosophy

Children are viewed in a holistic manner. Each facet of their development is addressed. It is believed that the attachment process is facilitated through intensive therapeutic interventions, which take place both in regular therapy sessions and on a daily basis within the treatment home.

The overall goal of the Family Attachment Center is to provide effective treatment for attachment-disordered children so as to prepare them to function as loving, contributing members of a family and, ultimately, the community. With the provision of a highly structured and nurturing environment, children successfully completing treatment will accomplish the following:

Develop trust
Assume responsibility for behavior
Learn to accept authority
Develop skills needed to function in a family
Learn how to communicate needs and feelings effectively
Accept and love themselves
Learn alternative ways of behaving
Develop the ability to listen
Develop self-awareness
Learn social responsibility, concern, and respect for others
Learn to participate in healthy, reciprocal relationships

In all aspects of the program, children will always be treated in a manner which conveys dignity and respect. This attitude is maintained by all members of the treatment team. Empathy toward children is sustained throughout treatment and they are continually encouraged to be active participants in their therapy. The more investment they have in gaining appropriate control over their lives, the more the treatment team members can join with them to help them overcome the problems and celebrate the victories. It is believed that children can be helped to heal and grow only through a judiciously applied therapeutic program.

Attachment and Bonding

Attachment and bonding describe the relationship that is established between an infant and his or her primary caretaker, usually the mother, during the first two years of life. Usually infants and mothers establish close and trusting relationships, upon which all subsequent developmental stages are based. When this close relationship is successfully established, a child is said to be bonded to his or her mother. In her book *Attachment and Separation* (1979), Vera Fahlberg, a pediatrician and expert in the area of infant bonding, states that "the bond that a child develops to the person who cares for him in his early years is the foundation for his future psychological development and for his future relationships with others."

Bonding is established by the repetition of a specific cycle, which Dr. Cline calls "the soul cycle." In the first step, a child has a need (i.e., hunger, pain, discomfort). The child then expresses the need by crying. This is referred to as a "rage reaction." Rage is said to be a combination of helplessness, hopelessness, and anger. In essence, the infant is saying, "I need something that I am totally helpless in obtaining, and right now I feel pretty hopeless that anyone will give me what I need. This makes me very scared and mad." The caretaker satisfies the child's needs, which is the third step of the cycle, by providing touch, motion, eye contact, smiles, and milk or food. These elements are important components of this "gratification" or "satisfaction" step. At this point, children begin to trust that their needs will indeed be met, and bonding takes place, thus completing the cycle.

This soul cycle is repeated thousands of times during the first two years of life. The uninterrupted completion of this cycle results in the formation of a strong, trusting bond between a child and his or her caretaker. This "basic trust," as Erickson called it, is the foundation for future development. Studies done by John Bowlby have determined that there exists "a strong causal relationship between an individual's experiences with his parents and his later capacity to make affectional bonds." The ability to trust, and the bond that results, enables children to develop relationships and to later accept limits and controls as they are imposed by their parents.

Treatment

Traditional interventions are ineffective with these children because most of these therapies have the client-therapist relationship as the foundation for treatment. Since unbonded children are unable to establish trusting relationships, they do not make progress with such therapy. Magid and McKelvey, in *High Risk: Children Without a Conscience,* state, "Most therapists in America don't know how [these] patients operate and are sucked into non-productive therapeutic sessions that seldom help the client and often have disastrous effects on the unwitting therapist."

During the therapy sessions, children are encouraged to express their anger and rage in a safe, accepting environment. They must express the rage before the feelings of sadness and emptiness can be successfully treated. The therapist does not allow them to exert usual control tactics. Instead, the trained therapist orchestrates control battles that end in win-win situations, something unfamiliar to these children. In the past, when children attempted to control a situation, either they pushed hard enough to win at all costs, or the adult, who is able to win the battle, had to do so at the expense of the child. All therapy sessions end in a good way, with positive resolution of the control issues and a feeling of warmth between the therapist and these children.

During therapy sessions, these children are encouraged to regress and re-experience the first-year-of-life cycle; only this time the cycle is successfully completed as they receive appropriate gratification and nurturing. It is through the positive outcome of this cycle that these children are able to release their anger, face their pain, and allow themselves to trust.

Magid and McKelvey describe the therapy as "physical holding and control of a patient who is confronted with his death-grip resistance to accepting love and acting responsibly. The therapy contains explosive dialogue as the psychopathic patient is encouraged to work through his unbelievable rage and anger while being forced to accept another's total control."

Specific Therapeutic Techniques

The therapy is divided into three phases: contracting, therapy, and discussion.

Contracting

Review of Problem: The purpose is to discuss with these children, in a conversational manner, their understanding of their problem. The amount of anger these children feel they have, and to whom it is directed, is discussed most often. How hard the child has tried to change is also a topic to review. This review is done with the child sitting, facing the therapist.

Engaging the Child: Contracting involves making an agreement with these children to work on their issues. They are shown the holding position and the therapy is explained. They understand that the therapist will help them get their anger out, first at the therapist, then toward the person to whom they feel anger. They must agree before the therapy can begin.

Therapy

Who's the Boss?: These children must understand that the therapist is in control. This is done by the therapist not allowing them to use their usual manipulative control tactics. The first step is to put them in the holding position and ask them to try to get up. This serves two purposes. First, it lets the children know that the therapist(s) has physical control. Second, it lets them know that they are safe and no matter how angry they become, they will not be allowed to hurt themselves or anyone else.

Activation: The therapist confronts the children on the way they are coming through (i.e., eye contact, voice inflection, body movement, etc.). The children are encouraged to express their anger toward the therapist. Usually, they are feeling very angry at being controlled and the anger is quickly accessed. The anger is encouraged and accepted by the therapist. These children are told to express their anger in loud, strong voices, while they are looking directly at the therapist.

If they get "stuck," the therapist may activate their resistances physically by having them perform straight-leg kicking, running in place, or jumping jacks. This serves to push them through their resistances, so that they are free to work on feelings.

During this phase, children express intense feelings of anger and rage. They are re-experiencing the rage reaction of the first year of life. Eventually, they are encouraged to just scream. Often, these screams have an infantile quality to them.

Bonding: Once children express their anger and rage, they move into the sad and painful feelings. The therapist changes pace and gives them love and nurturance and relief from the intense feelings of rage. This completes the "soul cycle." The therapist hugs them, which allows them to snuggle. This is the most important part of the therapy process, because these childen have re-experienced the rage reaction of infancy, only this time the cycle is complete with appropriate gratification.

Discussion

During the final phase, children, therapists, and any others involved discuss any pertinent issues brought up during the session. Patients give themselves a grade (A, B, C, etc.) on how they think they did during the session. They also give feedback as to how much anger they feel they got out and how much they feel they still have inside. Any homework is then assigned by the therapist. Finally, the reflective team that has been watching from behind the one-way mirror gives feedback to the child and the therapist. Feedback may also be given during the session.

The treatment team is cognizant that in some circumstances a series of intensive holdings may not be initially indicated. In such situations, the team will decide the most effective and supportive approach to take. Flexibility and creativity are central to the overall therapeutic approach, which advocates effective treatment in the least-restrictive manner.

Informed Consent

Prior to placement of children, placing parents or a representative of the placing agency will be given specific orientation to the treatment program. Written material as well as verbal description of the rationale, procedures, and safeguards for treatment will be included. The placing parent or agency representative will be placed in the holding position and many of the various techniques will be demonstrated. This serves to give the parent or representative a clear understanding of a child's experience during the sessions. Videotapes of actual holding sessions will also be viewed.

The placing parents or representative will be asked to sign a document asserting that the treatment program and holding techniques have been thoroughly explained. It is also made clear that the placing parents or representative can request that intensive work be discontinued or may remove a child from the program at any time.

Following admission of a child, placing parents or agency representatives will be required to participate in training seminars similar to those attended by professional parents. They will also be required to attend the initial treatment plan meeting and quarterly treatment reviews. The parents or representative will have continuous input into treatment.

Variance Request

The Minimum Standards for Child Placing Agencies, Appendix IX, state that the child cannot be restrained except in an emergency in order to protect other children or adults from harm. During the two-week intensive, these children are restrained in a reclining position, but for therapeutic reasons rather than for protection from immediate harm. Great care is given to assure that they are in no way injured or harmed during the sessions. During lengthy sessions, they are allowed to get up to stretch, go to the bathroom, or have a drink.

Other techniques used during the session and within the treatment home might be considered aversive. These include physical activation (such as straight-leg kicking, running in place), covering children's mouth or eyes with the hand, rolling their head from side to side, the volume and directness of the therapist's voice, the proximity of the therapist's face to their face, and the use of chores within the treatment home. Each will be individually explained, with procedures, rationale, and safeguards addressed.

Physical Activation

Unattached children have a great network of defense mechanisms that they have carefully constructed to prevent them from dealing with their intense feelings of emptiness, fear, and anger. During a holding session, this network is slowly replaced with more functional behavior patterns. At times, a child becomes entrenched within these defense mechanisms and requires additional help from the therapist to break free. When the verbal techniques fail to help them move through the resistances, the therapist may have them kick their legs, which serves to move the children past the resistances physiologically rather than psychologically.

Kicking is done with straight legs, without shoes, up and down on the cushions of a couch for several minutes. The children are asked to kick, and to say "Ready" when they are ready to work. The duration of the kicking is left up to the children. However, the quality of kicking is up to the therapist.

Other physical activation modalities, such as running in place or jumping jacks, are handled in a similar manner, with children determining the duration. At no time are they asked to perform physical tasks that are beyond their ability or for an unreasonable period of time. Once their resistances are activated and they are available to continue working, the physical activity ceases.

Covering the Child's Mouth or Eyes

As mentioned earlier, unattached children possess an inordinate need to control people and situations. One of the main purposes of the holding therapy is to take charge of these children and help them feel okay about allowing another person to "be the boss." A therapist must be able to control as many aspects of the therapy session as possible in order to help children regress. Covering their mouth when they give an inappropriate response or covering their eyes when they refuse to give eye contact are techniques that can be used to establish positive control.

Therapists may cup their hand over these children's mouth to prevent biting. The nose is never covered, so breathing is not impaired. Eyes may be covered by the therapist's hand for only a brief period. At no time is excessive pressure or force used.

Rolling the Head

Again, since control problems are one of the primary issues addressed in holding sessions, facilitating this occurs when a therapist takes as much charge of these children as possible. Rolling their head from one side to the other is one way a therapist can demonstrate physical control.

This technique is usually used only a few times during the session, if at all. With one hand over the children's mouth, the therapist slowly turns their head from side to side. No jerking or abrupt motion is used, nor is the children's head ever shaken.

Therapist's Voice

Expression of anger and rage is another vital aspect of holding therapy. In order to facilitate these children's expressions, therapists model volume and inflection. As one can imagine, it would be difficult to yell out feelings of anger when the request is made in a soft, gentle voice. Therefore, loud and direct statements and requests are made by the therapist.

Even though volume and intensity of voice are at a high level, at no time should the therapist come across as punitive or angry. As mentioned earlier, a secondary therapist, as well as a reflective team of trained staff members behind the mirror, are present to assure that the therapist stays on track and that the interaction remains therapeutic.

Proximity

Eye contact is an essential element of the bonding cycle. Studies show that newborns focus at an optimal point of about fifteen to eighteen inches, the approximate distance from their eyes to those of their nursing mother. During holding sessions, these children's head is cradled in a similar manner, with the therapist having close eye contact. This close proximity between children and therapist is maintained throughout the session, which includes the expression of anger as well as sadness and nurturance.

Pressure over the Thorax

[The following section was not included in the state-accepted proposal. However, it is included here because it is a necessary technique with selected sociopathic and noncompliant children. It must be used very carefully. In a letter to me, one of the authors of this proposal noted, "We will not be able to reach the more severely disturbed children because we did not talk about pressure over the thorax. However, as the state sees our success with the less severely disturbed children, we will ask for this in a future request for variance."]

Occasionally, children are extremely passively noncompliant and refuse to kick, work, maintain eye contact, or verbally respond during a holding session. Verbal encouragement and behavior modification may not be effective in gaining control and helping them to accept a therapist's authority. At such times, brief pressure over the thorax, above one rib, may be applied with the "pulp" of the finger to provide enough discomfort for them to be encouraged to respond. This pressure will not continue when they comply with a reasonable request to work or respond. Painful poking with the tip of the finger or knuckling is not allowed.

Pressure over the thorax may also be used for brief moments at times of intensive confrontive activation to help these children express, deal with, and resolve feelings of deep-seated rage and anger.

Possible Negative Effects of Treatment

Every therapeutic intervention has some risks. Great care has been taken to build in as many safeguards as possible, which assure that all aspects of the program remain therapeutic. The most common negative consequence of holding therapy is the sensation of sore or achy muscles following a session, for both the therapist and the children. Other possible negative effects may include an irritated throat from yelling, skin irritations, or slight bruising around the wrist from a therapist's restraint. These effects are common with any form of restraint, but they are not experienced after all sessions and are directly related to the amount of physical resistance children display. Care is given to assure that children are as comfortable as possible during the session and no unnecessary pressure or force is used.

One of the goals of holding sessions is to encourage children to regress. At times, this regression extends into their lives outside therapy sessions. For example, they may become enuretic or encopretic. These behaviors are temporary and are handled in a supportive manner.

In looking at all possible negative effects of treatment, one must consider the possibility of the children becoming psychotic. This is a rare phenomenon, but as with any other form of psychotherapy, a possibility. Great care is given to prevent this from occurring. First, the staff psychiatrist gives children complete psychiatric evaluations prior to treatment and assesses any evidence of psychosis. Next, if children at any time show any symptoms of detachment, holding sessions would not be scheduled, and if in progress, would be immediately stopped. If there are evidencing signs of psychosis or detachment, immediate attempts are made to reintegrate the children and the staff psychiatrist is called. Further treatment would be discontinued until a complete re-evaluation was made.

Review of Program Safeguards

Treating unattached children presents a unique and extraordinary challenge. The therapeutic interventions outlined here represent a new and innovative approach to working with very difficult chidren. Due to the somewhat controversial nature of the treatment, the team has been careful to incorporate ongoing safeguards. These safeguards assure that the program remains therapeutic and that dignity is maintained. Below is a summary of the safeguards.

ADMISSION

　　Adherence to admissions criteria

　　Psychiatric evaluation to ensure appropriate diagnosis and recommendations

　　Previous conventional treatment failure

　　Informed consent by placing parents or agency representative

　　Evaluation of placing family to assure reintegration

　　Clear permanent plan upon dismissal

TRAINING AND SUPERVISION

　　Extensive training for professional parents and placing parents or agency representative

　　Close supervision of the treatment home through regular therapy sessions, home visits, and contacts

　　Ongoing in-service training for parents and staff

　　Close coordination of the reintegration process

　　Follow-up outpatient treatment to families post-dismissal

THERAPY

　　Contracting with the child

　　Two treatment team members present at all holding sessions

　　Placing parents or agency representatives are allowed to view all sessions

　　All sessions are videotaped

　　Pre-session and post-session conferences to discuss issues

　　Flexibility of therapeutic approach

　　All sessions end in a positive way

　　Individual treatment plan

　　Review of treatment plan every ninety days

Guidelines for Educational Seminars and
Training for Intrusive Techniques and High Confrontation

1. Train those who use these techniques. Training must take place over many months by participating in a number of cases. Merely attending a workshop and then doing the therapy, while bold and sometimes helpful to the client, may be dangerous, ineffective, and legally unwise.
2. Emphasize proper diagnosis.
3. Encourage the careful analysis of all failures.
4. Teach others to always use the least-intrusive techniques first.
5. All of us must keep our methods open for others to see, comment upon, and provide feedback.
6. Emphasize the importance of providing patients with information about the heavier techniques before they are engaged in them. Informed consent is usually a must. (It often helps patients to view videotapes of others in therapy prior to their own. This may decrease the effectiveness of therapy, but it may be a worthwhile trade-off.)
7. Teach that the decision to use heavy confrontation is a *team* decision.
8. Emphasize that heavy confrontation requires ongoing education, just as does the use of electroshock therapy.
9. Teach that those using the heavier techniques, even with all the above safeguards, must expect to be misunderstood and have their motives and techniques questioned. Aspersions may be cast on professionalism and even personality. It is important to note here that all people cannot be reached by any therapy all the time.
10. Emphasize that holding and bonding therapy, in and of itself, is a door opener to enable children to form a therapeutic alliance, and must be used in conjunction with "usual" good therapeutic techniques, including family therapy, structured environments, behavior modification, and use of medication. The therapy is never to be conceptualized as *instead of,* but rather as *to open to.*

Institutional Guidelines for Holding

The following guidelines for holding children were developed by a large inpatient treatment center. These guidelines have been successfully followed to reach many children who did not respond to traditional techniques.

REASONS TO HOLD
1. To obtain reciprocity: trains for reciprocal response, i.e., we ask questions, they answer; sharing/give and take of control; smile leads to smile; showing our sorrow and empathy leads children to recognize and feel sorrow.
2. Closeness and intimacy: leads to positive relationship rather than pain; obtains the corrective emotional response from corrective emotional experience. All holdings begin with contract.

TYPES OF HOLDING
1. Provocative
2. Nurturant
3. Containment

PARAMETERS FOR HOLDING—TEAM DECISIONS (ALL PARAMETERS MUST BE "GO")
1. History
2. Symptoms
3. Permanency planning
4. Environmental circumstances
5. Supportive milieu, parents, school, adequate trial of conventional therapies
6. Diagnosis

CONTRAINDICATIONS
1. Time is not sufficient
2. Expertise is lacking
3. Low intellectual functioning (except in cases of pure compliance)

PREPARATION OF FAMILY/STAFF FOR HOLDING

1. Talking about it with family and child
2. Contract
3. Demonstration of holding
4. Discuss range of emotions
5. Examples of behavior
6. Are you unhappy? Contract may be obtained in days/weeks prior to holding.
7. Is part of it you?
8. Do you want to do something about it?
9. With me?
10. Videotape of holding; informed consent

HOLDING POSITIONS

1. Don't hold onto joints
2. Hold hands at palm, but controlling fingers
3. Hold forehead

PROVOCATIVE HOLDING

1. Contract
2. Explore early relationships
3. Explore how easily child gives and takes control; reciprocity in a light way—smiles, eye contact
4. Testing: try to get up (may begin to start to exert control in a heavier manner; first indication of seriousness)
5. Match reciprocal response: give support when compliant; meet resistance with resistance; "You're hurting me" response very typical at this stage—therapist checks nonverbally and relates this to degree of self-hurt
6. Kicking or squirming: asking child for what he or she is behaviorally giving anyway; if child is totally resistant, ignore the child and talk to other holders on nonrelated issues
7. Return to quick, unpredictable response: "I asked you to kick"; loud tones, varying voice tones ("What did I ask you to do?"); keep child off-balance to avoid lapses into usual resistances

8. Gross motor compliance at this point: if unable to get compliance bodily, utilize facial responses
9. Double bind
10. You can't get right verbal responses until you are able to get compliant physical responses
11. Check feelings toward therapist
12. Who have you been ticked off at all your life?
13. Once a child gives and maintains the appropriate emotional response, ask for appropriate voice tone—say again in a soft/loud way
14. Once a child is crying and you're sure he or she is feeling appropriate emotions, then give nurturance/hugs
15. Follow-up
    a. Usually two to three days after first big push, then four to five days after that
    b. Push can be lighter but enough to get child back into a good spot
    c. Touch, tickles in a small way can restimulate holding in a less-intrusive manner
    d. Challenge expression, behavior, attitude until you get reciprocal response
    e. Staff uses terminology and dynamics that came out of holding; avoid overuse
    f. Comments "how sad" if child resorts to resistance
    g. Therapist makes choice to pursue or just comment

CONTAINMENT HOLDING
1. Goal: reciprocal response and contract
2. Check resources: time, staff, control, team decision
3 Helping a child *through,* not *into,* feeling; child is already into feeling
4. Avoid secondary gain such that child wants to repeat process
5. Push and the soft, repeat process until bodily relaxation occurs
6. End with contract: "Interesting to see how you do this afternoon"

7. Don't ask for calmness
8. Give safety, caring, respect, assurances you are in control messages
9. Do not use "you can get up when you're in control"; this places the child in control
10. Respond to something that you can therapeutically grasp
11. Automatically back off (without verbal warnings) when child is being verbally responsive; let go of hand and check response
12. Follow-up later in the milieu by modeling appropriate touch and response, making attention and hugs available without demand

NURTURANT HOLDING
1. Team decision
2. Discuss with child
3. Contract: when you were young, you missed out on hugs; contract for missing lost time
4. Talking over the day: check body relaxation, eye contact
5. Watch: the heavier you push for compliance, the more resistance you may encounter

AN OFFICER AND A GENTLEMAN: A MOVIE ABOUT BONDING AND ATTACHMENT

The 1982 movie *An Officer and a Gentleman* made stars out of its leading players—Richard Gere and Debra Winger—and an Oscar-winner out of its major supporting actor—Louis Gossett, Jr. To most of the millions of people who saw the blockbuster, the movie was a love story involving a young man coming of age. For those who work with severely disturbed children, it was a study in intrusive therapy, bonding, and attachment.

In the opening sequence, flashbacks reveal the protagonist's background. We learn that Zack Mayo's mother committed suicide when he was six years old. Zack then writes to his father for four months before his father finally answers. Zack goes to live with his father in the Philippines, but the first thing his father announces is, "I don't have any time for this 'Daddy' stuff," shouting that he is too old to be a father. Zack's father speaks with a distinct alcoholic slur, and he lives with two concubines. We learn that Zack's father was often gone after Zack was born, and his absences and other behaviors played a role in Zack's mother's suicide.

We see a little boy with many reasons for problems with intimacy. In one final flashback, Zack is walking down the street with three other boys whom he appears to trust. All of a sudden they begin to beat him unmercifully for money he doesn't even have. As the others run away, Zack looks dazed and confused, and faces an almost certain unhappy future.

Later, young Zack puts himself into "therapy." He signs up for treatment in an adolescent group home—the Naval Air Academy. His therapist is his drill instructor, Master Sergeant Emil Foley.

We meet the drill instructor-therapist for the first time as he confronts the newly arrived youths. Foley is demeaning and demanding. For basic trust to develop, the youths must be stripped of all control. It is a simple matter for the therapist to lead most of the kids to feel helpless and hopeless; we can see it in their eyes as Foley goes down the line. Foley brings one boy to solid hopelessness and helplessness by accusing him of being gay: "Only two things come from Oklahoma—steers and queers. I don't see no horns, so you must be a queer!"

However, the most disturbed, and the most controlling, of all is Zack. Always in control, he just snickers at the others' discomfiture. He is probably thinking, "What a bunch of Navy crap." At this, the therapist directs his attention to Zack and does his best to make him feel helpless and hopeless, too: "You laughing at me, dick brain? You better quit eyeballing me. Boy, I'll rip your eyeballs out of your skull and fuck you to death!"

These comments, delivered with the right inflection and with close eye contact, would cause the average young person at least some discomfort. But Zack isn't even fazed. He maintains control, and the therapist, losing the encounter, turns to go. Just as he does, though, he notices a bandage on Zack's arm, and seizes the opportunity. "Do you have an injury there, Mayo?" When Mayo answers "No, sir," Foley rips off the bandage, revealing a tattoo of an eagle. (Zack had been so concerned about the eagle that he tried to hide it. But like so many psychopaths, he was somewhat obvious about it.) Now the therapist has some ammunition: "You better be proud of them wings, Mayonnaise. They're the only ones you're going to leave here with!" Now Zack's expression reveals an air of uncertainty.

As the movie continues, Zack's narcissism and inability to care for others is revealed in several ways. It is obvious that he is going to love and leave his girlfriend, Paula Pokrifki. His entitlement issues are obvious: Zack insists on being first on the obstacle course. And when another cadet, an African American, warns him that the whole squad could be kicked out because of Zack's sneaky contrabanding, Zack sneers and says, "I don't see anyone else complaining." In short, Zack is narcissistic, unable to love others, conscienceless, and uncaring.

The Weekend Therapy Session

Mayo and the others are in their barracks awaiting inspection. Foley enters, comes in front of Zack, and uses a stick to push up the ceiling panel above him. Contraband cascades from the ceiling. Foley notes, "In every class there is someone who thinks they are smarter than me, and in this case it's you, isn't it, Mayonnaise?"

The therapist could have dismissed Zack from therapy right then, and few would have disagreed. After all, Zack was being a jerk.

If Foley simply kicked Zack out of the service, how would Zack have reacted? He would probably say something along these lines: "Go ahead and kick me out—I don't care. I hate the fucking Navy; I don't know why I ever signed up in the first place. Go screw yourself! Someday you'll be sorry for this. . . ." He would have experienced one more loss, and his psychopathic personality would have continued unabated. He would have been discharged into a loveless civilian life, with practically no chance of securing long-term loving relationships.

However, Foley is not an average therapist. He is willing to spend a difficult long weekend to help Zack reach the point of capitulation, when Zack will lose all control, express his deeply buried rage, and admit his helplessness and hopelessness. Only then can the therapist show him acceptance and love, and the "gentleman" can be born.

The weekend therapy session begins with Zack running in place (physical activation of feelings) while Foley sprinkles water on him with a hose. During this session, therapist Foley makes Zack sing his "life-script"—a life of using people: "Casey Jones was a son of a bitch, rolled his train in a thirty-foot ditch.

Came all out with his stick in his hand, said, 'Listen, ladies, I'm a hell of a man.'"

Then Foley points out why he is helping Zack: "Say goodbye to your buddies, Mayo. Oh, I forget, you don't have any buddies, only customers." Looking over at a female cadet (Seger) struggling to do chin-ups, Foley says, "Look over there, Mayo. She may not make it through the program, but she has more heart and more character than you'll ever have."

This is the point of the movie. For Zack to have character or a heart, he has to be rebuilt from the ground up. He needs to experience the first-year-of-life bonding cycle. However, when a person is as heavily defended as Zack, it takes much more than an hour's therapy. It takes much more than talk-it-out therapy. Even unending, unqualified positive regard would not help him.

Foley then interprets Zack's problems in a way that would make any professional psychoanalyst smile. In a symbolic gesture, he gets down in the dirt with Zack. With his eyes ten inches away from Zack's face, Foley says this:

> Life sure has dealt you some shitty cards, hasn't it, Mayo? I done some checking. I've looked through your files. I read about your mama, and . . . don't you eyeball me . . . and your dad was an alcoholic and a whore chaser. That's why you don't mesh, Mayo, 'cause . . . and don't you eyeball me . . . way down deep inside you think these other boys and girls are better than you. [Grabs Mayo by the arm] Don't you, Mayo!

If Foley were a therapist, his words would have come out this way: "Zack, I've read your hospital chart. I understand your problems. Your mother committed suicide and your father has problems with intimacy. So way down deep inside, maybe you don't feel you're as good as other people. Do you think that could be the problem?" Foley uses excellent paradoxical technique, too; first telling Zack not to eyeball him, then grabbing his arm and physically forcing Zack to look him in the eyes!

Zack replies stridently, "No sir, no sir!" but his armor is cracking and he is starting to lose his cool—the first small step toward health. In the next scene, Foley has Zack running in a circle on the beach, rifle held high over his head, and is pushing the crack wider. As Zack stumbles around in the circle, Foley says, "Getting tired, Zack? I'm not! Move it, boy! This is where the fun starts. We got all day tomorrow to look forward to! Come on!"

The point of capitulation is reached on the second day. Zack is lying on a concrete slab with his feet raised sixteen inches off the deck. He is physically exhausted. Foley uses paradoxical techniques again. He asks Zack why he ever signed up for this abuse. He tells Zack that he might as well quit now, and that he will take Zack to a nearby bar for a beer. Breaking, Zack sobs out that he wants to fly jets. "My grandma wants to fly jets!" sneers Foley. Finally, with exquisite timing, Foley says, "Okay, Zack, you're out!" Zack shouts, "Don't you do it! Don't you do it! I got nowhere else to go. I got nowhere else to go. I got nothin'!" He is in total rage. He feels hopeless, helpless, and angry. Finally, the first-year-of-life cycle can begin.

After the capitulation, his voice softening, Foley says, "Come on, Zack, get up. You have some urinals to clean." Zack knows he has been accepted and his hard times are over. All he had to do was relinquish control. Basic trust is locked in, and Zack bonds with his therapist.

Down in the bay in a motorboat, other of the group home kids moon the therapist, yelling, "Keep it up, Zack, you got the queer on the run. Foley got his balls shot off in the war!" Foley, like all good therapists, doesn't take this adolescent nonsense personally. He ignores the kids, but asks Zack the essential diagnostic question: "Those friends of yours, Zack?" When Zack smiles a "Yes," Foley knows for sure that he made a wise choice to work with this cadet, for the ability to make and maintain friends is one of the best of prognostic signs.

Immediately after the capitulation scene, Zack gives his first "Thank you" to his friend. He also *gives* a pair of shined shoes and belt buckles to the African American cadet to whom he was so derisive before. Further, Zack helps others through the obstacle course, forgoing the honor of being first. He is showing exactly the type of love shown by Foley—a tough type of caring love.

The Follow-Up

Once a lesson has been learned, life always seems to provide the postgraduate course. Zack's mother killed herself and his father never cared about him. Now Zack's first friend, another cadet named Sid, commits suicide when he washes out of the program.

On discovering the body, Zack says, "Why didn't you come to talk to me about it? You didn't try." And shortly thereafter, when Paula tries to make contact with him, Zack will have nothing to do with her. This experience has thrown him back to his previous non-intimate self. He simply wants to be left alone, and even goes back to the therapist, who has a group in session, and demands to quit.

Foley, as all good therapists do when children are acting out, first tries to active listen. "We all know about your friend, Zack, and we're sorry." When this goes nowhere, he tries to ignore the acting out. This doesn't work either, and so Foley tries to give Zack alternative behavior; "Go back and get yourself cleaned up." Finally, when it is apparent that Zack is going to quit therapy with or without permission, the therapist realizes that Zack must re-experience the bonding cycle to re-establish trust.

Foley tells Zack to meet him down at the blimp hanger, where martial arts classes are held. In Foley's mind, the postgraduate corrective cycle will be quick and easy—a few moments of simple karate and Zack will be on the floor capitulating, and then the therapist will give him the gratification of being allowed the choice of quitting.

There are three important rules when working with disturbed children: (1) Avoid control battles at all costs. (2) If you can't avoid a control battle, win the battle at all costs. (3) Pick the issue for the control battle carefully. Foley made a mistake by overlooking Zack's history—he had learned karate while growing up in the Philippines. Therefore the choice of karate was a poor one, for Zack was too strong on this issue. The result is that Foley has to pull out all the stops, and he does win at all costs. When Zack is on the deck, unable to breathe, Foley says the essential words: "Now you can quit if you want, Zack. It's up to you." This "gift," again given at the moment of capitulation, locks in bonding. Zack does not quit.

Later, at the graduation ceremony, the school commander says, "Well done, Sergeant Foley!" This short line emphasizes the importance of administrative backup. The commander does not say, "What the hell is wrong with you, Foley! You just kicked hell out of this kid!"

Unfortunately, one of the main difficulties in using confrontive techniques is the lack of community understanding and professional backup. In some states, foster parents working with severely disturbed children cannot even ask them to stand in the corner or do push-ups. In other states, even a simple sixty-second scolding would be thought abusive. Although the children we are seeing are more disturbed than ever, the techniques we can use with them are becoming increasingly restricted.

The Gift of Autonomy

Following the establishment of basic trust, autonomy must develop. This is shown beautifully at the graduation ceremony. All of the graduates want their first salute (symbolic of the going-away kiss) from Sergeant Foley. Now they love him!

It is a heart-warming experience when the female cadet, Seger, takes her salute from Foley. The terse military exchange goes like this:

> "Congratulations, Ensign Seger."
> "Thank you, sir."
> "Gunnery Sergeant, Ensign Seger . . . *Sir!*"

In therapist-speak, Foley has said, "Dear child, you take your wings, for I have none, and fly farther than I ever will. I love you."

As Zack steps up for his salute, he correctly says, "I'll never forget you, Sergeant. I wouldn't have made this if it weren't for you." As Zack prepares to leave the group home, he stops and reflects for a moment on the sight of Sergeant Foley with a new group of children:

> "Where are you from, boy?"
> "Tucson, Arizona, sir."
> "Ah. Only two things come from Arizona—steers and queers. Which are you? I don't see any horns, so you must be a queer."

Again Zack smiles at this, but not sneeringly, as he did at the beginning of his time in the group home. Now he smiles in recognition—of where he came from, of where he might have ended up, and of the role his therapist played in saving his life. Then he rides away from the group home on his motorcycle, a loving and caring individual.

BIBLIOGRAPHY

Abel, E. L. *Fetal Alcohol Syndrome and Fetal Alcohol Effects.* New York: Plenum, 1987.

Ainsworth, M. and D. Salter. "The Development of Infant-Mother Attachment." In B. M. Caldwell, H. N. Ricciuti (eds). *Review of Child Development Research.* New York: Russell Sage Foundation, 1969.

Appell, G. and David, M. "A Study of Mother-Child Interaction at Thirteen Months." In B. M. Foss (ed). *Determinants of Infant Behavior,* vol. 3. New York: Wiley, 1965.

Banham, K. M. "The Development of Affectionate Behavior in Infancy." In M. L. and N. R. Haimowitz (eds). *Human Development: Selected Readings.* New York: Crowell, 1960.

Bauer, Gary. *Washington Watch,* June 1992.

Birtchnell, J. "Early Parent Death and Psychiatric Diagnosis." *Social Psychiatry* 7:202-210, 1972.

Benedek, Elissa. "Juvenile Homicide." *Psychiatric News* 3 (15 June), 1990.

Bettelheim, Bruno. *Love Is Not Enough.* New York: Free Press, 1950.

Bleiberg, Efrain. "Stages of Residential Treatment: Application of a Developmental Model." In *Psychoanalytic Approaches to the Very Troubled Child.* Haworth Press, 1989.

Bowlby, John. *Attachment.* New York: Basic Books, 1948.

———. *Child Care and the Growth of Love.* Baltimore: Penguin Books, 1953.

———. *Attachment and Loss. III. Sadness and Depression.* New York: Basic Books, 1980.

Brown University Child Behavior and Development Letter 6 (3): March 1990.

Casriel, Daniel. *A Scream Away from Happiness.* New York: Grosset & Dunlap, 1980.

Chasnoff, Ira. "Cocaine Addiction in Pregnant Women Creating a 'Lost Generation.'" Grand Rounds Review #2. *Psychiatric Institutes of America,* 1991.

Children's Defense Fund. *A Children's Defense Budget. An Analysis of the FY1987 Federal Budget and Children.* Children's Defense Fund, 1987.

Cleckey, Harvey. *The Mask of Sanity.* St. Louis: Mosby, 1964.

Cline, Foster. *Understanding and Treating the Severely Disturbed Child.* Evergreen, CO: Evergreen Consultants in Human Behavior, 1979.

————. *The Parent Education Text.* Evergreen, CO: Evergreen Consultants in Human Behavior, 1979.

Cline, Foster and M. B. Rothenberg. "Preparing a Child for Surgery." In C. Schaefer and H. L. Millman (eds). *Therapies for Children.* San Francisco: Jossey-Bass, 1977.

Conger, John and Paul Mussen. *Child Development and Personality.* New York: HarperCollins, 1956.

Associated Press. "12 Teens See Killing Victim, Keep Silent." *Denver Post,* 12 November 1981.

————. "One of Every 6 Births Illicit." *Denver Post,* 16 November 1981.

David, M. and G. Appell. "Mother-Child Relation." In J. G. Howells (ed). *Modern Perspectives in International Child Psychiatry.* Edinburgh, 1969.

Dorris, Michael. *The Broken Cord.* New York: HarperCollins, 1989.

Duchschere, Kevin. *Minneapolis Star Tribune,* 20 January 1990.

Erikson, Erik. *Childhood and Society,* 2nd ed. New York: Norton, 1950.

Fahlberg, Vera. *Attachment and Separation.* Deerfield Beach, FL: Health Commission, 1979.

Fanshel, D. *Far from the Reservation.* Metuchen, NJ: Scarecrow, 1972.

Feigelman, W. and A. R. Silverman. *Chosen Children: New Patterns of Adoptive Relationships.* New York: Praeger, 1983.

Fontana, Vincent. *Save the Family, Save the Child.* 1991.

Gergen, David. "An Age of Indifference." *U.S. News & World Report,* 25 June 1990.

Goldfarb, W. "Infant Rearing as a Factor in Foster Home Placement." *American Journal of Orthopsychiatry,* 14:162-167, 1944.

Haley, Jay. *Uncommon Therapy: The Psychiatric Techniques of Milton J. Erickson, M.D.* New York: Norton, 1973.

Hamill, Pete. "City of the Damned—New York Has Become an American Calcutta." *Esquire,* December 1990.

Hampden-Turner, Charles. "The Dramas of Delancey Street." *Journal of Humanistic Psychology,* 16 (1): 5-54, 1976.

Hartring, Barbara. *Uncharted Waters: Parenting an Attachment Disordered Child*. 2 Bogren Lane, Waylan, MA 01778.

Hartring, Barbara and C. M. Heinicke. "Some Effects of Separating Two-Year-Old Children from Their Parents: A Comparative Study." *Human Relations*, 9: 105-176, 1956.

Hayes, R. M. *Horse Breaking*.

Heinicke, C. M. and I. Westheimer. *Brief Separations*. New York: International Universities Press, 1966.

Hollandsworth, Skip. "Can Kids on Drugs Be Saved?" *Texas Monthly*, June 1990.

Jewett, C. *Adopting the Older Child*. Cambridge, MA: Harvard Common Press, 1978.

Kadushin, A. *Adopting Older Children*. New York: Columbia University Press, 1970.

Kadushin, A. and F. W. Seidl. "Adoption Failure: A Social Work Postmortem." *Social Worker*, 16: 32-38, 1971.

Karen, Robert. "Becoming Attached." *Atlantic Monthly*, February 1990.

Koontz, Dean. *Midnight*. New York: Putnam, 1989.

McKelvey, Carole and JoEllen Stevens. *Suffer the Children*.

Magid, Ken and Carole McKelvey. *High Risk: Children Without a Conscience*. Golden, CO: M & M Publishing.

March, William. *The Bad Seed*. New York: Dell, 1954.

Moss, Desda. *USA Today*, 9 June 1992.

Moss, H. A. "Sex, Age and State as Determinants of Mother-Infant Interaction." *Merrill-Palmer Quarterly*, 13: 19-36, 1967.

Oliver, Boyd and L. W. Sandler. "Adaptive Relationships in Early Mother-Child Interaction." *Journal of the American Academy of Child Psychiatrists*, 1: 141-166, 1964.

Payne, Roger. *National Geographic*, March 1976.

Pelled, N. "On the Formation of Object-Relations and Identifications of the Kibbutz Child." *Israeli Annals of Psychiatry*, 2: 144-161, 1964.

Pesce, Carolyn. *USA Today*, 21 October 1991.

Prechtl, H. F. R. "The Mother-Child Interaction in Babies with Minimal Brain Damage." In B. M. Foss (ed). *Determinants of Infant Behavior*, vol. 2. New York: Wiley, 1963.

Purdy, Jane. *He Will Never Remember: Caring for the Victims of Child Abuse*. Atlanta: Susan Hunter, 1989.

Purpura, Dominick. *Behavior Today*, 2 June 1975.

Robertson, J. A. *A Guide to the Film "A Two-Year-Old Goes to Hospital."* New York: NYU Film Library, 1953.

Rodning, C., L. Beckwit, and J. Howard. "Characteristics of Attachment Organization in Prenatally Drug-Exposed Toddlers." *Development and Psychopathology,* 1 (4): 277, 289, 1990.

Rule, Ann. *The Stranger Beside Me.* New York: Signet, 1988.

Schiff, Jacqui with Beth Day. *All My Children.* New York: M. Evans.

Schorr, Lisbeth. *Within Our Reach.* New York: Doubleday, 1988.

Shand, A. F. *The Foundations of Character,* 2nd ed. London: Macmillan, 1920.

State of Colorado Department of Social Services. Letter to Barbara Mattison, M.Ed., 8 January 1990.

Smith, D. F., G. G. Sandor, et al. "Intrinsic Defects in the Fetal Alcohol Syndrome: Studies on 76 Cases from British Columbia and the Yukon Territory." *Neurobehavioral Toxicology,* 3(2): 145-152, 1981.

Sontag, Lester. "Somatophysics of Personality and Body Function." *Vita Humana,* November 1963, 1-10.

Spitz, Renee and W. G. Cobliner. *The First Year of Life.* New York: International Universities Press, 1965.

Steiner, Claude. *Scripts People Live.* New York: Bantam, 1975.

Stott, Dennis. "Follow-up Study from Birth of the Effects of Prenatal Stresses." *Developmental Medicine and Child Neurology,* 15: 770-787, 1973.

Streissguth, A. P. "Alcoholism and Pregnancy: An Overview and Update." *Journal of Substance and Alcohol Actions/Misuse,* 4: 149-173, 1983.

Tinbergen, Niko and Elizabeth Tinbergen. *Autistic Children: New Hope for a Cure.* London: Allen & Unwin, 1983.

Tizard, B. and J. Hodges. "The Effect of Early Institutional Rearing on the Development of Eight-Year-Old Children." *Journal of Child Psychology and Psychiatry,* 19: 99-118, 1978.

Tizard, B. and A. Joseph. "Cognitive Development of Young Children in Residential Care: The Study of Children Aged 24 Months." *Journal of Child Psychology and Psychiatry,* 11: 177-186, 1970.

Tizard, B. and J. Rees. "A Comparison of the Effects of Adoption, Restoration to the Natural Mother, and Continued Institutionalization on the Cognitive Development of Four-Year-Old Children." *Child Development,* 45: 92-99, 1974.

———. "The Effect of Early Institutional Rearing on the Behavior Problems and Affectional Relationships of Four-Year-Old Children." *Journal of Child Psychology and Psychiatry,* 16: 61-74, 1975.

Tizard, Jan. "Trends." In *Adoption: A Second Chance,* vol. 6. New York: Free Press, 1977.

Tucker, Cyntia. *Denver Post,* June 13, 1992.

Ucko, L. E. "A Comparative Study of Asphyxiated and Nonasphyxiated Boys from Birth to Five Years." *Developmental Medicine and Child Neurology,* 7: 643-657, 1965.

Verny, Thomas with John Kelly. *The Secret Life of the Unborn Child.* New York: Bantam Doubleday Dell, 1981.

Waite, Helen. *Helen Keller and Anne Sullivan: Valiant Companions.* Philadelphia: MacRae Smith, 1959.

Ward, A. J. "Early Infantile Autism: Diagnosis, Etiology and Treatment." *Psychological Bulletin,* 73: 350-362, 1970.

"We Education Reformers Have New Respect for Catholic Schools." *Wall Street Journal,* 28 March 1991.

INDEX

Other materials by Dr. Cline on the subject of parenting diffi-cult children are available! For a catalog of books, audiocassettes, and videotapes, contact The Love and Logic Press, Inc., 2207 Jackson Street, Golden, CO 80401 (800-338-4065).

If you are searching for someone to talk to about therapies for unbonded children, contact Evergreen Consultants in Human Behavior (303-674-5503) or the Attachment Center at Evergreen (303-674-1910).